Managerial Statistics: A Case-Based Approach

Peter Klibanoff,

Kellogg Graduate School of Management, Northwestern University

Alvaro Sandroni,

Kellogg Graduate School of Management, Northwestern University

Boaz Moselle,

Principal, The Brattle Group, Brussels

Brett Saraniti,

Hawaii Pacific University

SOUTH-WESTERN
CENGAGE Learning

Australia • Brazil • Japan • Korea • Mexico • Singapore • Spain • United Kingdom • United States

Managerial Statistics: A Case-Based Approach, First Edition

Klibanoff, Sandroni, Moselle, Saraniti

VP/Editorial Director:
Jack W. Calhoun

Editor-in-Chief:
Alex von Rosenberg

Acquisitions Editor:
Charles E. McCormick, Jr.

Sr. Developmental Editor:
Alice Denny

Sr. Marketing Manager:
Larry Qualls

Production Project Manager:
Kelly N. Hoard

Manager of Technology, Editorial:
Vicky True

Technology Project Editor:
Kelly Reid

Web Coordinator:
Scott Cook

Manufacturing Coordinator:
Diane Lohman

Production House:
GEX Publishing Services

Printer:
Courier
Westford, MA

Art Director:
Stacy Jenkins Shirley

Internal Designer:
Joe Pagliaro

Cover Designer:
Bethany Casey

Cover Images:
©Getty Images

Library of Congress Control Number:
2005927132

For more information about our
products, contact us at:
Cengage Learning,
Customer & Sales Support,
1-800-354-9706

Cengage Learning
5191 Natorp Boulevard
Mason, OH 45040
USA

Brief Contents

Contents

Acknowledgements

Many people have helped shape this text and influence our thinking about or presentation of the topics therein. The book grew out of a redesign of the core statistics course in the MBA curriculum at the Kellogg School of Management, Northwestern University. Initially, Peter Klibanoff and Boaz Moselle undertook this redesign. Alvaro Sandroni joined soon after in helping implement it. Brett Saraniti joined us more recently to help turn the notes into a text, while Boaz had left for the government and private sectors by this time and was less involved in the final phases. We owe great thanks to the many current and former colleagues who developed some of the early material from which the redesign grew and who provided us with pedagogical advice and encouragement early in our careers. Larry Jones especially stands out in this regard and we also greatly valued the help from Matt Jackson, Alejandro Manelli, Tzachi Gilboa, and Bob Weber. Don Jacobs, former Dean of Kellogg, deserves credit for motivating the redesign and for insisting on Microsoft Excel-based tools. We want to thank those colleagues who have taught Kellogg courses along with us based on our notes, and who also helped improve the content and form of the material. Peter Esö, Christoph Kuzmics, Karl Schmedders, Eilon Solon, and Rakesh Vohra helped make our teaching more successful and more fun by being an active part of our "teaching team." Karl and Eilon jointly developed with us some of the material Chapter 2 is based on. Peter Esö was extremely helpful in developing some of the Chapter 9 material and in creating the current form of Chapters 8 and 9. Bob Weber was generous enough to let us adopt and expand his KStat collection of macros for Microsoft Excel. Two of Peter Klibanoff's former doctoral students helped in producing the notes on which the book is based: Emre Ozdenoren helped integrate the use of KStat and Excel throughout, and Sayan Chakraborty helped with the material in Chapter 1. Piotrek Kuszewski helped with the test bank materials. We thank the numerous doctoral students who have been our teaching assistants for their help and contributions. Finally, this text literally would not exist without the joy and challenge of teaching our many MBA students at Kellogg over the years. It was they who motivated the whole orientation of the text and whose feedback convinced us that not only were we on the right track, but that students elsewhere could benefit from, learn from, and enjoy a text based on our approach to managerial statistics.

We would like to thank the team at South-Western Cengage Learning responsible for our text. We thank Charles McCormick, Jr., Alice Denny, and George Werthman for believing in the project enough to take us on and for their patience as it developed. We thank our production manager at Cengage Learning, Kelly Hoard, and our production manager at GEX Publishing Services, Sarah McKay, for their great work, communication skills, and patience in seeing this through to the final product.

Finally, we all thank our families for bearing with the time and energy that this project took away from them.

Peter Klibanoff
Alvaro Sandroni
Boaz Moselle
Brett Saraniti

Preface

This book is different from any other textbook involving managerial statistics, but we feel that it is more than just different: it's better. The purpose of this book is to make established statistical methods relevant and accessible to management students. Managers don't need to know matrix algebra. They don't need to know how to mindlessly plug numbers into innumerable formulas by hand or in a spreadsheet. Managers need to be able to build models from scratch and understand what they mean. They need to be able to detect and mend common problems that arise in real-world applications of regression. They need to be able to know intuitively and substantively what statistical outputs mean and what they do not mean. The ability to generate, interpret, use, and understand results is our focus, and we use cases to motivate everything.

While an electrical engineer-turned-manager (a rare find) will further her statistical intuitions by studying mathematical relationships and formulas, most management students would be better served by our case-based approach. Tools and modeling skills are developed by seeing how they can be used in real-world cases. Students become well versed at using statistics to make better managerial decisions. All of the material is motivated by showing how it can be used to help managers make better choices in an uncertain world. This contrast with the traditional approach is remarkable in many ways, but most notably in its effectiveness. It works. It's awesome. We're sure.

To concentrate the students on understanding how to use statistics properly without the unnecessary distractions of mastering new software or unfamiliar Excel functions, we have integrated an Excel macro program called KStat into the text. KStat is simple and menu-driven, so students can quickly learn its functions and spend more time on meaning and comprehension. Furthermore, it's streamlined, focusing on a limited set of functions to reduce the cluttered appearance of many common software outputs. Courses that rely on sophisticated software often degenerate into tedious number crunching, as do classes that overemphasize formulas and hand calculations. KStat gives us all the necessary computational power … and it's free!

We cover the major topics presented in traditional texts, but we place stronger emphasis on techniques for detecting and overcoming problems with regression models. Many of the topics that are not covered in great detail in the main text are explored in the various cases, which are an integral part of this book. We feel that students usually learn material better when they don't know all of the necessary techniques ahead of time. Rather than including this content in the main text, we have added extensive teaching notes for the cases, which contain significant supplemental coverage that can be used in the class discussions.

A Road Map...

Traditional Topics	Covered in:
Probability Review	Chapter 1
Sampling Distributions	Chapter 1
Confidence Intervals	Chapter 1
Prediction Intervals	Chapter 4
Hypothesis Testing	Chapter 2
Simple Regression	Chapters 3 and 4
Multiple Regression	Refrigerator Case, Colonial Broadcasting Case, Chapters 7, 8 and 9, Nopane Advertising Case, Baseball Case
Dummy/Slope and Dummy Variables	Chapter 5
Non-Linear Regression	Chapters 6 and 8
Spurious Correlation[1]	Chapter 6
Multicollinearity[1]	Chapter 7, Nopane Advertising Case
Generalized F-test	Chapter 7
Modeling[2]	Chapters 6, 7, 8, Colonial Broadcasting Case, Nopane Advertising Case
Omitted Variable Bias[1]	Refrigerator Case, Colonial Broadcasting Case, Chapter 7, Nopane Advertising Case
Heteroskedasticity	Chapter 8
Forecasting/Time Series	Chapter 9, Harmon Foods Case
Interaction Variables	Chapter 5, Nopane Advertising Case

Key Emphases and Features

CASE MOTIVATED

This book presents a case- and example-based curriculum. Topics are motivated by managerial choices that can be aided using the new tools introduced in each chapter. For instance, rather than introducing multiple regression with mathematical theory, a case is posed in which simple regression proves inadequate. Specifically, in the example, simple regression produces misleading results through an omitted variable bias. Multiple regression is then introduced as a means of overcoming the failings of the current set of tools that have been developed at that point in the class. Additional tools and troubleshooting techniques are methodically brought in through subsequent cases and are balanced by traditional content.

Teaching notes are included for instructors for the major case inserts, as are detailed answer keys for the case exercises used in the end-of-chapter materials.

---

1. These techniques are not usually covered as thoroughly as we have done in this text.
2. Mindless computational modeling techniques such as best subsets and stepwise regression are *not* covered. Many of the cases provided show the weaknesses of such machine-gun approaches.

INTEGRATED, USER-FRIENDLY SOFTWARE

The text is built around the KStat Regression Package, which was created exclusively for use with this material. The streamlined functionality allows students to focus on the concepts of the course without wasting significant time and energy learning a particular commercial software package. KStat is a custom set of pull-down menu functions that runs within Microsoft Excel, making it simple, familiar, and extremely easy to learn. It is free to students, who may keep and use it as long as they wish.

APPLIED MANAGERIAL FOCUS

The material is concentrated on managerial decision making. Each case presents the students with a realistic scenario in which statistical techniques can facilitate the task at hand. Topics from finance, marketing, and other management fields are incorporated into the text, as well as problems to demonstrate additional relevancy to the students.

NON-TECHNICAL DEVELOPMENT

Students from non-technical backgrounds learn especially well using this material because of its concentration on tangible applications and its de-emphasis on formulas and hand calculations. Rather than watering down standard material that turns off the more mathematically savvy students, this textbook develops the topics in an innovative way that maintains the interest of the entire spectrum of abilities. The approach fully supports the trend in management education toward the relegation of mechanics to the computer and has worked incredibly well with our diverse groups of students.

Objectives

To make the topic of applied statistical regression both accessible and relevant.

To equip students with a practical understanding of how to use statistical tools and methods for managerial decision making.

To develop an understanding of what regression is and how to apply it in a variety of decision-making contexts.

To introduce business statistics as a compelling and invaluable element of management education.

Pedagogy

NARROW FOCUS

We have streamlined the content of the text to vastly reduce time spent on uninteresting and ultimately unimportant mechanics and formulas. The topics covered are limited to a standalone review of basic probability followed by hypothesis testing and regression analysis. This book's depth and detail in the coverage of regression is unparalleled in a text of this size.

SCREEN CAPTURES

Screen captures are used throughout the text, though not superfluously. The integration of the KStat program becomes particularly valuable with this feature. Unlike other texts that straddle multiple software packages or wrestle with the unnecessary vastness of Excel, the customized package developed for this text allows for a seamless combination of textbook and technology.

KSTAT SOFTWARE

KStat, which is included in the Student CD packaged with new texts, is the foundation of most examples and homework problems. The program adds simple menu-driven capabilities to Excel and offers useful comment boxes that intuitively define and qualify all statistical terminology.

DATA FILES

Students have access to the extensive collection of data files used in textbook examples and homework exercises on the Student CD included with each new text. The data is almost entirely from real-world sources except for a handful of special cases used to illustrate exceptional conditions.

CASE EXERCISES

Each chapter contains lengthy case exercises to allow students the opportunity to plunge deeper into the material. Rather than merely providing simple computational exercises, these problems create a focus on generating, interpreting, and ultimately applying the results. Four major standalone cases with extensive teaching notes included in the instructor's manual are interspersed between the relevant chapters. Traditional exercises with more limited goals are also included with each chapter under a separate heading.

Instructor Ancillaries

INSTRUCTOR'S MANUAL

An instructor's manual designed to aid new adopters with the teaching of these materials will be included with the other teaching supplements. The manual includes chapter-by-chapter discussions of frequently asked questions, additional examples, and useful organizational suggestions. Teaching notes for the case inserts are also included with these materials to aid in discussion of the cases. This, coupled with the other ancillary materials that follow, enable an easy transition to the text.

Solutions are provided in a complete, detailed manner. Answers to the case exercises in particular are thorough and comprehensive.

POWERPOINT SLIDES

An extensive set of PowerPoint slides is also available for use with the text. These slides are classroom-tested at Kellogg and have proved to be quite successful for multiple instructors. Samples of the slides are included in the appendices to this package.

TEST BANK

The instructor materials include a test bank. The test bank is built from actual exams used by the authors and others and is supplemented with additional questions as well as detailed answer keys. The answer keys provide exhaustive solutions to each problem, written in clear, unambiguous English. Samples of test bank questions and solutions are also included at the end of the package.

Chapter Outline

CHAPTER 1   THE DOUBLE E (EE): INTRODUCTION TO PROBABILITY DISTRIBUTIONS AND ESTIMATION

The first chapter reviews the basics of probability and sampling distributions. The EE company's various needs focus the content on applicability and helps students realize the potential of basic tools to aid in decision making. More importantly, the material lays the foundation for later chapters.

CHAPTER 2   CONSUMER PACKAGING: CONDUCTING AND USING HYPOTHESIS TESTS

This chapter introduces the concept of hypothesis testing through a marketing research example. The case involves making a decision concerning whether or not to go ahead with a new initiative based on a sample of data from the company's test marketing. Standalone Excel and the KStat package are both used throughout the case to minimize traditional hand calculations. A formal analysis summarizes the lessons from the case and extends them to more generic circumstances. Later in the chapter, the case is extended to compare two possible alternatives to the simpler choice posed earlier. Two sample hypothesis tests are then shown to help quantify the decision. A pair of additional examples follows to allow students to apply these lessons in measuring a political gender gap and testing for a difference in asset returns.

CHAPTER 3   THE AUTORAMA: INTRODUCTION TO REGRESSION THROUGH INVENTORY PLANNING

Rather than developing the theoretical ideas of regression first and then presenting interesting applications, we first pose a problem where regression is used to help make a complex decision. Pieces of the theory are inserted into the discussion of the case, but most are postponed until the end of the chapter. The case itself involves an auto dealership that wants to optimally stock its inventory of cars in a new location with a different underlying population than its original one. That is, the distribution of income levels is very different between the two locations. By relating income to purchase price through regression analysis, students can estimate the price levels of cars likely to sell at the new dealership.

CHAPTER 4   BETAS AND THE NEWSPAPER CASE: USING THE REGRESSION EQUATION

In this chapter we further demonstrate the value of regression analysis through two realistic case studies. The first case shows the value of understanding the coefficients in a regression equation, while the second focuses on using the equation to make predictions.

First, we propose a new investment in a fast food chain that is not publicly traded. The investment is wise if the appropriate cost of capital is not too high, but we are unaware of the appropriate beta to use with CAPM to compute it. Using a simple linear regression, we can compute the beta for a comparable company (McDonald's) and then determine our own cost of capital. A more extensive analysis is then done on the estimated beta, including constructing a confidence interval and an estimate of the probability of a positive NPV for the project. This is an excellent introduction to an examination of the coefficients in the regression equation, and the integration of a well-known topic from finance demonstrates relevance to the students.

The second case in this chapter illustrates the use of regression to make predictions and the evaluation of those predictions. The case involves the choice of a newspaper owner to possibly add a Sunday edition of his paper, which currently runs only six days a week. A dataset containing daily and Sunday circulations of major newspapers is used to establish the relationship between the two. A break-even level of sales is known and the case involves estimating the chances of surpassing this figure. After using the regression equation to make a prediction, the students assess the value of this point estimate by looking at a KStat-generated prediction interval. The interval is gigantic, proving the simple regression to be of little value despite having what most consider a large R-squared.

CASE INSERT 1   ENERGY COSTS AND REFRIGERATOR PRICING

This case insert introduces multiple regression with the refrigerator case. The case poses a decision regarding the investment in a new energy-efficient refrigerator that costs more to build but saves customers money through lower energy bills. Rational consumers ought to pay more for the new fridge and the dataset allows us to regress energy costs onto price with surprising results. Energy costs have a significant positive relationship with price.

The subject of omitted variable bias is then introduced (in the instructor's manual) to explain this curious result. A more extensive dataset, which includes additional data such as the refrigerator size and features, is then used to conduct a multiple regression that yields results more appropriate for the decision problem presented in the case.

CHAPTER 5   CALIFORNIA STRAWBERRIES: DUMMY AND SLOPE DUMMY VARIABLES

Dummy variables and slope dummy variables are used in this chapter's California Strawberries case. The case examines two bottling processes with different rates that can be measured and compared using the techniques introduced in the text. Students learn how to determine if differences between slopes are significant.

CHAPTER 6   FORESTIER WINE: GRAPHICAL ANALYSIS, NON-LINEAR REGRESSION AND SPURIOUS CORRELATION

This chapter illustrates the need to supplement regression analysis with graphical analysis through the Forestier Wine case. The case relates income levels to wine sales for four different brands of wine. The regression equations are *identical* for all four wines, but the underlying data are not. One reflects a solid linear relationship, one is perfectly quadratic, another is heavily influenced by an outlier, and the last is solely driven by one data point. Graphical analysis forces students to question the appropriateness of the linear regression model for these applications.

Additionally, the idea of spurious correlation is introduced through a classic example of snowfall in Amherst, Massachusetts, and the U.S. unemployment rate. Regressing either one on the other results in a 96.7% R-squared.

CHAPTER 7   THE HOT DOG CASE: MULTIPLE REGRESSION, MULTICOLLINEARITY AND THE GENERALIZED F-TEST

This chapter poses an economic analysis explaining the market share of a hot dog company based on its price and the prices of three rivals obtained from supermarket scanner data. Two of the rivals are Ball Park regular and special all-beef hot dogs, which are almost perfectly correlated, resulting in an apparent lack of significance for either product. The text shows students how to detect this multicollinearity by observing correlation coefficients or variance inflation factors (both of which are introduced or reviewed in the chapter). The generalized F-test is also introduced to test for joint significance of the two Ball Park variables.

The Dubuque Hot Dog case also involves establishing a proper multiple regression model and then using that model to make predictions and evaluate the relative importance of each competitor to Dubuque. The idea of hidden extrapolation is introduced by hypothesizing possible forecasts based on rivals' pricing.

CASE INSERT 2   COLONIAL BROADCASTING

This HBS case covers a discussion of the Colonial Broadcasting Company. The case involves the A.C. Nielson Ratings of "made for TV" movies. The case forces students to interpret the coefficients of certain variables under the inclusion of various subsets of these variables. The presence or absence of different variables and the implicit assumptions made in each selection are discussed in detail in the instructor's manual, which contains teaching notes for the case.

CHAPTER 8   THE ADVERTISING CASE: HETEROSKEDASTICITY AND LOGARITHMS

This chapter presents a review of logarithms and demonstrates their use as both a modeling technique and a potential relief from heteroskedasticity. Initially, a homework exercise that compares advertising expenditures to sales is reintroduced to students as a good candidate for a non-linear regression due to the diminishing marginal returns. Various forms of non-linearities are described and approaches for modeling these relationships are discussed. Next, the detection, possible cure, and limitations created by heteroskedasticity are presented and motivated by revisiting the hot dog case.

CHAPTER 9   SODA SALES AND HARMON FOODS: DEALING WITH TIME AND SEASONALITY

Two forecasting cases are used in this chapter to demonstrate different techniques for modeling seasonality. Quarterly data in the Dada Soda case visually depict a clear seasonality as summer sales outpace winter sales. Multiple dummy variables are used to additively model and measure the seasonal impact on sales.

Next, the longer Harmon Foods HBS case uses a multiplicative seasonality model to forecast sales of the company's breakfast cereal. The case also introduces the technique of lagging predictive variables to model lingering effects.

Finally, we delve further into forecasting with a discussion of time series and other techniques for analyzing this type of data.

CASE INSERT 3   NOPANE ADVERTISING STRATEGY

One last HBS case is used to explore the ideas of interaction variables and to better understand the use of slope dummy variables in the context of multiple regression. Again, the variable selection and the possibility of omitted variable bias are emphasized in the teaching notes contained in the instructor's manual.

CASE INSERT 4   THE BASEBALL CASE

This final case uses data from several years of BK Lions' games at Singha Field to develop forecasting models and measure the effect of scheduling, seasonality, rival matchups, and additional factors on attendance at the games. The case is broad enough to cover several of the themes from previous chapters and to further the discussion on modeling techniques and the tradeoffs involved in variable selections. For instance, the coarse simplicity of a weekend/weekday dummy variable can be contrasted with the relatively complex precision of using six separate dummies to compare attendance on each day of the week.

Acknowledgements

We would like to acknowledge the work of our reviewers who provided comments and suggestions of ways to continue to improve our text. Thanks to:

Suryapratim Banerjee, Vanderbilt University

Bruce Barrett, University of Alabama

Bernard Dickman, Hofstra University

Walter J. Mayer, University of Mississippi

David R. McKenna, Boston College

Muhammad A. Obeidat, Southern Polytechnic State University

Alan Olinsky, Bryant College

Victor R Prybutok, University of North Texas

Helen M. Roberts, Montclair State University

Subarna K. Samanta, The College of New Jersey

Edward D. White III, Air Force Institute of Technology

Finally, we are also acknowledge our senior acquisitions editor Charles McCormick, Jr., our senior developmental editor Alice Denny, our production project manager, Kelly Hoard, our senior marketing manager Larry Qualls, and others at South-Western Cengage Learning for their editorial counsel and support during the preparation of this text.

Peter Klibanoff
Alvaro Sandroni
Boaz Moselle
Brett Saraniti

About the Authors

PETER KLIBANOFF

Peter Klibanoff is currently Associate Professor of Managerial Economics and Decision Sciences at the Kellogg School of Management, Northwestern University. He completed his Ph.D. in economics at Massachusetts Institute of Technology, and also holds a Bachelor of Arts degree in applied mathematics from Harvard University. Recent work is published in *Economic Theory*, *Econometrica*, *The Journal of Economic Theory*, *The Journal of Finance*, and *The Review of Economic Studies*. His research interests span a broad range of topics in economic theory. Some topics of special interest include game theory and decision theory, especially issues related to modeling uncertainty; the effect and mitigation of externalities; optimal regulation; and behavioral finance. He teaches statistics at the MBA level and a Ph.D. course on decision theory. He is also the author of Kellogg's Online Statistics Essentials web-based course.

ALVARO SANDRONI

Alvaro Sandroni is Mechthild Esse Nemmers Professor of Managerial Economics and Decision Sciences at the Kellogg School of Management, Northwestern University. He completed his Ph.D. in Economics at the University of Pennsylvania as well as a Ph.D. in mathematics at the Instituto de Matematica Pura e Aplicada, Brazil. He has works published in *Review of Economic Studies*, *Journal of Economic Theory*, *Games & Economic Behavior*, *International Journal of Game Theory*, *Mathematics of Operations Research*, and *Econometrica*. He has received research grants from the National Science Foundation, as well as Bergmann Memorial Research Grants. His primary teaching interests are in microeconomics.

BOAZ MOSELLE

Boaz Moselle is a former Assistant Professor of Managerial Economics and Decision Sciences at the Kellogg School of Management, Northwestern University. He has worked as Chief Economist in the U.K. energy regulator Ofgem, and is currently a Principal of consulting firm The Brattle Group, where he heads its Brussels office. He holds a Ph.D. in economics from Harvard University, a Ph.D. in mathematics from London University, and a B.A. in mathematics from Cambridge University.

BRETT SARANITI

Brett Saraniti holds a Ph.D. in Managerial Economics and Decision Sciences from the Kellogg School of Management, Northwestern University. He is currently Associate Professor of Economics and Quantitative Methods at Hawaii Pacific University. He is also an Adjunct Associate Professor at the Kellogg School of Management where he teaches every summer. He has held visiting teaching positions at Brisbane Graduate School of Business, Brisbane Australia; the Sasin Graduate Institute of Business, Bangkok; and the Helsinki School of Economics and Business Administration. He has also worked on projects for Cantor Fitzgerald & Co., Chevron Corporation, and UNext, Inc. Brett spends most of the year on the North Shore of Oahu where he surfs and enjoys time with his wife, Samantha, and their children Francesca and Carlo.

CHAPTER 1

DOUBLE E (EE): AN INTRODUCTION TO PROBABILITY DISTRIBUTIONS AND ESTIMATION

This chapter introduces us to the Double E (EE) chain of consumer electronics stores and their struggle to improve operations by using some basic statistical analysis. EE's main problem is dealing with pseudo customers who utilize its sales staff's time and expertise and then buy the products online or elsewhere. The case motivates the use of data to diagnose and help construct solutions to the company's issues. The topics introduced include means, standard deviations, variances, proportions, normal and t-distributions, sampling, the sampling distribution of the sample mean, confidence intervals for means and proportions, and some associated Excel functions.

The techniques developed in this case will establish a foundation for more sophisticated analysis discussed later.

1.1 EE: Uncertainty and Probability

EE is a chain of stores selling consumer electronics in the United States. Over the last decade, it has expanded to more than 4,000 stores spread across the country, thereby becoming one of the largest retailers of consumer electronics in the country. However, of late, EE's profits have been declining. The primary reasons for this are suspected to be falling quality of service and growing competition. EE has decided to deal with the problems aggressively and wants to come up with fast and effective solutions. In this chapter, we will see how probability and basic statistics will be useful to EE in a number of areas. Furthermore, many topics introduced in this chapter will be used and referred to repeatedly throughout the remainder of the book.

PROBABILITY DISTRIBUTION

Much of what EE deals with, or encounters in the course of its operations, involves fluctuating quantities. For example, it experiences variations in its weekly sales, the number of items turned in for repair each week, the number of items a customer buys during one visit, the length of time a salesperson spends with a single customer, the end-of-quarter profits, etc. One convenient way of summarizing the fluctuations is to use a **probability distribution**. A probability distribution makes possible the calculation of the chance that a variable lies in a given range. For example, a probability distribution for weekly sales allows us to calculate the chance that the weekly sales will be in a given range (e.g., weekly sales between $10,000 and $50,000).

A **continuous probability distribution** is one in which the variable can assume any value within a range. This means that if a variable can take the values, a and b, it can assume any value between a and b. Graphically, a continuous probability distribution can be represented by a curve (see Figure 1.1).

Figure 1.1 Graph of probability distribution describing the daily sales (in dollars) at an EE store.

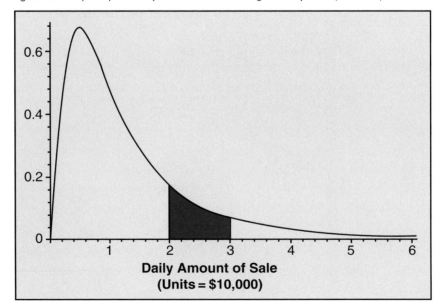

One variable that would typically be described by a continuous distribution is the dollar amount of sales in a day at an EE outlet. The area under the curve within a given range gives the probability of sales falling in that range. For example, in Figure 1.1, the probability that the dollar amount of sales on a given day is between $20,000 and $30,000 is equal to the area of the shaded region. Since something always has to happen, the total area under the curve for any probability distribution is equal to one.

A **discrete probability distribution** is one in which the variable takes on only a certain countable number of values. For instance, the number of customers who buy flat-panel televisions tomorrow in a given store follows a discrete probability distribution with possible values of {0, 1, 2, 3, 4, 5 or more}. The tools developed in this text will rely on continuous distributions. In fact, though the dollar amount of sales is discrete (we cannot divide pennies any further), we have assumed for simplicity that it is described by a continuous distribution. We will frequently use this standard trick to our advantage. For purposes of convenience, it often pays to approximate discrete distributions by continuous distributions.

1.2 The Mean

We will now introduce three of the most widely used attributes of a probability distribution, namely, the mean, the variance, and the standard deviation. We start with the mean. The mean of a distribution measures the average (or expected) value of that distribution. The mean is often our best single prediction for a variable's value. Consider the sales manager of an EE store. He knows that the weekly sales of desktop personal computers (PCs) can be described by a probability distribution. The mean sales provide him with a single number around which the actual weekly sales will vary. It is usually denoted by the Greek letter μ ("mu").

What the mean does for a probability distribution is similar to what the average does for a group of numbers. The mean is also calculated much like the average of a group of numbers. Before learning how this is done, let us review how one computes the average of a group of numbers. Suppose the sales manager at an EE store observes the sales of desktop PCs for 5 weeks in succession. Let us take them to be 19, 25, 20, 25 and 27. To get the average sales of desktops per week during this period, she needs to sum up these numbers and divide by five. The average weekly number sold is equal to the following:

> Average sales = (19+25+20+25+27)/5 = 116/5 = 23.2

This means that, on average, 23.2 desktop PCs were sold each week at the store during this time period.

1.3 The Variance and Standard Deviation

Knowing the mean is not always enough to compare two probability distributions. If a particular distribution has a higher mean than a second one, all the values of the first one are not necessarily higher than the second one. To illustrate this, consider the dollar amounts of sales in two of EE's stores. Suppose they can be represented by the probability distributions shown in Figure 1.2. The means of the

Figure 1.2 μ_1 = mean of distribution 1; μ_2 = mean of distribution 2.

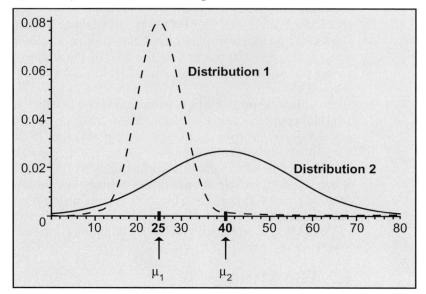

distributions are labeled μ_1 and μ_2. Though the mean of distribution 2 (μ_2) is higher than that of distribution 1 (μ_1), a value drawn from distribution 2 may be lower than one drawn from distribution 1. In fact, because distribution 2 is so spread out there is a greater probability of obtaining very low values than there is with distribution 1. This shows that having a measure of the spread around the mean is useful in addition to knowing the mean itself.

The variance is the most frequently used measure of variation or spread of a distribution around the mean. The higher the variance of a distribution, the more likely it is for the variable to assume values far from the mean. Mathematically, the variance is the average squared deviation from the mean (i.e., for each possible value, subtract the mean, square the resulting number, and calculate the mean of these numbers using the probability distribution) and is usually denoted by σ^2 ("sigma squared"). Basically, it measures on average how "far" the actual sales are from their average.

Why is a number like the variance useful? Consider, for example, the sales manager at an EE store who is in charge of ordering inventories. To order inventories in the right quantities, she needs to account for the variability in weekly demand for different items sold at the store. She knows that probability distributions can be used to understand the demand fluctuations. To set the right inventory levels, knowing the mean is generally insufficient. She also needs to know how spread out the distribution for demand is about its mean. In other words, she needs to measure the variability in demand for that particular item. The variance and standard deviation of the probability distribution can do this for her.

THE MEAN AND VARIANCE OF FINANCIAL SECURITIES

One important application of mean and variance lies in finance. The return on any financial security fluctuates and can be described by a probability distribution. A security with a higher mean return than a second one provides higher returns on average. Obviously, any investor would prefer a higher mean return all else equal.

However, this is not the only factor that influences the investment decisions of most investors. Investors' behavior suggests that they like high returns but dislike huge fluctuations or variations in the returns. Huge fluctuations suggest significant possibilities of very high or very low returns. This makes the security risky or volatile. The variance of the probability distribution used to describe the returns on a security is one measure of the risk associated with the security. The higher the variance becomes, the more risky the security is. A risk-sensitive individual takes into account both the means and the variances of securities while making investment decisions.[1]

STANDARD DEVIATION

One drawback of the variance is that, as a number, it can be hard to interpret. This is because it is measured in the square of the original variable's units. For example, the distribution of weekly sales measured in dollars will have a variance measured in dollars squared. Interpreting dollars squared is difficult. For this reason, it is common to use the square root of the variance, called the standard deviation, instead of the variance itself. The standard deviation is a measure of spread that is always in the same units as the original variable. Since the standard deviation is the square root of the variance, it is usually denoted by σ ("sigma").

1.4 Proportions

Working with variables with only two possible outcomes can sometimes be helpful. Consider the customers who come to an EE store. Some of them buy at least one product and some leave without buying any. The variable "customer buys at least one item" has two possible outcomes: YES or NO. To use this variable numerically, we can say the variable takes the value 1 if the customer buys at least one product and 0 if he or she does not buy any. If we use 1 and 0 in this way, then the average, or mean, of the variable is the **proportion** of customers who buy at least one item. A specific illustration is the following. We look at any five EE customers. We observe if each customer buys an item or not on his or her visit to the store and assign the value 1 and 0 accordingly. For example (see Figure 1.3), customers 1, 4, and 5 do not buy any items, and customers 2 and 3 do.

Let us take the average of the values in the right-hand column. The average is 0.4. Notice that 0.4 (or 40%) is the proportion of these five customers who bought at least one item. Hence, the average of this variable gives the proportion of the five customers who bought at least one item.

Figure 1.3 This table shows if a customer bought an item.

Customer Identity	Value of variable showing if an item is bought
Customer 1	0
Customer 2	1
Customer 3	1
Customer 4	0
Customer 5	0

---

1. In Chapter 4, we will revisit the connection between variance and risk in the context of capital budgeting and the CAPM model.

When dealing with a variable with two outcomes coded as 0 and 1, instead of talking about the mean, we will sometimes use the proportion, which we denote by p. The proportion is always between 0 and 1. When p is the mean of the distribution of such a variable, $p(1-p)$ and $\sqrt{p(1-p)}$ will be its variance and standard deviation, respectively. So, for a variable with only two outcomes, 0 and 1, knowing the proportion tells you the mean, the variance, and the standard deviation.

1.5 The Normal Distribution

The normal distribution is one of the most common distributions in statistics. There is a whole family of normal distributions, one for each pair of means and standard deviations. Each normal distribution can be uniquely characterized by those two parameters.

Characteristic features of a normal distribution are its bell shape and symmetry (see Figure 1.4). Symmetry of the distribution implies that if a vertical line is drawn along the middle of the distribution, the left and right halves will be mirror images of one another. The tails of a normal distribution approach, but never touch, the X-axis. Though they are possible, values far above or below the mean occur with small probability. Normal distributions with large standard deviations have shorter peaks and fatter tails than most. Distributions with smaller standard deviations have taller peaks with thin tails.

Figure 1.4 Normal distribution is symmetric and bell-shaped.

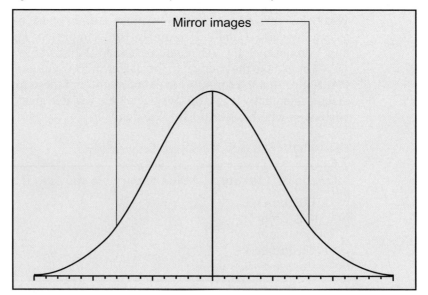

EXCEL FUNCTIONS

<u>NORMDIST</u>: The NORMDIST function in Excel calculates the area within a given range under a particular normal distribution. Directly, this function gives us the area to the left of a given value, but because the total area under the curve is equal to one, we can use the function to determine any area or probability for a normal distribution.

For example, suppose we want to find the area to the right of 36.5 under the normal distribution with mean of 28 and standard deviation of 7 (the area A as shown in the Figure 1.5).

To calculate this area, open a worksheet in Excel. Select **INSERT>FUNCTION** from the menu and choose **Statistical** from the **Function Category** window. Then choose **NORMDIST** from the **Function Name** window as shown below.

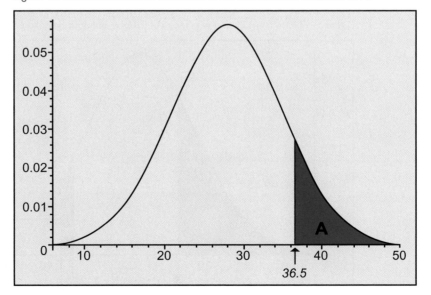

Figure 1.5 Normal distribution with mean of 28 and standard deviation of 7.

When you click **OK**, you will see a dialog box like this, and you can fill in the boxes with the appropriate values.

Function Arguments		? X
NORMDIST		
X 36.5	▦	= 36.5
Mean 28	▦	= 28
Standard_dev 7	▦	= 7
Cumulative true	▦	= TRUE

= 0.887680617

Returns the normal cumulative distribution for the specified mean and standard deviation.

Cumulative is a logical value: for the cumulative distribution function, use TRUE; for the probability mass function, use FALSE.

Formula result =   0.887680617

Help on this function   OK   Cancel

Click **OK** to get the area to the left of 36.5. This area turns out to be 0.888 (rounding off to three decimal places). Since we wish to find the area to the right of 36.5, we have to calculate 1 minus 0.888. This means that area A, which equals the probability of being at least 36.5, is 1–0.888 = 0.112.

How can we find the area between two values under a normal distribution using the NORMDIST function? Suppose we want to find the area lying between 36.5 and 38 under the normal distribution with mean of 28 and standard deviation of 7. This is the region marked B in Figure 1.6. Observe that the area of B is equal to the area to the left of 38 minus the area to the left of 36.5. Therefore, you should find these two areas using Excel and subtract the smaller one from the larger. Earlier, we found that the area to the left of 36.5 is 0.888. (Typing =**NORMDIST(36.5, 28, 7, TRUE)** into a blank cell will also give you the same result.) Proceeding similarly, the area to the left of 38 is 0.923. Therefore, the area between 36.5 and 38 is 0.923–0.888 = 0.035.

Figure 1.6 Normal distribution with mean of 28 and standard deviation of 7.

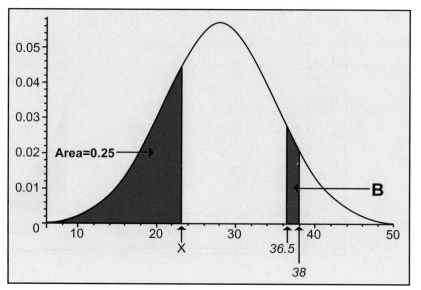

NORMINV: Consider once again the normal distribution with mean of 28 and standard deviation of 7. Suppose we want to find the value for which the probability of falling below that value is 0.25. In Figure 1.6, this is the point denoted by X. To find this value, select **INSERT>FUNCTION** from the menu and choose **Statistical** from the **Function Category** window. Then choose **NORMINV** from the **Function Name** window. When you click **OK**, you will see a dialog box like this (once we have filled in some of the boxes):

Function Arguments

NORMINV

Probability 0.25 = 0.25
Mean 28 = 28
Standard_dev 7 = 7

= 23.27857332

Returns the inverse of the normal cumulative distribution for the specified mean and standard deviation.

Standard_dev is the standard deviation of the distribution, a positive number.

Formula result =   23.27857332

Help on this function   OK   Cancel

In the dialog box, type in the probability that you want to the left of the value (0.25 in this example). Type the mean and standard deviation of the normal distribution corresponding to **Mean** and **Standard_dev**, respectively. When you click **OK**, Excel returns the value of X as 23.279. In other words, the probability of obtaining a value below 23.279 from a normal distribution with mean of 28 and standard deviation of 7 is 0.25.

To calculate the value having a given probability to the right, you will need to input 1 minus that probability into NORMINV. For example, if you enter 0.75 as the probability, you find that the probability of obtaining a value above 32.721 from a normal distribution with mean of 28 and standard deviation of 7 is 0.25. The NORMINV function tells you what value will give you a certain probability to its left. At 32.721, we find 75% of the area to the left leaving 25% of the area under the curve to the right.

Function Arguments

NORMINV

Probability 0.75 = 0.75
Mean 28 = 28
Standard_dev 7 = 7

= 32.72142668

Returns the inverse of the normal cumulative distribution for the specified mean and standard deviation.

Standard_dev is the standard deviation of the distribution, a positive number.

Formula result =   32.72142668

Help on this function   OK   Cancel

Notice how both of these values we calculated with NORMINV are the same distance from the mean of 28. That is, $|32.721-28| = 4.721$ and $|23.279-28| = 4.721$.

The symmetry of the normal distribution makes the distance from the mean (needed to get 25% of the area under the tail) the same in either direction.

THE STANDARD NORMAL

The normal distribution with mean of 0 and standard deviation of 1 is called the standard normal or the z-distribution. Any normal distribution can be converted into the standard normal. The method of transforming a normal distribution into the standard normal is referred to as *standardization*. If a variable, X, has a normal distribution with mean of μ, and standard deviation of σ, then the variable $z = (X - \mu)/\sigma$ has a standard normal distribution. The new variable, z, measures the number of standard deviations X is away from the mean. For example, consider the weekly sales of microwaves at an EE store. Suppose that it is described by a normal distribution with mean of 25 and standard deviation of 5. If X denotes the variable *weekly sales of microwaves*, then the variable, $z = (X–25)/5$, will have the standard normal distribution.

Standardizing a normal variable is useful because it converts distances from the mean into units of standard deviations. This is important and helpful in drawing conclusions insensitive to the original units the variable was measured in. For example, stores A and B have weekly inventories of 30 and 20 microwaves, respectively. The weekly demand for microwaves in store A is normally distributed with mean of 25 and standard deviation of 5 (see Figure 1.7). For store B, the weekly demand is normally distributed but with mean of 16 and standard deviation of 3.5 (see Figure 1.8). Given this information, management wants to know which store has a higher probability of a stock out, i.e., running out of microwaves.

One way of answering this question is to do the following: To find the probability of a stock out in Store A, we look at the normal distribution with mean of 25 and standard deviation of 5 and find the area to the right of 30. Similarly, in Store B, we find the area to the right of 20 under the normal distribution with mean of 16 and standard deviation of 3.5. We can compare these two probabilities and see which store has a bigger chance of a stock out.

Figure 1.7 Shaded area represents the probability of a stock out in store A.

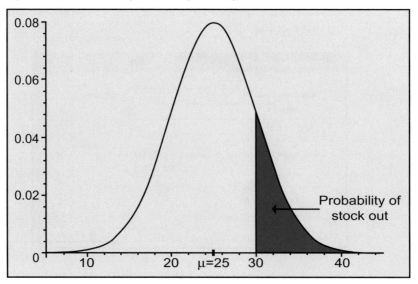

Figure 1.8 Shaded area represents the probability of a stock out in store B.

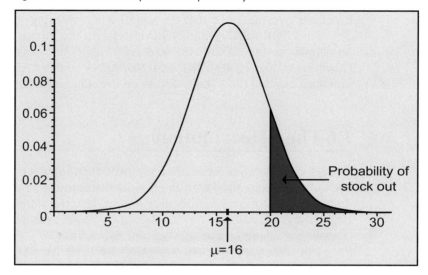

A simpler and more intuitive way of answering the above question would be to standardize the two distributions and compare them directly. This will give us the number of standard deviations 30 and 20 are away from their respective means. In store A, an inventory level of 30 is $z_1 = (30-25)/5 = 1.00$ standard deviation above the mean. For store B, the inventory level of 20 is $z_2 = (20-16)/3.5 = 1.14$ standard deviations above the mean (see Figure 1.9). The probability that a store suffers a stock out increases the fewer standard deviations its inventory level is above the mean. Since 1.00 is less than 1.14, the probability of a stock out in store A will be higher than that in store B. Standardization allows us to answer our question without finding the actual probabilities of stock outs in each store.

Figure 1.9 The standard normal distribution. The shaded area represents the probability of a stock out in store A. The dotted area represents the probability of a stock out in store B.

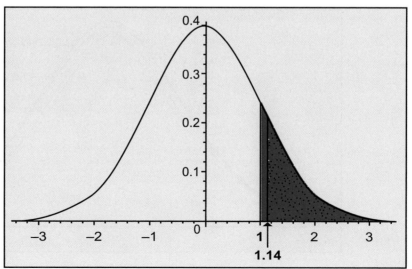

EXCEL FUNCTIONS

Excel has two functions that are useful when working with the standard normal. These are **NORMSDIST** and **NORMSINV**. As the names suggest, these functions are similar to the NORMDIST and NORMINV functions we encountered earlier. However, unlike NORMDIST and NORMINV, the NORMSDIST and NORMSINV functions assume the distribution to be the standard normal.

1.6 The t-Distribution

The t-distributions are a common family of distributions in statistics. In fact, we will use them far more often than the normal distributions. The curve of a t-distribution is similar to a standard normal distribution. Like the standard normal, it is symmetric, bell-shaped, and has a mean of 0; however, all t-distributions have more area in the tails (i.e., fatter tails) than the standard normal.

t-distributions are characterized by a positive number called *degrees of freedom*. A t-distribution with a few degrees of freedom has very fat tails, and one with many degrees of freedom looks much like a standard normal. This is evident in Figure 1.10, where, as the degrees of freedom of a t-distribution increases (from 10 to 25 to 100), its shape resembles the standard normal.

(The determination of the appropriate of degrees of freedom will be discussed further later on when we use t-distributions in connection with estimation.)

EXCEL FUNCTIONS

TDIST: The TDIST function gives the area under a t-distribution within a given range. Suppose we want to calculate the area to the right of 1 under a t-distribution with 20 degrees of freedom. This is the area marked A in Figure 1.11.

In Excel click **INSERT>FUNCTION** and choose **Statistical** from the **Function Category** window. Then choose **TDIST** from the **Function Name** window. When

Figure 1.10 t-distributions converging to the standard normal as the degrees of freedom increases.

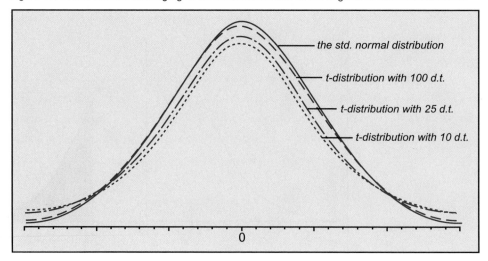

you click **OK**, you will see a dialog box like this (once we have filled in some of the boxes):

Function Arguments	? X
TDIST	

x	1	= 1
Deg_freedom	20	= 20
Tails	1	= 1

= 0.164628289

Returns the Student's t-distribution.

Tails specifies the number of distribution tails to return: one-tailed distribution = 1; two-tailed distribution = 2.

Formula result =   0.164628289

Help on this function   OK   Cancel

In the dialog box, we choose the number, which is 1 in this case, to the right of which we want to find the area. Next, we must plug in the degrees of freedom of the t-distribution (in this case, 20). Since we want to find the area in one of the tails of the t-distribution, we type in 1 corresponding to **Tails**. Clicking **OK** now gives the area of region A to be about 0.165.

Suppose we want to find the area to the left of −1 (B in Figure 1.11). To do this, we have to make use of the symmetry of t-distributions since Excel does not accept a negative number as the first entry in the dialog box for TDIST. Symmetry ensures that for a variable Y with a t-distribution, Prob (Y<−1) = Prob (Y>1). In other words, the area to the right of 1 is the same as the area to the left of −1, i.e.,

Figure 1.11 The t-distribution with 20 degrees of freedom. What are the areas of regions A and B?

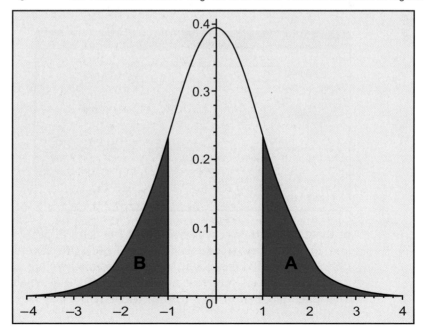

the area of A is equal to area of B. Once we have realized this, we can determine the area of B by finding the area of A. Hence, the area of B = area of A = 0.165.

We might also be interested in knowing the area to the right of −1 under a t-distribution with 20 degrees of freedom. Since we cannot enter a negative number as the first entry of a TDIST dialog box, we cannot calculate this area directly. However, we can see from the symmetry in Figure 1.11 that Prob(Y>−1) = Prob(Y<1) = 1 − Prob(Y>1).

In English, that means the area to the right of −1 is equal to 1 minus the area to the right of 1. We know how to calculate the area to the right of 1 under a t-distribution with 20 degrees of freedom. In fact, we did this earlier. It is equal to the area of A in Figure 1.11, which we calculated to be 0.165. Therefore, the area to the right of −1 under a t-distribution with 20 degrees of freedom, equals 1 − 0.165 = 0.835.

Suppose we need to find the total area to the right of 1 and to the left of −1 for the t-distribution with 20 degrees of freedom. This is equal to the sum of areas A and B. You can do this by finding the area to the right of 1 and multiplying by 2. The required area becomes (2)(0.165) = 0.33. A more automatic way of doing this is to utilize the option of 2-Tails in the TDIST function. In the TDIST dialog box, type in **X** equal to 1, **Deg_freedom** equal to 20, and **Tails** equal to 2. Clicking **OK** gives the sum of the areas A and B, which is 0.329. The difference between 0.329 and 0.33 is solely due to round-off error.

TINV: Like the NORMINV and NORMSINV functions, the TINV function returns a number for a given probability/area. However, the TINV function operates in a different manner. Given an area under a t-distribution with a specified number of degrees of freedom, the TINV command returns a number to the right of which lies half the area entered. For example, referring to Figure 1.11, an area of about (0.5)(0.329) = 0.0165 lies to the right of 1 under a t-distribution with 20 degrees of freedom. To see how TINV returns the desired number, click **INSERT>FUNCTION**, **choose Statistical** and choose **TINV** from the **Function Category** and click **OK**. The following dialog box appears (after filling in the values):

In the dialog box, you will type 0.329 (the sum of areas A and B) for **Probability** and 20 as the **Deg_freedom**. When you click **OK**, Excel returns the value 1.0005. (Since we rounded 0.329 a little bit, the results here are off a little bit as well.) The function, therefore, returns a number to the right of which lies half the given area. The remaining half of the area lies to the left of the negative of the same number (in this case, −1).

Suppose we want to find the number to the right of which is an area of 0.0225 under a t-distribution with 14 degrees of freedom. To find the number using Excel, open the TINV dialog box and type in 0.045 [= (2)(0.0225)] as **Probability** and 14 as **Deg_freedom**. Excel returns the value 2.201. The usefulness of the TINV command will become clearer below when we study confidence intervals.

1.7 Estimating with Data

One of the reasons for EE's declining profits is the stiff challenge posed by its rivals. EE is facing increasingly tough competition from online retailers. Managers at EE suspect that a number of customers who come to an EE store get help from the salespeople in understanding and comparing different products but often stop short of buying the product. They would rather buy the chosen product from an online retailer. Online retailers, with lower operating expenses, overhead costs, and often a tax-advantage can afford to sell the product at a cheaper price than a brick-and-mortar retailer like EE. Such a phenomenon adds nothing to EE's revenues and reduces the quality of service provided to customers who buy from EE.

To cut down on the service provided to pseudo customers (customers who use EE to learn about a product but do not buy from EE) and increase the quality of service for its true customers, managers at EE have suggested several possible strategies. One of the suggested solutions is to set a refundable service charge for all customers seeking advice from a salesperson at EE. This service charge will be refunded in full if the customer goes on to buy the product from EE; otherwise, it will not be refunded. Before spending time debating the merits of various strategies such as these, EE must ascertain whether and to what extent such a problem exists. The manager might want to know the average time spent by a salesperson with pseudo customers per day, the average waiting time for a true customer (waiting time is defined by the length of time a true customer waits before being attended by a salesperson), and the proportion of pseudo customers. For instance, if pseudo customers do not take up much of the salespeople's time, then the problem of the sales force spending unproductive time with pseudo customers would not be so serious. Specifically, EE management, based on costs and industry benchmarks, has concluded that if less than 20% of a salesperson's day (approximately 1 hour and 36 minutes of an 8-hour day) is spent with pseudo customers, then the drain on service personnel by pseudo customers will not be considered a serious problem.

To estimate the average time spent with pseudo customers, the manager could chart the daily time spent by each salesperson with pseudo customers by going to (or contacting) each of the 4,000+ EE stores and subsequently find the average of those times. In practice, observing the service time spent by each salesperson with pseudo customers across all EE stores is costly. Even in situations where all the historical data could be collected, it is never possible to collect data on future service times. Thus, in all such situations, we will need to draw conclusions from a **sample** of the elements of interest rather than looking at the entire **population** of interest (here, time spent by salespersons with each past, present, and future pseudo customer).

> **Sample Size:**
>
> The sample size is the number of observations in the sample. This is denoted by n, i.e., n = 100 means there are 100 observations in the sample. In general, the larger the sample size, the more precise are the estimates based on that sample. When deciding on the size of the sample, one trades off the cost and time involved in collecting each observation against the value of more precise estimates.

ESTIMATING THE MEAN

The management team at EE would like to know the average time a salesperson spends attending to pseudo customers. However, all it has is the information in the sample. What is the best way to use the sample to estimate the population (or "true") mean? The best estimate of the true mean is the **sample mean**. The sample mean is calculated by adding all the values in the sample and dividing by the sample size.

It is important to distinguish between the population mean and the sample mean. Notationally, the population mean is denoted by μ, and the sample mean is denoted by $\bar{x}$("x-bar"). $\bar{x}$ is the estimator that we'll use to estimate μ.

COMPUTATION OF THE SAMPLE MEAN

Consider a sample of service times that the service manager has collected. It is stored in the file **service.xls**. This file provides the observed service times spent with pseudo customers in a day by 100 salespersons. The size of the sample is 100. Service times have been measured in seconds and stored in the column named **servicetime**. To calculate the sample mean, we can rely on the **Univariate statistics** command in KStat. To do this, after opening Kstat.xls, import the data into KStat using the **Import data** command on the **Statistics** drop-down menu. Now select **Univariate statistics** from the **Statistics** drop-down menu (see Figure 1.12).

Click on **Univariate statistics** to get the sample mean, $\bar{x}$ (as well as a number of other values to be explained later), on a new worksheet named **Univariate**. The sample mean is the number corresponding to mean in the Univariate worksheet (the selected cell in Figure 1.13). The sample mean is given as 4880.03 seconds.

How does this compare with the 1 hour 36 minutes threshold set by management? Since the threshold is 5760 seconds (equal to 1 hour 36 minutes), we see the sample mean is below it. We hope that this is because the sample mean reflects the actual mean, but we are unsure. Maybe we were lucky (or unlucky if it means we make a bad decision) with the sample we used. We must continue the analysis to quantify more precisely our confidence that the population mean is below management's threshold.

ESTIMATING THE STANDARD DEVIATION

The sample mean provides an estimate of the population mean. Is the time spent by most salespersons with pseudo customers similar to the mean? Are a few spending a long time while the others are spending a short time? To answer these questions,

Figure 1.12 KStat's Univariate statistics function.

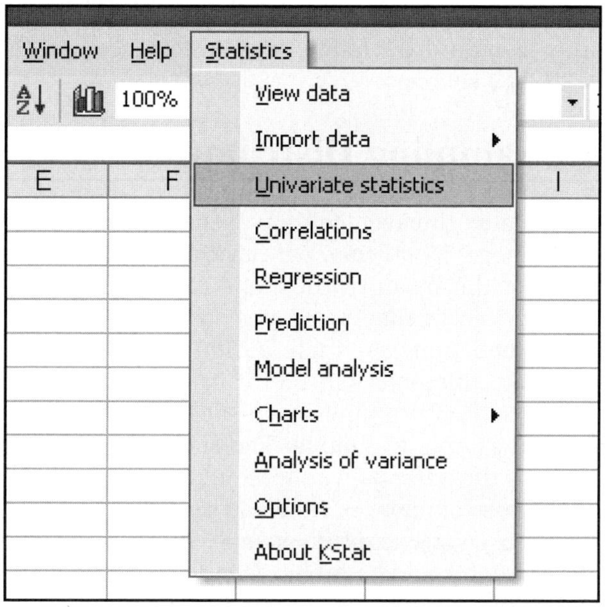

we must estimate the distribution's variance or the standard deviation. Since we'll mostly be working with the standard deviation later on, we'll focus on that now. The best estimate of the true standard deviation is the **sample standard deviation**. The sample standard deviation, s, is the estimator we use to estimate the population standard deviation, σ.

Figure 1.13 Univariate statistics for servicetime (mean).

	A	B	C
1		**Univariate statistics**	
2			**servicetime**
3		**mean**	4880.03
4		**standard deviation**	2610.62218
5		**standard error of the mean**	261.062218
6			
7		**minimum**	562
8		**median**	4700
9		**maximum**	11921
10		**range**	11359
11			
12		**skewness**	0.268
13		**kurtosis**	-0.872
14			
15		**number of observations**	100
16			
17		**t-statistic for computing**	
18		**95%-confidence intervals**	1.9842

The Univariate statistics command in KStat calculates the sample standard deviation. Import the data into KStat and select **Univariate statistics** from the **Statistics** drop-down menu. The sample standard deviation is the number corresponding to standard deviation (the selected cell in the Figure 1.14). For this data, s = 2610.62 seconds.

1.8 The Sampling Distribution

We have estimated the average time spent by an EE salesperson each day serving pseudo customers. To do this, we have used a sample of 100 observations. Our estimate, $\bar{x}$, of the mean, μ, depends on the particular sample we have used. Naturally, the average time spent per day by a salesperson to serve pseudo customers calculated from a sample of 100 randomly observed times of EE salespersons will be different from the $\bar{x}$ calculated from a different sample of 100 randomly selected service times of EE salespersons. The value of the sample mean, $\bar{x}$, varies from sample to sample. The source of the variation in the value of the sample mean is the potential variation in the sample drawn from the population. In other words, since many samples could be drawn from a population, there are correspondingly many values of the sample mean $\bar{x}$. Thus, we can view the sample mean as a variable having a probability distribution. This distribution is called the **sampling distribution of the sample mean**.

In general, any estimator based on a sample will have a sampling distribution. There are sampling distributions for the sample variance, the sample standard deviation, as well as for the sample mean. Sampling distributions are important since they give us an idea about the accuracy of an estimator. The

Figure 1.14 Univariate statistics for servicetime (standard deviation).

A	B	C
1	**Univariate statistics**	
2		**servicetime**
3	mean	4880.03
4	standard deviation	2610.62218
5	standard error of the mean	261.062218
6		
7	minimum	562
8	median	4700
9	maximum	11921
10	range	11359
11		
12	skewness	0.268
13	kurtosis	-0.872
14		
15	number of observations	100
16		
17	t-statistic for computing	
18	95%-confidence intervals	1.9842

estimators that we commonly consider are all unbiased. An estimator is unbiased if the mean of the sampling distribution of the estimator is equal to what is being estimated. For example, the mean of the sampling distribution of $\bar{x}$ is μ, the population mean. Thus, $\bar{x}$ is an unbiased estimator of μ. Unbiased estimators are desirable because, on average, they are right. They are not consistently too high or too low.

A sampling distribution tightly concentrated around the mean tells us that the estimator is likely to be much more accurate (i.e., closer to the true value) than one that has a sampling distribution widely dispersed around the average. This is evident if one looks at Figure 1.15. Estimator 1 is more accurate than estimator 2 since estimator 1 has a higher probability of falling within any given distance from the true population value than estimator 2. This occurs because the standard deviation of the former is less than that of the latter. An unbiased estimator with a smaller standard deviation of its sampling distribution will be more accurate than one with a larger standard deviation.

At this point, you might be thinking we have to draw all possible samples from the population to get a sampling distribution of an estimator. Fortunately, statistics tells us that a single sample is enough to allow us to approximate the sampling distribution of most estimators. We will make use of this fact whenever we want to determine the sampling distribution of an estimator.

HOW ACCURATE AN ESTIMATOR IS THE SAMPLE MEAN?

The accuracy of $\bar{x}$ is determined by its sampling distribution. What is the sampling distribution of $\bar{x}$? Since $\bar{x}$ is an unbiased estimator of μ, its sampling distribution has a mean of μ, the population mean. The standard deviation of the sampling distribution of $\bar{x}$, denoted $\sigma_{\bar{x}}$, is equal to the population standard deviation divided by the square root of the sample size, i.e.,

$$\sigma_{\bar{x}} = \frac{\sigma}{\sqrt{n}}$$

Figure 1.15 The sampling distributions of the two estimators show that estimator 1 is more accurate than estimator 2.

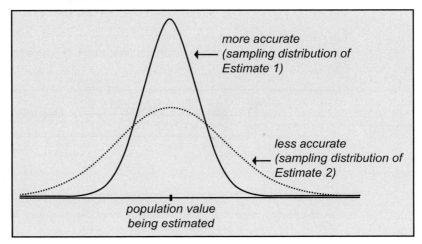

more accurate
(sampling distribution of
Estimate 1)

less accurate
(sampling distribution of
Estimate 2)

population value
being estimated

Furthermore, as long as the sample size is not too small, the sampling distribution of $\bar{x}$ is approximately a normal distribution.[2] In sum, $\bar{x}$ has a sampling distribution that is normal with a mean of μ and a standard deviation of $\sigma_{\bar{x}}$. Equivalently,

$$z = \frac{\bar{x} - \mu}{\sigma_{\bar{x}}}$$

has a standard normal (or z) distribution.

ESTIMATING THE SAMPLING DISTRIBUTION OF THE SAMPLE MEAN

Since the population standard deviation is never observed, we must estimate it. The best estimator of the standard deviation of the sampling distribution of $\bar{x}$ (i.e., $\sigma_{\bar{x}}$) is denoted by $s_{\bar{x}}$, and is usually referred to as the **standard error of the mean.** $s_{\bar{x}}$ equals the sample standard deviation divided by the square root of the sample size

$$\left(\frac{s}{\sqrt{n}} \right)$$

Since the standard error of the mean is only an estimate based on the sample, it introduces some additional sampling error into our calculations. This causes

$$\frac{\bar{x} - \mu}{s_{\bar{x}}}$$

to have a t-distribution with n−1 degrees of freedom[3], whereas as we saw above,

$$\frac{\bar{x} - \mu}{\sigma_{\bar{x}}}$$

has the standard normal (or z) distribution. The additional sampling error is reflected in the fatter tails of the t-distribution compared to the standard normal. This is why the t-distribution will appear so often in this text and in statistics. We will often use the notation

$$t = \frac{\bar{x} - \mu}{s_{\bar{x}}}$$

because this quantity has a t-distribution.

COMPUTING THE STANDARD ERROR OF THE MEAN

You can calculate the standard error of the mean, $s_{\bar{x}}$, in two different ways. Once you know the sample standard deviation, s, dividing it by the square root of the sample size $\left(\sqrt{n} \right)$ yields $s_{\bar{x}}$. Proceeding in this fashion, we have the following:

$$s_{\bar{x}} = \frac{s}{\sqrt{n}} = \frac{2610.62}{\sqrt{100}} = \frac{2610.62}{10} = 261.06 \text{ seconds}$$

---

2. It is exactly a normal distribution only when the population is normally distributed. However, as long as the sample size is not too small, a result known as the Central Limit Theorem tells us that the sampling distribution is approximately normal.
3. This is exactly true only when the population is normally distributed but is often a good approximation if it is not.

We can alternatively calculate $s_{\bar{x}}$ using the **Univariate statistics** command in KStat. Import the data into KStat and select **Univariate statistics** from the **Statistics** drop-down menu. The number corresponding to **standard error of the mean** is the desired number (the selected cell in Figure 1.16). KStat calculates this number to be 261.06 seconds.

Side Comments:

In the above discussion of the sampling distribution of $\bar{x}$, we have been implicitly assuming that the sample from which $\bar{x}$ was calculated was gathered using a good sampling procedure. What makes a sampling procedure good? In a good sampling procedure, each observation should be randomly selected from the population of interest and each observation should be chosen independently of any other. Choosing observations independently means that the probability of choosing a particular observation does not depend on other observations. Such a sample is often referred to as **independently and identically distributed (i.i.d.)**.

1.9 Confidence Intervals

Having obtained an estimate, we will be interested in ascertaining its accuracy, i.e., how close the estimate is to the true value. The service manager at EE has calculated the estimated mean time spent by an EE salesperson attending to pseudo customers

Figure 1.16 Univariate statistics for servicetime (standard error or the mean).

	A	B	C
1		Univariate statistics	
2			servicetime
3		mean	4880.03
4		standard deviation	2610.62218
5		standard error of the mean	261.062218
6			
7		minimum	562
8		median	4700
9		maximum	11921
10		range	11359
11			
12		skewness	0.268
13		kurtosis	-0.872
14			
15		number of observations	100
16			
17		t-statistic for computing	
18		95%-confidence intervals	1.9842
19			

per day to be 4880.03 seconds. It is important for him to know how precise this estimate is. He would be happy if his estimate came within, for example, 120 seconds of the true mean. On the other hand, he might be unhappy and the estimate would be quite misleading if the estimate were 1500 seconds away from the mean. Therefore, we would like to know the probability that the estimate will be within or beyond a certain distance of the mean.

What is the probability that the estimate meets the service manager's accuracy needs? In other words, what is the proportion of samples of size n for which our estimate (the sample mean, $\bar{x}$) is within 120 seconds of the population mean, μ. In probability terms, we would like to know the probability that the sample mean is within 120 seconds of the true mean. Using the notation for probability statements, we can write this as $\text{Prob}(-120 \leq \bar{x} - \mu \leq 120)$.

From the previous sections, we know that

$$t = \frac{\bar{x} - \mu}{s_{\bar{x}}}$$

has a t-distribution with n–1 degrees of freedom. We can use this to do the following simplification of the above probability statement:

$$\text{Prob}\left[-120 \leq \bar{x} - \mu \leq 120\right]$$
$$= \text{Prob}\left[-120/s_{\bar{x}} \leq (x - \mu)/s_{\bar{x}} \leq 120/s_{\bar{x}}\right]$$
$$= \text{Prob}\left[-120/s_{\bar{x}} \leq t \leq 120/s_{\bar{x}}\right]$$
$$= \text{Area between } -120/s_{\bar{x}} \text{ and } 120/s_{\bar{x}} \text{ under a t-distribution}$$
$$\text{with n–1 degrees of freedom}$$

In going from the first line to the second line in the above box, we divided through by $s_{\bar{x}}$. From the sample, we can calculate $s_{\bar{x}}$ by using KStat. In fact, we did compute its value previously as 261.06 seconds. Hence, in this example:

$$120/s_{\bar{x}} = 120/261.06 = 0.46$$
$$-120/s_{\bar{x}} = -120/261.01 = -0.46$$

Since n = 100, the t-distribution has 99 degrees of freedom (100–1 = 99). Therefore, the required probability is the area between –0.46 and 0.46 under a t-distribution with 99 degrees of freedom. This is the shaded area in Figure 1.17.

We can use the TDIST command to calculate this. In the TDIST dialog box, type in 0.46 corresponding to **X**, 99 corresponding to **Deg_freedom**, and 2 corresponding to **Tails**. Excel returns the value 0.65. So the required probability is 0.35, i.e.,

$$\text{Prob}\left[-0.46 \leq (\bar{x} - \mu)/s_{\bar{x}} \leq 0.46\right] = 1 - 0.65 = 0.35.$$

This implies that the service manager's estimate of the average time spent by an EE salesperson interacting with pseudo customers per day has a probability of 0.35 of being within 120 seconds of the true average time spent with pseudo customers by a salesperson daily.

Figure 1.17 t-distribution with 99 degrees of freedom.

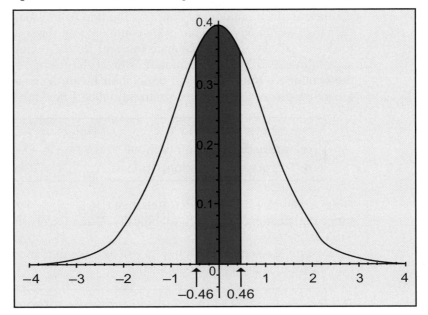

In the form of an equation, we have shown the following:

$$\text{Prob}\left[\bar{x}-120 \leq \mu \leq \bar{x}+120\right]=0.35$$

In other words, we calculated the probability of selecting a sample of size 100 that gives a sample mean time within 120 seconds of the true mean. However, once we have the sample, the sample mean either is within 120 seconds of the true mean or it is not. For this reason, it would be incorrect to plug in $\bar{x} = 4880.03$ seconds (as calculated previously) and conclude that the probability the true mean, μ, is between 4760.03 seconds and 5000.03 seconds is 0.35. Instead, we say that we are 35% [= (0.35)(100)%] *confident* the true mean is between 4760.03 seconds and 5000.03 seconds. Specifically, if our sample is one of the 35% of possible samples having a sample mean that is within 120 seconds of the population mean, then the interval we calculated for μ will contain the true mean.

Why do we say that we are 35% confident that the true mean is between 4760.03 seconds and 5000.03 seconds rather than saying the probability the true mean is between 4760.03 seconds and 5000.03 seconds is 0.35 or 35%? This distinction between confidence and probability emphasizes that the randomness lies in which elements of the population are observed in the sample and not in the value of the population mean. Informally, any given sample you observe may be more or less representative of the population as a whole. If the sample happens to be more representative, the sample mean will be close to the population mean. On the other hand, if the sample is unrepresentative, then the sample mean will lie far from the population mean. Of course, one can never tell whether a particular sample is representative. The best you can do is know the probability of obtaining such a sample.

We have just seen how to calculate how confident we are that the population mean is in a given range. We can also reverse the procedure and find the range that we have a given confidence contains the population mean. For example, what is the range within which we are 95% confident that the true mean falls? The answer to this is called a 95% **confidence interval** for the population mean, μ. Once the sample mean, $\bar{x}$, and the standard error of the mean, $s_{\bar{x}}$, are known, computing the confidence interval for the population mean, μ, is straightforward. However, before we proceed, it is necessary to introduce a new notation.

> For α between 0 and 1, $t_{\alpha/2, (n-1)}$ is the value such that there is a $\alpha/2$ probability of being above that value in a t-distribution with **n–1** degrees of freedom. In Excel, $t_{\alpha/2, (n-1)} = \text{TINV}(\alpha, n-1)$.

For example, if $\alpha = 0.05$ and $n = 100$, then $t_{0.05/2, (100-1)} = t_{0.025, 99}$. Figure 1.18 illustrates the meaning of $t_{0.025, 99}$ graphically. Using Excel, we can calculate $t_{0.025, 99} = \text{TINV}(0.05, 99) = 1.98$.

Using the above notation, a $(1-\alpha)(100)\%$ confidence interval for the population mean, μ, is given by the following:

> The $(1-\alpha)(100)\%$ Confidence Interval for μ
>
> is $\left[\bar{x} - t_{\alpha/2, (n-1)} s_{\bar{x}}, \ \bar{x} + t_{\alpha/2, (n-1)} s_{\bar{x}} \right]$

$(1-\alpha)(100)\%$ is called the level of confidence (or confidence level). A 95% confidence interval for μ tells us that 95% of the time a sample of size n is drawn from the population and used to calculate a 95% confidence interval that interval will contain μ. For a graphical representation, see Figure 1.19.

Figure 1.18 A t-distribution with 99 degrees of freedom with $t_{0.025,99}$ indicated.

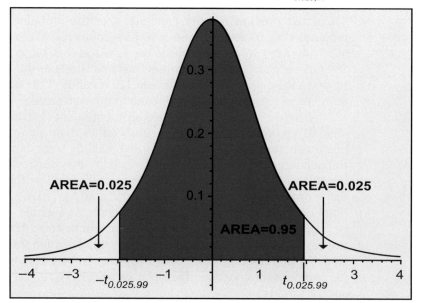

Figure 1.19 95% confidence interval.

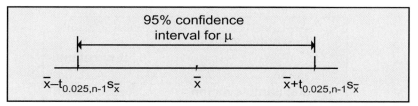

We will see how to calculate confidence intervals with the help of an example. Suppose we want to find the 95% confidence interval for the mean service time for pseudo customers. As we have seen above, to calculate the confidence interval, we will need to know the values of the following three quantities: $\bar{x}$, $s_{\bar{x}}$, and $t_{\alpha/2,(n-1)}$ = $t_{0.05/2,(100-1)}$ = $t_{0.025, 99}$.

We know that $\bar{x}$ and $s_{\bar{x}}$ are equal to 4880.03 seconds and 261.06 seconds, respectively. To calculate $t_{0.025, 99}$ using Excel, we could use the TINV command with 0.05 for the **Probability** and 99 for **Deg_freedom**. As above, TINV(0.05, 99) = 1.98.

Therefore, the 95% confidence interval for the mean service time for pseudo customers is the following:

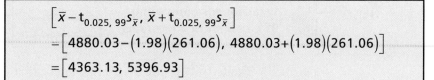

This means we are 95% confident the average time spent by a service person interacting with pseudo customers in one day is between 4363.13 seconds and 5396.93 seconds.

The value of $t_{0.025, 99}$ can also be calculated using the Univariate statistics command in KStat. Import the data into KStat and select **Univariate statistics** from the **Statistics** drop-down menu. The number corresponding to **t-statistic for computing 95% confidence intervals** is the value of $t_{0.025, 99}$ (the selected cell in Figure 1.20). It is the same as we calculated earlier using the TINV command, i.e., 1.98.[4]

The standard error of the mean plays a crucial role in determining the width of a confidence interval. This makes sense since we learned previously that the smaller the standard deviation of the sampling distribution, the more accurate an estimator is.

Confidence intervals can identify reasonable best (or worst) case scenarios regarding the mean value. For example, since the 95% confidence interval for the mean service time for pseudo customers is (4363.13 seconds, 5396.93 seconds), we can say, "We are 95% confident that salespeople spend at least an average of 4363.13 seconds interacting with pseudo customers per day and at most an average of 5396.93 seconds per day with pseudo customers." Furthermore, we can say, "We are 97.5% confident that salespeople spend at most an average of 5396.93 seconds

---

4. The Univariate statistics command always provides the t-statistic for computing a 95% confidence interval only. To calculate the t for a different level of confidence, you must use the TINV command.

Figure 1.20 Univariate statistics for servicetime (t-statistic for 95% confidence interval).

	A	B	C
1		**Univariate statistics**	
2			**servicetime**
3		mean	4880.03
4		standard deviation	2610.62218
5		standard error of the mean	261.062218
6			
7		minimum	562
8		median	4700
9		maximum	11921
10		range	11359
11			
12		skewness	0.268
13		kurtosis	-0.872
14			
15		number of observations	100
16			
17		t-statistic for computing	
18		95%-confidence intervals	1.9842
19			

per day"[5]. Similarly, "We are 97.5% confident that salespeople spend at least an average of 4363.13 seconds per day with pseudo customers."

Now that management estimated the time spent with pseudo customers, what should its decision be? Since 5396.93 seconds is fewer than 5760 seconds (equal to the 1 hour 36 minutes cutoff that management decided on), management is 97.5% confident that average time spent by an EE salesperson serving pseudo customers is less than the threshold. Management, therefore, should conclude that pseudo customers are not a large enough drain on salespersons' resources to change policy given the costs and disruptions involved with these changes.

Confidence intervals may also be constructed for proportions and we briefly discuss them here. The special properties of proportions that we discussed earlier are useful in this regard. For instance, with a sample proportion of $\bar{p}$, the **standard error of the proportion** $s_{\bar{p}}$ is equal to $\sqrt{\bar{p}(1-\bar{p})/n}$. $\frac{\bar{p}-p}{s_{\bar{p}}}$ has approximately a standard normal (or z–) distribution. A $(1-\alpha)(100)\%$ confidence interval for the proportion is

$$\left[\bar{p} - z_{\alpha/2}s_{\bar{p}}, \ \bar{p} + z_{\alpha/2}s_{\bar{p}} \right].$$

---

5. How did we get 97.5% confidence when the 5396.93 seconds figure comes from a 95% confidence interval? A 95% confidence interval is constructed so the mean will be below the lower bound of the interval for 2.5% of samples, above the upper bound of the interval for 2.5% of samples, and between the interval limits for 95% of samples. If we want to say how confident we are that the mean will be below the upper bound without specifying whether it is above or below the lower bound, then our confidence level is 95% plus the 2.5% below the interval to make a total of 97.5%.

SUMMARY

In this chapter, we introduced several important ideas including discrete and continuous probability distributions, the mean, variance and standard deviation, proportions, and the normal and t-distributions. We worked extensively on integrating Excel into our understanding of these concepts. Later, we learned how to use KStat to estimate the mean and standard deviation and other aspects of probability distributions given a data sample. We learned how to use that same data to quantify the accuracy of these mean estimates using the standard error of the mean and confidence intervals for the mean. We also examined the special case of proportions.

NEW TERMS

Probability distribution A description of how probabilities are spread out over possible outcomes

Discrete probability distribution A distribution that can take on only a certain countable number of values

Continuous probability distribution A distribution that can take on any value within a given range or ranges

Mean The center or average of a distribution

Variance A measure of the spread around the mean determined by averaging the squared deviations from the mean

Standard deviation A measure of the spread around the mean determined by taking the square root of the variance

Normal distribution Any of the family of common bell-shaped probability distributions

Standard normal distribution A normal distribution with mean of 0 and standard deviation of 1

t-distribution Another family of distributions similar to the standard normal but with fatter tails

Degrees of freedom A parameter used to characterize the t-distribution

Population The entire set of values of interest

Sample The portion of the population that is observed

Sample size The number of observations in the sample

Sample mean The mean or average of the values in the sample, denoted by $\bar{x}$

Sample variance The variance of the sample, denoted by s^2

Sample standard deviation The standard deviation of the sample, denoted by s

Sampling distribution of the sample mean The probability distribution of $\bar{x}$

Unbiased An estimator whose mean is equal to the parameter being estimated

Standard error of the mean An estimate of the standard deviation of the sampling distribution of $\bar{x}$, denoted by $s_{\bar{x}}$ and equal to $\frac{s}{\sqrt{n}}$

independent and identically distributed (i.i.d.) A sampling procedure that creates a sample with desirable properties

Confidence interval A range of values that will contain the mean of the population with a certain specified level of confidence

NEW KSTAT AND EXCEL FUNCTIONS

KStat

Statistics>Univariate statistics

This command generates Univariate statistics for all variables contained in the current KStat data spreadsheet. These statistics include the sample mean, sample standard deviation, standard error of the mean, minimum, median, maximum, and range. It also generates some other measures of the variables' distributions such as skewness and kurtosis that we will not make use of here.

EXCEL

AVERAGE

Typing =AVERAGE(A2:A7) into a blank cell will return the average of the numbers in cells A2:A7. You can select **Insert>Function** and choose AVERAGE from the list of statistical functions.

NORMDIST

Typing =NORMDIST(20,25,10,1) into a blank cell will return the area to the left of 20 under the normal distribution with a mean of 25 and a standard deviation of 10.

NORMINV

Typing =NORMINV(0.318,25,10) into a blank cell will return a number such that the probability of obtaining a value less than that number from a normal distribution with a mean of 25 and standard deviation of 10 will equal 0.318.

NORMSDIST

Typing =NORMSDIST(−1.91) into a blank cell will provide you with the area under the standard normal curve to the left of −1.91. This area equals the probability of having an outcome from a standard normal less than −1.91. To find the probability of an outcome greater than +2.04 (the area under the curve to the right of 2.04), use =1−NORMSDIST(2.04).

NORMSINV

Typing =NORMSINV(0.42) into a blank cell will return a number such that the probability of obtaining a value less than that number from a standard normal distribution will equal 0.42.

TDIST

Typing =TDIST(1.76,48,1) into a blank cell will return the area above 1.76 in a t-distribution with 48 degrees of freedom. Typing =TDIST(1.76, 48, 2) will return the area above 1.76 plus the area below −1.76 in a t-distribution with 48 degrees of freedom. You may not enter a negative number for the first argument. You can select **Insert>Function** and choose TDIST from the list of statistical functions.

TINV

Typing =TINV(0.05,98) into a blank cell returns the value having area 0.025 above it in a t-distribution with 98 degrees of freedom. This tells you how far in each direction one would have to go from the mean to get an area of 1−0.05 = 0.95 underneath the t-distribution.

NEW FORMULAS

The $(1-\alpha)100\%$ confidence interval for a mean: $\left[\bar{x} - t_{\alpha/2,\ (n-1)} s_{\bar{x}},\ \bar{x} + t_{\alpha/2,\ (n-1)} s_{\bar{x}} \right]$

The $(1-\alpha)100\%$ confidence interval for a proportion: $\left[\bar{p} - z_{\alpha/2} s_{\bar{p}},\ \bar{p} + z_{\alpha/2} s_{\bar{p}} \right]$

CASE EXERCISES

1. Return to me

A Hawaiian hotel chain is interested in studying tourists who travel to the state. One question they are investigating is whether or not tourists who return to the islands stayed at the same hotel as in their previous trip. The data file **return.xls** lists the responses of 1,000 tourists who were involved in the study. A one (1) indicates they did return to the same hotel, whereas a zero (0) indicates they did not. Use Excel's average function to determine the proportion of tourists in the study who stay at the same hotel as they had at their previous trip. Using the formulas in section 1.4, calculate the variance and standard deviation of the proportion of tourists in the study who stay at the same hotel.

2. EE TV sales

The weekly sales of flat-panel televisions at one EE store (store A) follow a normal distribution with mean of 12 and standard deviation of 4. Store B usually has lower sales normally distributed but with mean of 9 and standard deviation of 3. If the two stores currently have 18 and 14 flat-panel televisions in stock, respectively, and neither will receive a new shipment for the next week, determine which store has the higher probability of running out of stock.

If the company has declared that each store should stock enough inventory so the chances of running out of stock are at most 2%, determine the minimum number of flat-panel televisions each store should keep in its weekly inventory to comply with the rule.

3. EE job applications

Certain data from EE's 4,000 stores are not entered into its electronic data base. For instance, employment applications are typically handwritten on paper forms and never re-entered into their computer system. EE would like to learn more about the acceptance rate for entry-level employees. Specifically, it feels that if stores are accepting more than half of their applicants, then the quality of the typical employee may suffer. Since entering these data for its hundreds of thousands of applicants would be expensive and time consuming, EE has decided to use sampling to learn about this issue. Access the data in the file **EESample.xls**, which contains information from a random sample of 55 EE stores.

   a. Use KStat to determine the sample mean, sample standard deviation, and the standard error of the mean.

   b. Construct a 95% confidence interval for the true mean acceptance rate of entry-level job applicants at EE stores.

   c. Construct a 90% confidence interval for the true mean acceptance rate of entry-level job applicants at EE stores.

   d. Assuming the true mean acceptance rate of entry-level jobs was 50%, determine the chances that the sample mean could have been as low as it is or even lower.

   e. What does your answer to part d tell you about the feasibility of the assumption about the true mean?

4. EE stores

The management at EE wants to investigate the consistency in hiring practices across all of its stores. Rather than learning whether the mean acceptance rate for all EE stores is less than 50%, it wants to know the probability that any given store has an acceptance rate above 50 percent. Access the data in the file **EESample.xls**, which contains information from a random sample of 55 EE stores.

   Create an additional column of data called **half plus** that is equal to one (1) if the acceptance rate is greater than 50 percent. (You can do this manually or you can use Excel's IF function which is much quicker.)

   a. Determine the sample proportion for the fraction of EE stores which hire more than half of their applicants.

   b. Provide a 95% confidence interval for the true proportion.

   c. Provide a 70% confidence interval for the true proportion.

   d. Assuming the true proportion of stores that accept over half of their applicants is 0.50, determine the chances that our sample proportion would have been as low as it is or even lower.

   e. What does your answer to part d tell you about the feasibility of the assumption about the true proportion?

5. Cashing out

A local mortgage bank in New Jersey is interested in knowing more about its customers. Specifically, it would like to understand how much home equity customers who refinance their homes are likely to cash out. A sample of 65 loans is contained in the file **njbank.xls**.

    a. Use KStat to determine the sample mean, sample standard deviation, and the standard error of the mean for the amount of home equity cashed out.

    b. Construct a 95% confidence interval for the true mean cash out value for customers at the bank

    c. Construct an 82% confidence interval for the true mean cash out value for customers at the bank.

The bank is interested in the proportion of customers who did not take any cash out when they refinanced. Make a new column of data titled **No Cash** that equals one (1) if the customer took no cash out and zero (0) for all other amounts.

    d. Determine the sample proportion of customers who did not take any cash out when they refinanced.

    e. Construct a 95% confidence interval for the true proportion of customers who did not take any cash out when they refinanced.

    f. If the true proportion of customers who did not take any cash out when they refinanced is equal to 0.5, determine the chances that the bank would have discovered a sample proportion as low as or lower than it did in its sample.

PROBLEMS

1. Given z follows a standard normal distribution, use Excel to determine the following:

    a. Prob(z < 2.8)

    b. Prob(z < 1.8)

    c. Prob(z < 0.8)

    d. Prob(z < −0.2)

    e. Prob(z < −1.2)

2. Given that z follows a standard normal distribution, use Excel to determine the following:

    a. Prob(z > 2.3)

    b. Prob(z > 1.3)

    c. Prob(z > 0.3)

    d. Prob(z > −0.7)

    e. Prob(z > −1.7)

3. Given that z follows a standard normal distribution, use Excel to determine the following:

   a. Prob(2.9 > z > 2.1)

   b. Prob(1.9 > z > 1.1)

   c. Prob(0.9 > z > 0.1)

   d. Prob(−0.3 > z > −1.1)

   e. Prob(−1.3 > z > −2.1)

4. Given that x follows a normal distribution with mean of 55 and standard deviation of 12, use Excel to determine the following:

   a. Prob(x < 90)

   b. Prob(x < 71)

   c. Prob(x < 57)

   d. Prob(x < 42)

   e. Prob(x < 25)

5. Given that x follows a normal distribution with mean of 7 and standard deviation of 20, use Excel to determine the following:

   a. Prob(x > 30)

   b. Prob(x > 9)

   c. Prob(x > 2)

   d. Prob(x > −12)

   e. Prob(x > −29)

6. Given that x follows a normal distribution with mean of 800 and standard deviation of 350, use Excel to determine the following:

   a. Prob(1000 < x < 1200)

   b. Prob(800 < x < 1000)

   c. Prob(600 < x < 800)

   d. Prob(400 < x < 600)

   e. Prob(200< x < 400)

7. Given that z follows a standard normal distribution, determine the value of z for the following examples:

   a. The area to the left of z equals 0.50

   b. The area to the left of z equals 0.18

   c. The area to the left of z equals 0.025

   d. The area to the right of z equals 0.29

   e. The area to the right of z equals 0.10

   f. The area to the right of z equals 0.05

8. For a t-distribution with 24 degrees of freedom, determine the following
   a. Prob(t > 1.25)
   b. Prob(t > 0.92)
   c. Prob(t > 0.58)
   d. Prob(t > 0.21)
   e. Prob(t > −0.25)
   f. Prob(t > −2.05)

9. For a t-distribution with 64 degrees of freedom, determine the following:
   a. Prob(t > 1.55)
   b. Prob(t > 0.72)
   c. Prob(t > 0.18)
   d. Prob(t > 0.04)
   e. Prob(t > −0.75)
   f. Prob(t > −1.99)

10. A recent Gallup Poll (*Will Investors Jump on the Optimism Bandwagon?* October 27, 2003) noted that 57% of investors say the economy has hit bottom. The article also states that the survey included a random sample of 802 adult investors. Determine a 95% confidence interval for the true proportion of investors who would say that the economy has hit bottom.

11. In response to concern by many of its clients, Nucleus Research reported findings from a recent study on spam and employee productivity (*Spam: The Silent ROI Killer* September 24, 2003) The article noted that the average employee in its survey of 117 workers spent 6.5 minutes per day dealing with unwanted emails or spam. Assuming the sample standard deviation, s, is 14 minutes per day, determine a 90% confidence interval for the true mean number of minutes per day that employees spend dealing with spam.

12. You are given a sample consisting of 83 data points with a sample mean of 37 and a sample standard deviation of 21.
    a. Construct a 90% confidence interval for the true mean
    b. Construct a 95% confidence interval for the true mean
    c. Construct a 99% confidence interval for the true mean

13. A sample of 43 data points results in a sample mean of 1.15 and a sample standard deviation of 0.482.
    a. Construct a 90% confidence interval for the true mean
    b. Construct a 95% confidence interval for the true mean
    c. Construct a 99% confidence interval for the true mean

CHAPTER 2

CONSUMER PACKAGING: CONDUCTING AND USING HYPOTHESIS TESTS

In this chapter, you will learn about one of the most important and widely applied statistical techniques: hypothesis testing. Hypothesis testing is a basic tool we will use throughout the course when we want to convince ourselves or others that our data provide evidence for some fact about the world. For example, we will use hypothesis testing to study the effectiveness of our test marketing, identify political gender gaps, and confirm stylized facts regarding stock market anomalies. We will also use it in later chapters as a central piece of the regression model.

2.1 Hypothesis Testing: How to Make Your Case with Data

In the first chapter, you learned some of the basics of how to use data to estimate important features of the world. For example, by observing sales in test markets, you can form an estimate of average sales in a full-product rollout by calculating the sample average in the test markets. Similarly, by collecting data on visitors to an e-commerce web site, you can form estimates of useful quantities, such as the proportion of visitors clicking on banner ads and the proportion arriving at the site through links on third-party sites. You also learned how to use confidence interval estimates to help assess the accuracy of your estimates.

One of the primary uses of statistical estimates is to convince others (or even ourselves) that something is true. Whether you are the one looking for an advantage by using statistics to bolster your argument or you are the person whom the presenter wants to convince, you must understand how estimates can be used as proof or evidence. The method used to prove or support arguments with statistics is called **hypothesis testing**. In this section, we will learn the fundamentals of hypothesis testing and see some applications with marketing and financial data using estimators you learned about in the previous chapter. As we move through this text and learn and apply new and more sophisticated estimation techniques, hypothesis testing will continue to play a prominent role.

A good, non-technical way to understand much of the logic and terminology associated with hypothesis testing is to think of a criminal trial in a court of law. Imagine for a moment that you are a prosecuting attorney in a murder case. Your goal is to prove to the jury that the defendant is guilty of murder. In hypothesis testing, what you would like to prove is called the **alternative hypothesis** (often denoted H_a or sometimes H_1). All the possibilities that are not in the alternative hypothesis are called the **null hypothesis** (denoted H_0). For example, for the lawyer, the null hypothesis is that the defendant is not guilty of murder, and the alternative hypothesis is that the defendant is guilty of murder. The null and alternative hypotheses do not overlap and, together, cover all possibilities. In other words, the null is true, or the alternative is true, but not both. The null and alternative must always be set up so this is the case.

What are the possible outcomes of the trial? Either the jury will find the evidence convincing enough to declare the defendant guilty or it will not, in which case the defendant is declared not guilty. Similarly, in a hypothesis test, either the evidence (based on the data) is strong enough for you to accept the alternative hypothesis as true, or it is not. For historical reasons, accepting the alternative is more commonly referred to as "rejecting the null hypothesis." Since at least one of the two hypotheses must be right, rejecting the null hypothesis is the same as accepting the alternative hypothesis. (Ensure you understand this.) Thus, the two possible outcomes of a hypothesis test are rejecting the null hypothesis and not rejecting the null hypothesis. A hypothesis test can never result in rejecting the alternative hypothesis or, equivalently, accepting the null hypothesis. If a jury finds the defendant not guilty, that means the evidence was not strong enough to prove the defendant guilty. It does not mean the evidence proved the defendant was innocent. Standard criminal trials are not set up to prove innocence. They can only prove or fail to prove guilt. The same is true of hypothesis tests. They can only reject the null or fail to reject the null. This is why you must ensure when setting up a hypothesis test that the alternative hypothesis is what you hope to prove; it is impossible to prove a null hypothesis using a hypothesis test.

What makes evidence strong or weak? In hypothesis testing, we say that evidence (in support of the alternative or, equivalently, against the null) is strong if, assuming the null hypothesis were true, the evidence would be unlikely to have been found. Two examples from the trial should make this clear. Suppose the victim had been strangled and fingerprints found on the victim's neck matched the defendant's fingerprints. Is this strong or weak evidence? To evaluate this, we must ask ourselves what the probability of a matching fingerprint appearing on the victim's neck would be if the defendant were not guilty. Assuming the defendant was not someone who had some other reason to be close to the victim (e.g., assume they were not spouses), then this probability would be small. This is what it means to have strong evidence. On the other hand, suppose we discover the murderer was wearing blue jeans. Furthermore, we discover the defendant owns a pair of blue jeans. Is this strong evidence? Well, what is the probability, assuming that the defendant is not guilty, that he or she would own at least one pair of blue jeans? This probability is high as many people who are not murderers wear blue jeans. Therefore, this is weak evidence and would be insufficient to prove guilt. The statistical measure of strength of evidence, expressed in probability terms, is called the p-value. As in the above examples, low p-values correspond to strong evidence against the null/supporting the alternative, and high p-values correspond to weaker evidence.

So, strong evidence favors rejecting the null (finding the defendant guilty) and weak evidence does not, but how strong should we require the evidence to be before we reject (or declare guilt)? Statistics, like the courts, cannot deliver perfection. Just as a jury will sometimes come to the wrong verdict, a hypothesis test will sometimes lead to an incorrect conclusion. A trial can have two types of errors: (1) The jury could find the defendant guilty when, in fact, he or she is innocent and (2) the jury could fail to find the defendant guilty when, in fact, the defendant is guilty. In hypothesis testing terms, error (1) is rejecting the null hypothesis when the null hypothesis is true. This is called **type I error**. As you might guess, errors like (2) (i.e., not rejecting the null hypothesis when the null is false) are called **type II errors**. Ideally, we would like the probability of making each of these errors to be small (in the courtroom and in hypothesis testing). In the court, we can control the probability of a type I error by setting the standard of proof required for a conviction. For example, many of you have probably heard the phrase "beyond any reasonable doubt" used in this regard. In many trials, the jury is not supposed to return a guilty verdict unless the evidence shows beyond any reasonable doubt the defendant is guilty. Of course, this verbal directive is vague and open to interpretation, but it suggests the jury should not convict unless it is convinced the probability of a type I error is small. In hypothesis testing, as in the courtroom, we have to set a standard of proof. We do this by choosing a **level of significance** (denoted by the Greek letter alpha, α) between 0% and 100% (0.00 and 1.00). The level of significance states the maximum probability of a type I error that is acceptable. So, if you conduct a hypothesis test using a small level of significance, it will take strong evidence for you to reject the null hypothesis. If you do reject the null in such a case, however, it is unlikely that you have done so in error. On the other hand, setting a higher level of significance allows you to prove your point (reject the null) more often but with a higher probability of making the point in error.

We will not say much about the type II error in this book, but you should know a few things about it. First, once the level of significance is set, the probability of making a type II error decreases as the sample size of your data increases. Therefore, the main tool in fighting against type II error is gathering more data. Second, the maximum probability of making a type II error is often denoted by the Greek letter beta (β) and $1-\beta$ is often called the **power** of a hypothesis test. So, if a test is said to be powerful, that means that the probability of a type II error is low. Conversely, a test that lacks power is one that may quite often fail to reject the null (i.e., be inconclusive) when the null is false. Again, increasing the sample size will make any test more powerful.

Now that you have learned the logic and terminology behind hypothesis testing, we turn to some examples to see how this works in practice. It may be helpful to refer back to this section if you find yourself getting confused at any point about what hypothesis tests are doing.

2.2 Test Marketing

Your company produces personal computers and is considering the introduction of new color options for the hardware in the hopes of boosting sales. Maintaining production of more than one color of computer is costly. For introducing new colors to be profitable, the company has set a sales goal of 275 units per week. The marketing department introduced and advertised the new colors in a test marketing experiment over 36 weeks. The weekly sales are given in the file **testmarket.xls**. Based on the sales in the test market, should the company adopt the new color options?

To answer this question let us take a look at the descriptive statistics for the sample data. Loading **testmarket.xls** into KStat.xls and then choosing **Statistics>Univariate Statistics** results in the output in Figure 2.1.

Figure 2.1 Univariate statistics for sales.

Univariate statistics	
	sales
mean	290.549537
standard deviation	53.0851979
standard error of the mean	8.84753299
minimum	168.143198
median	296.830109
maximum	411.650035
range	243.506837
skewness	−0.069
kurtosis	−0.015
number of observations	36
t-statistic for computing 95%-confidence intervals	2.0301

The sample mean of weekly sales $\bar{x}$ = 290.549, the sample standard deviation of weekly sales is s = 53.085, and the estimated standard deviation of the sample mean (called the standard error of the mean) equals $s_{\bar{x}}$ = 8.8475. We are going to need these numbers later.

We can rephrase the posed question: Do the sales in the test market indicate that the average sales per week will exceed 275 units? We are going to answer this question using hypothesis testing.

As a first step, determine the null hypothesis and the alternative hypothesis. To formulate the two hypotheses, focus on what you want to prove. The statement you want to prove should always appear as the alternative hypothesis. The way this hypothesis is established is by rejecting another hypothesis, namely the null hypothesis. Therefore, the null hypothesis is the statement you want to reject. Recalling the courtroom analogy, you prove that someone is guilty by showing that innocence can be rejected.

In our example, suppose we want to convince the management that the sales in the test market justify the introduction of the new colors. That is, we want to argue the average weekly sales if we go ahead with the color options will exceed 275 units. We define the alternative hypothesis as follows:

H_a: Average sales per week will exceed 275 units.

The opposite of the alternative hypothesis yields the null hypothesis.

H_0: Average sales per week will be less than or equal to 275 units.

Denote the average sales per week by μ. We can rewrite the hypotheses in formal terms:

$$H_0: \mu \leq 275$$
$$H_a: \mu > 275$$

The hypotheses concern the population average weekly sales, μ, rather than the sample average sales, $\bar{x}$, because μ determines sales going forward. If all we desired were to prove something about the sample average from the test market, there would be no need for hypothesis testing — the sample average is known and may be directly compared with 275. Hypotheses will always be about an unknown value or values.

The second step of hypothesis testing relates the sample data to the hypotheses. After all, we want to use the sample data to reject the null hypothesis. When would we do that? If the average sales of the new color PCs in the test market were much higher than 275, we would start to doubt that the null hypothesis is correct. On the other hand, if the average weekly sales were barely above or maybe below 275 units, we would not question the null hypothesis. By how much must sales exceed 275 units for us to reject the null hypothesis? To answer this question, we tentatively assume the null hypothesis is true with $\mu = 275$. This value for μ will be the most difficult to reject of any in the null hypothesis since it is closest to the values in the alternative hypothesis. If we can reject this assumption, we can reject the null hypothesis.

We want to evaluate how far away the observed weekly sales in the test market are from the target value of 275. To make a probability statement, it is convenient to measure this difference in units of estimated standard deviations of $\bar{x}$:

$$t = (\bar{x} - 275)/s_{\bar{x}}$$

This value measures the number of estimated standard deviations the sample mean, $\bar{x}$, is from the assumed mean, 275. This measure is called a **test statistic**. In our example, the test statistic takes on the following value:

$$t = (290.55 - 275)/8.8475 = 1.7575$$

The expression for the test statistic should look familiar to you. In the previous chapter,

$$\frac{\bar{x} - \mu}{s_{\bar{x}}}$$

had a t-distribution with n–1 degrees of freedom, where n is the sample size. We are tentatively assuming $\mu = 275$ and have a sample size of 36. So, in our example, the test statistic has a t-distribution with n–1 = 35 degrees of freedom. This fact is the reason we used t to denote the test statistic above.

The third step of hypothesis testing uses the test statistic to find the p-value. Assuming that the null hypothesis is true, the p-value is the probability of obtaining a sample result that is as least as unlikely as the one we have observed. In the context of our example, the p-value is the probability of obtaining a sample mean of $\bar{x} = 290.55$ or higher assuming the true mean is $\mu = 275$. This probability is the area above 1.7575 in a t-distribution with 35 degrees of freedom as shown in Figure 2.2.

We can determine the p-value using the Excel function TDIST. The probability of obtaining a sample mean of 290.55 or higher if $\mu = 275$ equals TDIST(1.7575,35,1) = 0.04379. Therefore, the p-value equals 0.04379. Instead of typing the TDIST formula into a cell in an Excel sheet, you could use the **Insert>Function...** command and select the TDIST function. This opens the dialog box below, which you can fill in.

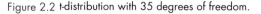

Figure 2.2 t-distribution with 35 degrees of freedom.

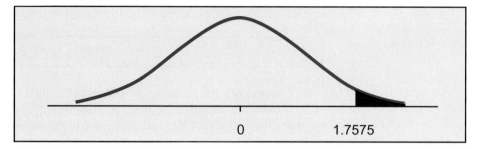

When the p-value is small, it is unlikely the sample results came from a population where the null hypothesis is true. The smaller the p-value, the stronger the evidence in favor of the alternative hypothesis.

The fourth step of hypothesis testing compares the calculated p-value to the level of significance (α, the maximum allowable probability of a type I error) that you have previously determined is appropriate for this test. In statistics, we can never be 100% sure when we make a conclusion based on sample data. Therefore, we have to decide on the probability with which it is acceptable to make an error.

The value for α will usually be given. So, choosing a value for α is not an issue, in particular when you perform a hypothesis test for someone else's use. Often, industry-specific standards and product-specific standards exist for α. In general, the costlier it is to claim that you have proved your claim when it is wrong, the smaller the α you should choose. Typical levels of α seen in practice will be between 0.01 and 0.1. For purposes of this text, if you need to specify α and have not been given any information to the contrary, you may assume $\alpha = 0.05$. However, the level of the p-value has its own meaning even if α is unspecified. Typically, a p-value will be clearly high or low; p-values over 0.3 would typically be considered high (and thus weak evidence for the alternative) in any application, and p-values less than 0.05 would typically be considered low (and thus strong evidence for the alternative). In between, judgment is needed.

The introduction of the color options entails much risk. If sales turn out to be mediocre, your company might face significant losses. Therefore, company policy is to be conservative in the evaluation of test data. Typically, the marketing department uses a level of significance of 5%, that is $\alpha = 0.05$.

The final step of hypothesis testing reaches a conclusion about the null hypothesis. The straightforward decision rule is this: If the p-value is smaller than or equal to the specified level of significance α, then we can reject the null hypothesis. If the p-value is larger than α, then we cannot reject the null hypothesis.

The p-value of 0.04379 is less than $\alpha = 0.05$. Therefore, we reject the null hypothesis. Based on the sales in the test market, we are convinced that the average weekly sales will exceed 275 units. Your company should introduce the new color PCs, and the procedure of the hypothesis test is complete.

Suppose, based on new information about costs, you find the sales for the new colors must exceed 285 units per week to be profitable. What would your recommendation be in that case?

The new hypotheses are the following:

$$H_0: \mu \leq 285$$
$$H_a: \mu > 285$$

The value of the test statistic for this new scenario equals:

$$t = (290.55 - 285)/8.8475 = 0.6273$$

The resulting p-value is TDIST(0.6273,35,1) = 0.2673. We cannot reject the null hypothesis because the p-value is larger than α. Your company should not introduce the new colors yet. (A good strategy might be to collect more data on the test market, which might enable us to get a better idea about the potential sales of the new color PCs.)

What would your conclusion be if sales must exceed 300 units per week for the colors to be successful? The sample mean, $\bar{x} = 290.55$, is smaller than 300. So, obviously you cannot conclude sales are going to exceed 300 units. In such a case, we do not need to perform a hypothesis test. It is clear that there is insufficient evidence to prove sales will exceed 300 units.

Before the marketing department started its test market campaign, it did extensive market research on the sales potential of the new colors. The research effort led to the projection that average weekly sales of the new color PCs would be 280 units. What do you think about the accuracy of this estimate now that you have sales data available from the test market?

We have some doubts about the marketing department's claim and will try to prove them wrong. The alternative hypothesis states that average weekly sales are not equal to 280. The opposite, namely that average weekly sales equal 280, is the null hypothesis. More formally, we define the hypotheses as follows:

$$H_0: \mu = 280$$
$$H_a: \mu \neq 280$$

The test statistic equals the following:

$$t = (290.55 - 280)/8.8475 = 1.1924$$

We are going to doubt the null hypothesis if the sample mean significantly deviates from the value of 280, i.e., when the sample mean is considerably smaller or considerably larger than the prediction of the marketing department. The p-value for this test equals the sum of two probabilities, namely the sum of the probability of a deviation by at least 1.1924 standard deviations above the assumed mean and of the probability of a deviation by at least 1.1924 standard deviations below the assumed mean. This value is given by the shaded area in Figure 2.3.

We can compute this p-value using the function TDIST:

$$\text{p-value} = \text{TDIST}(1.1924,35,2) = 0.2411$$

Figure 2.3 t-distribution and p-value for two-tailed test.

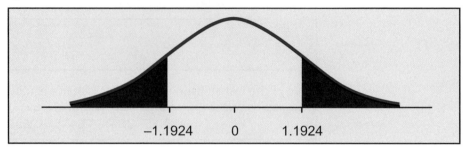

Using the significance level $\alpha = 0.05$, we conclude we cannot reject the null hypothesis that average monthly sales per district will equal 280 units. Therefore, we cannot claim on the basis of the test market data that the marketing department's forecast was wrong.

This last test differs from the previous ones since the null hypothesis is not an inequality but an equation. Tests of this form are called **two-tailed** hypothesis tests. Whenever the null hypothesis is an inequality, the hypothesis test is called **one-tailed**. The null hypothesis of a one-tailed test always contains the borderline case, that is, it contains a $\leq$ or a $\geq$ sign. The strict inequality sign ($>$ or $<$) always appears in the alternative hypothesis.

The test statistics for one-tailed tests and two-tailed tests have the identical form. The main difference in the analysis is in the calculation of the p-value. For a one-tailed test, the last parameter of the TDIST function equals 1 (TDIST(...,...,1)) because only the area in one tail is relevant. For a two-tailed test, the last parameter of the TDIST function equals 2 (TDIST(...,...,2)) because the p-value includes the area in both the upper and lower tails of the distribution.

2.3 Hypothesis Testing: A Formal Analysis

Now let us see what goes on behind hypothesis testing, review the mechanical calculations, and see why they really work.

The first formal step in hypothesis testing is writing down the two hypotheses. For example, in the last test marketing example the hypotheses that we developed were the following:

$$H_0: \mu = 280$$
$$H_a: \mu \neq 280$$

Hypothesis tests are always stated in terms of the true parameters we are interested in and not in terms of the estimators. Here, the parameter we are interested in is μ, the true average sales.

The estimate we derived for the average sales was $\bar{x} = 290.55$.

To evaluate the evidence in our data, we will initially assume the null hypothesis is correct. We then see if our observed result is likely or unlikely given the null. If it is likely, then it is not strong evidence in favor of the alternative, and we cannot reject the null. Conversely, if it is unlikely (less likely than the level of significance that we have set up in advance), we will reject the null hypothesis.

The null hypothesis determines the sampling distribution of our estimator, $\bar{x}$. What is this distribution? First, we make an assumption that this distribution is a normal distribution. (If our sample is large, this assumption is justified by the central limit theorem.) Any normal distribution has a mean and a standard deviation. The mean is the one given by the null hypothesis, e.g., 280. As you learned in the first chapter, the standard deviation of $\bar{x}$, which we will denote by $\sigma_{\bar{x}}$, is given by $\sigma / \sqrt{n}$.

Since we do not know σ, we must use the sample standard deviation, s, to estimate it. Therefore, the estimated standard deviation of $\bar{x}$ (which we will denote by $s_{\bar{x}}$, sometimes called the standard error of the mean) is given by $s / \sqrt{n}$.

To evaluate the strength of our evidence, we want to see how far away our observed estimator is from the value we would expect if the null hypothesis were true. To do this, we look at the quantity: estimator minus the value given in the null hypothesis. Since we would like to use this difference to make a probability statement, it is convenient to convert it into a number of standard deviations by dividing by the standard deviation of our estimator. Therefore, our test statistic will have the following form:

$$\text{test statistic} = \frac{\text{estimator} - \text{value given in the null hypothesis}}{\text{standard deviation of the estimator}}$$

This test statistic has the following interpretation: Our estimate is (insert value of test statistic) standard deviations away from the value given in the null hypothesis. In our example, our estimator is $\bar{x} = 290.55$, the value in the null hypothesis is 280, and the standard deviation of the estimator is $\sigma_{\bar{x}}$. Since we are using $s_{\bar{x}}$ (= 8.8475) to estimate $\sigma_{\bar{x}}$, our test statistic will have a t-distribution instead of a standard normal (or z) distribution. Finally, the degrees of freedom for this t-distribution is n−1, where n is the sample size.

In our example, the test statistic (often written t since it has a t-distribution) is t = (290.55−280)/8.8475 = 1.1924, which means that our estimator $\bar{x}$ is 1.1924 standard deviations above the value in the null hypothesis. We saw earlier that the corresponding p-value = 0.2411, which means that if the null hypothesis were true, there is about a 24% chance of getting a value of our estimator as far away as 1.1924 standard deviations (or further).

ONE-TAILED TESTS

The example above was a two-tailed test because the alternative hypothesis included values both above and below the value in the null. In general, if the null hypothesis is an equality, then the test is a two-tailed test. In other examples, we may want to prove that a parameter is above a certain value or prove that it is below a certain value instead of showing it is simply different from a certain value. This requires a one-tailed test. Such a test is called one-tailed because the values in the alternative hypothesis are all on one side of the values in the null hypothesis.

For example, if we want to prove that average sales are greater than 275, we would use the following hypotheses:

$$H_0: \mu \le 275$$
$$H_a: \mu > 275$$

Notice two things here. First, the "equals" value appears in the null hypothesis as, by convention, it always will. Second, when forming our test statistic we have to know what number to plug in for the value in the null hypothesis. The rule is we always use the equals value. In this example, the value of the test statistic is $t = (290.55-275)/8.8475 = 1.7575$. We used the equals value of 275 for the value in the null hypothesis. Since our alternative hypothesis has a greater than (>) sign, only positive values of the test statistic will provide evidence against the null hypothesis. Thus, the one tail we care about when calculating the p-value in this example is the upper tail or the one with positive values. This p-value is the area above 1.7575 in a t-distribution with 35 ($= n-1$) degrees of freedom. As you saw in the test marketing example, we can find this area using Excel's TDIST function as follows:

$$\text{p-value} = \text{TDIST}(1.7575, 35, 1) = 0.04379.$$

Similarly, if we wanted to prove that average sales were less than 275, we would use these hypotheses:

$$H_0: \mu \ge 275$$
$$H_a: \mu < 275$$

Here, the test statistic is again $t = (290.55 - 275)/8.8475 = 1.7575$ (the same as above!) Since the alternative hypothesis has a less-than sign, however, only negative values of the test statistic will provide evidence against the null hypothesis. Therefore, when calculating the p-value, the one tail we care about is the lower tail, or the one with negative values. So, the corresponding p-value is the one which gives the area below 1.7575 in a t-distribution with 35 ($= n-1$) degrees of freedom. Since the TDIST function always gives the area above a given number, we can find the area below 1.7575 by using p-value $= 1-\text{TDIST}(1.7575, 35, 1) = 0.9562$. The p-value came out large, indicating weak evidence against the null (or in favor of the alternative). We could have seen this without any calculation. Whenever you do a one-tailed test and the estimated value is on the wrong side of the equals value in the null (i.e., above the null value if the alternative looks at the lower tail or below the null value if the alternative looks at the upper tail), you automatically know the p-value is larger than 0.5. Since this is higher than any level of significance you would ever want to use, you know you cannot reject the null (or accept the alternative) using these data. In such a case, calculating the test statistic and exact p-value is not necessary.

Recall from the first chapter that Excel's TDIST function does not accept negative values. We rely on the symmetry of the t-distribution to handle such cases.

So, for example, suppose we want to show that average sales are below 310. The appropriate hypotheses are the following:

$$H_0: \mu \geq 310$$
$$H_a: \mu < 310$$

The test statistic is t = (290.55 − 310)/8.8475 = −2.1984. The correct p-value is the area below −2.1984 in a t-distribution with 35 degrees of freedom. This equals TDIST(2.1984, 35, 1) = 0.01731 (the area above 2.1984). It may help you to draw a picture in cases like this.

MECHANICS OF TESTS CONCERNING A POPULATION MEAN

Step 1: Choose the appropriate hypothesis test:

One-tailed tests		Two-tailed test
$H_0: \mu \geq \mu_0$	$H_0: \mu \leq \mu_0$	$H_0: \mu = \mu_0$
$H_a: \mu < \mu_0$	$H_a: \mu > \mu_0$	$H_a: \mu \neq \mu_0$

Step 2: Calculate the test statistic:
    We have the same test statistic whether we face a one-tailed test or a two-tailed test.
    The test statistic is computed using the following formula:

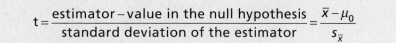

$$t = \frac{\text{estimator} - \text{value in the null hypothesis}}{\text{standard deviation of the estimator}} = \frac{\bar{x} - \mu_0}{s_{\bar{x}}}$$

It has a t-distribution with n−1 degrees of freedom[1].

Step 3: Calculate the p-value:
    One-tailed test, less-than sign in alternative: p-value = TDIST(|test statistic|, n − 1, 1) if test statistic is negative. Otherwise p-value > 0.5.
    One-tailed test, greater-than sign in alternative: p-value = TDIST(test statistic, n − 1, 1) if test statistic is positive. Otherwise p-value > 0.5.
    Two-tailed test: p-value = TDIST(|test statistic|, n − 1, 2).

Figure 2.4 Symmetry of t-distribution.

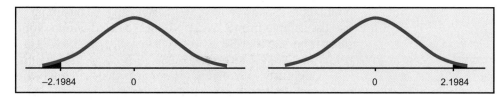

| −2.1984 | 0 | | 0 | 2.1984 |

---

1. Rarely, you may be given a value for σ, the population standard deviation. In this case, use $\sigma_{\bar{x}}$ in place of $s_{\bar{x}}$, and use the standard normal (z) distribution in place of t.

|test statistic| means the absolute value of the test statistic. That is, it is equal to the test statistic if the test statistic is positive, and it is equal to -test statistic if the test statistic is negative.

Step 4: Final decision:

Suppose our designated level of significance is α (e.g. $0.05 = 5\%$).

If p-value $\leq \alpha$, we reject the null hypothesis (and accept the alternative hypothesis).

If p-value $> \alpha$, we cannot reject the null hypothesis (and cannot accept the alternative).

TESTS CONCERNING THE POPULATION PROPORTION

Just as we have done hypothesis tests where the parameter is the population mean, we can do tests about the population proportion. We form the test statistic in the same way as above. However, in this case, since our estimator is the sample proportion, $\bar{p}$, instead of the sample mean, we need a different formula for the standard deviation of the estimator. We will not make use of tests concerning proportions until the next section on two population problems.

2.4 Consumer Packaging

The marketing department at a large consumer products firm is considering changing the packaging of one of its primary sales items. Two alternatives are being considered. To assess the relative strengths of these two alternatives, the marketing research department is directed to test which package sells better. Accordingly, a collection of 72 sales districts (similar in terms of demographic characteristics) is selected; 36 are assigned for testing package 1, and the other 36 are used to test package 2. Sales figures for a one-month test period are collected (in the file **package.xls**). The variables pack1 and pack2 contain the observations on sales for the districts assigned to packages 1 and 2, respectively. Each variable has 36 observations. First, we will look at the descriptive statistics.

Now think conceptually for a moment. What are our two populations here? One is any store where the product is sold in package 1, now or in the future, and the other is stores where it is sold in package 2, now or in the future. The variable of interest for each population is sales, and specifically we want to compare average monthly sales from the two populations, i.e., average monthly sales if we adopt package 1, to average monthly sales if we adopt package 2. Call these numbers μ_1 and μ_2, respectively. The first 36 districts in our experiment give us a sample from population 1, and the next 36 districts give us a sample from population 2. We can use the sample from each population to estimate its population parameters. Mean sales from the first 36 stores (written $\bar{x}_1 = 290.55$) give our estimate of μ_1, and, using the other 36 stores, $\bar{x}_2 = 262.75$ is our estimate of μ_2.

Obviously, our estimates suggest that sales will be higher on average with package 1 since we can estimate the difference $\mu_1 - \mu_2$ by $\bar{x}_1 - \bar{x}_2 = 27.80$. So, if you had to make the choice right now between the two packages, the rational

Figure 2.5 Univariate statistics for pack1 and pack2.

STATISTICS>UNIVARIATE STATISTICS		
Univariate statistics		
	Pack 1	**Pack 2**
mean	290.543889	262.746667
standard deviation	53.0855902	47.8475435
standard error of the mean	8.84759837	7.97459058
minimum	168.14	163.95
median	296.825	265.115
maximum	411.65	350.13
range	243.51	186.18
skewness	−0.069	−0.269
kurtosis	−0.015	−0.460
number of observations	36	
t-statistic for computing 95%-confidence intervals	2.0301	

decision (assuming that the packages cost the same to produce, etc.) would be to go with package 1. However, you have other options. You could choose to continue or expand the marketing experiment, postponing your final decision until you have more data. So, it is worth asking how confident you are that package 1 is the better of the two. After all, a month is not a long time, and 36 stores might not be a big enough sample. In other words, it might be that package 1 is inferior, and unfortunately, you hit an atypical sample. Hypothesis testing can help by telling you how strong the evidence you have is for a particular proposition. In this case, since you have the option of continuing the experiment, you want to be fairly certain of the superiority of package 1 before concluding that it is the better one. You make the alternative hypothesis the statement that packaging 1 is better in terms of average monthly sales. (Recall that the alternative hypothesis is the one you want to prove — here you want to see if the data convincingly show that package 1 is better).

$$H_0: \mu_1 - \mu_2 \leq 0$$
$$H_a: \mu_1 - \mu_2 > 0$$

How do we perform this test? For the purposes of this example, we will have Excel do it. (You can see it done "by hand" in the next section, which explains the statistical theory of two-sample tests.)

Switch to the **Data** worksheet. **INSERT>FUNCTION...** gives us a window like this:

Choose **Statistical** from the **Function category** window and **TTEST** from the **Function name** window. When you click **OK**, you will see a dialog box like this (once we have filled in some of the boxes):

In the dialog box, we choose the range of variables 1 and 2. In our example, variable 1 corresponds to the variable pack1, and variable 2 corresponds to the variable pack2. Since we have a one-tailed test, we enter 1 for **Tails**. We choose 3 for the **Type** of the test since we assume unequal variances for the two samples.

The formula result gives us the p-value (p = 0.01126) associated with this one-tailed test. It tells us that if package 1 is no better than package 2 (i.e., if the null hypothesis is true), there is at most a probability of .01126 of seeing as big a difference favoring package 1 in the sample averages as we have obtained. Thus, we may be highly confident that package 1 is better than package 2. For any significance level, α, above 1.126%, we can say that package 1 has (statistically) significantly greater average sales than package 2.

A final important point here is that you should distinguish between statistical significance and economic significance. That the difference in average sales across the two kinds of packaging is statistically significant means we have strong evidence of a difference. It does not tell us how important that difference is, i.e., whether it is economically significant. In this case, the estimated difference does seem economically significant: Going from package 2 to package 1 is estimated to increase sales on average by (290.55–262.75)/262.75 = 10.58 percent. However, think about the following scenario: Imagine you must choose between two alternative packages and suppose that you are currently using package 1, so you will incur some costs if you switch to package 2. Suppose further you conduct a marketing experiment as above (but with a larger sample size), and find that sales with package 2 are higher by an estimated 0.3%, and this difference is statistically significant. In that case, you would likely choose not to change over (at least for the time being) because the estimated difference, though statistically significant, may not be economically significant. It may be too small to justify incurring the costs of switching over.

2.5 Two Populations

This section expands on the example above and explains the statistical techniques used to compare two populations. This material follows from what you learned about one-population testing though the formulas may look a little more complicated. Consider the following: We have a sample from population 1, giving a sample mean of $\bar{x}_1$, and a sample from population 2, giving a sample mean of $\bar{x}_2$. We will assume both samples are not too small (say n_1 and n_2 are at least 30). For small samples, some extra issues arise (see the note at the end of this section). If population 1 has a mean of μ_1 and a standard deviation of σ_1, and population 2 has a mean of μ_2 and a standard deviation of σ_2, then the first sample mean, $\bar{x}_1$, is approximately normally distributed with a mean of $\mu 1$ and a standard deviation of

$$\sigma_{\bar{x}_1} = \sigma_1 / \sqrt{n_1}.$$

The second sample mean, $\bar{x}_2$, is (approximately) normally distributed with a mean of μ_2 and a standard deviation of

$$\sigma_{\bar{x}_2} = \sigma_2 / \sqrt{n_2}.$$

Two properties of random variables are important to us here. If X and Y are independent random variables, the mean and variance of their difference, $X-Y$, are given by the following:

$$\mu_{X-Y} = \mu_X - \mu_Y$$
$$\sigma^2_{X-Y} = \sigma^2_X + \sigma^2_Y$$

We apply these formulas to $\bar{x}_1$ and $\bar{x}_2$, giving the following:

$$\mu_{\bar{x}_1-\bar{x}_2} = \mu_1 - \mu_2$$

$$\sigma^2_{\bar{x}_1-\bar{x}_2} = \sigma^2_{\bar{x}_1} + \sigma^2_{\bar{x}_2} = \frac{\sigma^2_1}{n_1} + \frac{\sigma^2_2}{n_2}$$

So, $\bar{x}_1 - \bar{x}_2$ is (approximately) normally distributed with a mean of $\mu_1 - \mu_2$ and a standard deviation of the following:

$$\sigma^2{}_{\bar{x}_1 - \bar{x}_2} = \sqrt{\left(\sigma_1^2 / n_1\right) + \left(\sigma_2^2 / n_2\right)}$$

As in the case of one population, because σ_1 and σ_2 are unknown, we will need to estimate them using sample standard deviations s_1 and s_2 instead. Thus, we use

$$s_{\bar{x}_1 - \bar{x}_2} = \sqrt{\left(s_1^2 / n_1\right) + \left(s_2^2 / n_2\right)} \text{ to estimate } \sigma_{\bar{x}_1 - \bar{x}_2}.$$

An approximate $(1-\alpha)(100)\%$ confidence interval for $\mu_1 - \mu_2$ is given by the following:[2]

$$\bar{x}_1 - \bar{x}_2 \pm t_{\alpha/2, n_1 + n_2 - 2} s_{\bar{x}_1 - \bar{x}_2}$$

The test statistic for hypothesis tests concerning $\mu_1 - \mu_2$ is the following:

$$t = \frac{\bar{x}_1 - \bar{x}_2 - \left(\mu_1 - \mu_2\right)_0}{s_{\bar{x}_1 - \bar{x}_2}}$$

The equals value in the null hypothesis tells us what to insert for $(\mu_1 - \mu_2)_0$.

Recall the consumer packaging example on the previous section. The univariate statistics were the following:

Figure 2.6 Univariate statistics for pack1 and pack2.

Univariate statistics	Pack 1	Pack 2
Mean	290.543889	262.746667
standard deviation	53.0855902	47.8475435
standard error of the mean	8.84759837	7.97459058
Minimum	168.14	163.95
Median	296.825	265.115
Maximum	411.65	350.13
Range	243.51	186.18
Skewness	−0.069	−0.269
Kurtosis	−0.015	−0.460
number of observations	36	
t-statistic for computing 95%-confidence intervals	2.0301	

2. The use of $n_1 + n_2 - 2$ degrees of freedom for the t in the confidence interval formula is only strictly correct if the variances of the two samples are the same. If the variances differ, the approximate degrees of freedom to use is given by:

$$df = \frac{\left(s_{\bar{x}_1 - \bar{x}_2}\right)^4}{\frac{\left(s_{\bar{x}_1}\right)^4}{n_1 - 1} + \frac{\left(s_{\bar{x}_2}\right)^4}{n_2 - 1}}$$

So, we have $\bar{x}_1 = 290.55$, $s_1 = 53.086$, $\bar{x}_2 = 262.75$, $s_2 = 47.848$. Our estimate for the difference in means $\mu_1 - \mu_2$ is 290.55–262.75 = 27.80. We estimate the standard deviation of $\bar{x}_1 - \bar{x}_2$ by using the equation below:

$$s_{\bar{x}_1 - \bar{x}_2} = \sqrt{\left((53.086)^2 / 36\right) + \left((47.848)^2 / 36\right)} = 11.91$$

Now we may, for example, construct an approximate 95% confidence interval for our point estimate. It is given by $\bar{x}_1 - \bar{x}_2 \pm t_{\alpha/2, n_1 + n_2 - 2} s_{\bar{x}_1 - \bar{x}_2}$ = 27.80± TINV $(\alpha, n_1 + n_2 - 2)(11.91)$ = 27.80±(1.9944)(11.91) = (4.04, 51.55). We also can do the hypothesis test that we had Excel perform for us previously. The null and alternative hypotheses were as listed below:

$$H_0: \mu_1 - \mu_2 \leq 0$$
$$H_a: \mu_1 - \mu_2 > 0$$

The test statistic is equal to:

$$\frac{27.80 - 0}{11.91} = 2.334$$

Calculating the area above 2.334 in a t-distribution with 70 degrees of freedom gives a p-value of TDIST(2.334, 70, 1) = 0.01124. How does this compare with the computer output? Excel's TTEST function gave us a p-value of 0.01126[3]. The reason for the slight discrepancy is our use of $n_1 + n_2 - 2 = 70$ as the number of degrees of freedom for the t-distribution. As explained in the footnote to the formula for the confidence interval for $\mu_1 - \mu_2$, when the variances of the populations are not equal there is a more exact formula for degrees of freedom. In this example, this formula gives 69 rather than 70 and TDIST(2.334, 69, 1) = 0.01126. This how Excel calculated the p-value.

POPULATION PROPORTIONS

Analogous formulas for differences in population proportions can be summarized briefly as follows. We will again assume the samples are large. (In practice, estimating population proportions from small samples is unusual.) Given sample proportions $\bar{p}_1$ and $\bar{p}_2$, we estimate the standard deviation of their difference using the following:

$$s_{\bar{p}_1 - \bar{p}_2} = \sqrt{\frac{\bar{p}_1(1 - \bar{p}_1)}{n_1} + \frac{\bar{p}_2(1 - \bar{p}_2)}{n_2}}$$

A $(1 - \alpha)(100)\%$ confidence interval for $\bar{p}_1 - \bar{p}_2$ is given by the following:

$$\bar{p}_1 - \bar{p}_2 \pm z_{\alpha/2} s_{\bar{p}_1 - \bar{p}_2}$$

---

3. Look back at the previous section to see the Excel dialog box that produced this.

The test statistic for hypothesis tests concerning $\bar{p}_1 - \bar{p}_2$ is the following:

$$z = \frac{\bar{p}_1 - \bar{p}_2 - \left(p_1 - p_2\right)_0}{s_{\bar{p}_1 - \bar{p}_2}}$$

The comparison of proportions is the only type of hypothesis test or confidence interval for which we will use a standard normal (z) distribution rather than a t-distribution.

NOTE ON SMALL SAMPLE SIZES

When doing two population statistics when one or both samples are small (fewer than 30, say), some additional issues arise. First, as in the single population case, we cannot assume that our estimators (the sample means) are normally distributed unless we think the populations follow distributions close to normal. Second, if for some reason we believe that the two populations have the same standard deviation, then we can make use of that fact to obtain estimates that (in the case of small samples) are significantly more efficient. Though we will not cover techniques for dealing with these special cases, you should be aware these issues arise when you have small sample sizes.

Example: Political Gender Gaps

Men and women may have significantly different opinions on political candidates. One month before the 2003 California governor's recall ballot, a Field Poll[4] noted several gender gaps among the top candidates including Cruz Bustamante, Arnold Schwarzenegger, and Tom McClintock. According to their press release, we are told that Cruz Bustamante is the first choice to replace Governor Gray Davis by 26 percent of likely male voters and 35 percent of likely female voters. Is this gender difference in support for Bustamante statistically significant? A difference is statistically significant only if we can prove it is not equal to zero using a hypothesis test. To try to do so, we use the following hypotheses (where p_m and p_w are the true proportions of men and women, respectively, supporting Bustamante):

$$H_0: p_m - p_w = 0$$
$$H_a: p_m - p_w \neq 0$$

To carry out this test, we need to know the sample sizes. The last page of the press release tells us that the total sample size was 505, so assume 252.5 men and 252.5 women. (This should be approximately right since they were sampled randomly.)

(continued)

---

4. The Field Poll, Tuesday, Sept 9th, 2003.

Then we get an estimated standard deviation of the difference in proportions:

$$s_{\bar{p}_m - \bar{p}_w} = \sqrt{\frac{.26(1-.26)}{252.5} + \left(\frac{.35(1-.35)}{252.5}\right)} = 0.041$$

and a test statistic:

$$z = \frac{.26 - .35 - 0}{.041} = -2.207$$

The above test statistic gives a p-value of 0.027 (=2*NORMSDIST (−2.207)), i.e., there is only a 2.7% chance that a difference this large could be due to sampling error rather than a genuine difference in the proportions of men and women supporting Bustamante. If we were using a 5% level of significance, we would conclude that the gender gap in support for Bustamante was significant.

The exercises at the end of this chapter should give you plenty of practice in using these techniques.

Further information from the Field Poll, Tuesday, Sept 9th, 2003:

Replacement candidate preferences by subgroup

...There is a significant gender gap in voter preferences in the replacement election. Bustamante holds a thirteen-point advantage over Schwarzenegger among women voters, 35% to 22%, while men are slightly favoring Schwarzenegger (29% to 26%)....

[table 3 reports that 16% of men and 10% of women voters prefer Tom McClintock. while table 7 shows that in the vote to recall Governor Davis, 38% of men and 41% of women support the governor and would vote against the recall.]

About the Survey Sample Details

The findings in this report are based on a telephone survey conducted September 3–7, 2003, in English and Spanish among a random sample of likely voters in California. A representative sample of [505 likely voters was selected].... According to statistical theory, results from the overall likely voter sample have sampling error of ±4.5 percentage points at the 95 percent confidence level. Results from subgroups have somewhat larger sampling error ranges. There are other possible sources of error in any survey in addition to sampling variability. Different results could occur because of differences in question wording, sampling, sequencing, or through omissions or errors in interviewing or data processing. Extensive efforts were made to minimize such potential errors.

2.6 Asset Returns

Another interesting application comes from finance. The dataset here consists of 20 years of monthly data (1926–1945) on the returns for various different asset classes: the S&P500, portfolios of small stocks (the bottom 20% of market capitalization of the New York Stock Exchange (NYSE)), of corporate bonds, of government bonds, and of Treasury bills. (The data can be found in the file **capm.xls**.) Investment decisions are often based in part on past performance, so a natural question to ask is whether performance has been stable over time. In this example, we will try to determine if the average return on an asset class changed over the period.

This will be a hard question to answer. For example, could one ever reject a theory that said that every month is unique with a different average return? Furthermore, if you define the asset class closely enough, it is highly likely that the characteristics of the return distribution change across time due to, for example, industry-specific changes in regulations or technical innovations.

Because of this, we will start with a simpler idea. We take our 20-year sample and ask if the data suggest that average returns are stable over the period for the broad asset classes about which we have data, by comparing average returns in the first 10 years with average returns in the second 10 years.

We begin by taking a closer look at the dataset. We can graphically examine the performance of one of these portfolios, the S&P500:

Figure 2.7 S&P 500 monthly returns (0.1 = 10%).

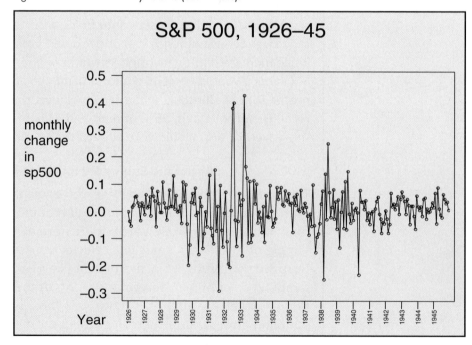

Market returns in this period displayed extraordinarily high variance compared with today.

To carry out our test, first click **Insert>Function...**. Then choose **Statistical** as your function category and choose **TTEST** as your function name. In the following dialog box choose the range for the first 10 years of S&P500 series as **Array 1** and the range for the last 10 years of S&P500 series as **Array 2**. In the **Tails** row, enter 2 for a two-tailed test, and in the **Type** row, enter 3 (for unequal variances).

The average monthly return for the first 10 years of the S&P500 is 1.18%, and the average monthly return for the last 10 years is 0.65%. Notice the substantial difference between the two sample average returns. A monthly return of 1.18% gives 15.11% annually, and 0.65% per month gives 8% a year. Nonetheless, since the p-value for the test with the null hypothesis that the two means are identical is large (p = 0.628), we cannot reject the hypothesis that the mean monthly return is the same in both halves of the sample. That may seem like a surprising conclusion. but the lesson is that with so much variation in the month-to-month performance, as shown in the graph above, drawing any conclusions is difficult. Mathematically, the variation in returns makes the standard error, $s_{\bar{x}_1 - \bar{x}_2}$, larger, which, in turn, makes the test statistic closer to zero and the p-value larger.

If we do the same hypothesis test for the small stock portfolio, we get a p-value of 0.669397. The average monthly return for the first 10 years of the small stock portfolio is 1.2%, and the average monthly return for the last 10 years is 2.0%. Again, despite our large estimate of the difference, we conclude that it is not statistically significant. That is, though the average returns in the first decade seemed to be higher, there is no strong evidence that this difference was real, so you would not want to rely on this difference as a basis for decision making.

SUMMARY

In this chapter, we learned how to support or reject a claim with data. Hypothesis testing allows us to ascertain the strength of the evidence provided by our data in support of an alternative hypothesis (against a null hypothesis). After learning how to structure and conduct one-tailed and two-tailed tests for a population mean or proportion, we learned how to conduct the same types of tests for the difference between two means or proportions. We learned how to use KStat and Excel to handle much if not all of the computational aspects of hypothesis testing. When we apply hypothesis testing to regression analysis later on, the computer will anticipate our interest in conducting certain important tests and will report back information about these tests making the computational aspects of testing almost effortless. Therefore, understanding how to interpret key numbers such as test statistics and p-values and how to choose approporiate hypothesis tests will be central to our study.

NEW TERMS

Hypothesis testing The method used to prove or support arguments with statistics

Null hypothesis (H_0) The default assumption; the opposite of the alternative hypothesis

Alternative hypothesis (H_a) The statement you are trying to prove or show is true

Type I error Rejecting the null hypothesis when it is true

Type II error Failing to reject the null hypothesis when it is false

Level of significance (α) The maximum acceptable probability of making a type I error

Test statistic The number of standard deviations that our estimator is away from the equals value in the null hypothesis

P-value The maximum probability of obtaining a test statistic value that is at least as unlikely as the observed one if the null hypothesis is true; used to determine the strength of the data's support for the alternative hypothesis

One-tailed test A hypothesis test where the alternative hypothesis uses a > or < sign.

Two-tailed test A hypothesis test where the alternative hypothesis uses the ≠ sign

NEW FORMULAS

Generically, the test statistic is computed using this formula:

$$\frac{\text{estimator} - \text{value in the null hypothesis}}{(\text{estimated}) \text{ standard deviation of the estimator}}$$

Specifically, we learned the test statistics for the following circumstances:

Test statistics having a t-distribution

For a test concerning a population mean when the standard deviation must be estimated:

$$t = \frac{\bar{x} - \mu_0}{s_{\bar{x}}}$$

follows a t-distribution with n−1 degrees of freedom if $\mu = \mu_0$

     For a test concerning the difference of two population means when the standard deviations must be estimated:

$$t = \frac{\bar{x}_1 - \bar{x}_2 - \left(\mu_1 - \mu_2\right)_0}{s_{\bar{x}_1 - \bar{x}_2}}$$

follows a t-distribution with approximately $n_1 + n_2 - 2$ degrees of freedom if

$$\mu_1 - \mu_2 = \left(\mu_1 - \mu_2\right)_0$$

Test statistics having a standard normal distribution (assuming a large sample size)

For a test concerning a population proportion:

$$z = \frac{\bar{p} - p_0}{s_{\bar{p}}}$$

where

$$s_{\bar{p}} = \sqrt{\frac{\bar{p}\left(1 - \bar{p}\right)}{n}}$$

For a test concerning the difference of two population proportions:

$$z = \frac{\bar{p}_1 - \bar{p}_2 - \left(\bar{p}_1 - \bar{p}_2\right)_0}{s_{\bar{p}_1 - \bar{p}_2}}$$

where

$$s_{\bar{p}_1 - \bar{p}_2} = \sqrt{\frac{\bar{p}_1\left(1 - \bar{p}_1\right)}{n_1} + \frac{\bar{p}_2\left(1 - \bar{p}_2\right)}{n_2}}$$

NEW KSTAT AND EXCEL FUNCTIONS

EXCEL

TTEST

Typing =TTEST(A2:A57,B2:B34,2,3) into a blank cell will return the p-value for the hypothesis test with alternative hypothesis that the difference in two population means is not equal to zero using the data in the cells A2:A57 and B2:B34 and will not assume equal variances between the two populations. To conduct a related one-tailed test using the same data with alternative hypothesis that the mean from the population with the higher sample average is greater than the mean from the population with the lower sample average, type =TTEST(A2:A57,B2:B34,2,3).

CASE EXERCISES

1. The gender gap

Look at the Field poll numbers in the Gender Gap example starting on page [52].

  a. Justify the claim in the last paragraph that "According to statistical theory, results from the overall likely voter sample have sampling error of ±4.5 percentage points at the 95 percent confidence level."

  b. The last paragraph notes that "Results for subgroups have somewhat larger sampling error ranges." Estimate the "larger sampling error range" for the approval ratings of Arnold Schwarzenegger among likely women voters.

  c. Test using a 5% level of significance if a gender gap exists in the approval ratings of Arnold Schwarzenegger.

  d. Test using a 5% level of significance if a gender gap exists in the approval ratings of Tom McClintock.

  e. Do the same for Gray Davis. In his case, would the gap have been significant if the sample proportions were the same but the sample had included 1,000 likely voters? What about if it had included 10,000 likely voters? What lesson do your answers suggest?

2. The January effect

To carry out this exercise, you need to access the **capm.xls** dataset. Look for a "January effect" in small stocks, i.e., test if the average returns on a portfolio of small capitalization companies are different in January than in the rest of the year. Finance experts are particularly interested in looking for this kind of effect. (In finance, the efficient markets hypothesis suggests that any such anomaly is a profit opportunity.) To carry out this test you will need to use the TTEST function of Excel. An easy way to do this is to first create a "dummy variable" for January, i.e., in the data worksheet, you will need to make a new column that contains a 1 whenever the cell is in a row which corresponds to January (look for the date in column 1) and a 0 for any other month. One way to do this is to type the 1 and the eleven zeros for the first year, and then cut and paste all the other years. Use **Data>Sort...** to sort the data with respect to the January dummy. This way you will separate the January data from non-January data, and you can use the TTEST function of Excel to do a two-sample t-test. Report the p-value and explain what it suggests about the existence of a January effect for small stocks. Repeat the exercise for the S&P500. Finally, test to see if the return on T-bills was different in U.S. presidential election years than in other years. To do this, you need to sort the data with respect to the date column to get it back to its original form. Then, you need to create a new dummy variable for the election years, and sort the data with respect to this variable.

3. Fast food nation

A recent Gallup Poll (July 7–9, 2003) addressed the idea of holding the fast food industry responsible for the social costs of obesity in the United States. One question divided those surveyed into people who thought that fast food was good for you and those who disagreed. Two hundred thirty-six of the 1,006 people surveyed believed that fast food was good for you, and 770 of the 1006 surveyed thought that fast food was not good for you.

The survey examines if people should accept responsibility for their dietary behavior. The poll asked people how frequently they ate at fast food restaurants. Half of those who believed that fast food was not good for them ate fast food at least once a week. That is, 50% of the "not good for you" group ate fast food at least once per week. This compares with 62% for those who think that fast food is good for them.

    a. Does this data show that people who believe that fast food is good eat fast food more often than those who believe that it is not good? Justify your answer.

The same survey asked infrequent fast food diners (less than once per month) if they would be more likely to eat at fast food restaurants if the restaurants offered new healthier menu options. A major fast food company has decided to go ahead with such a plan because it believes at least half of the infrequent diners would respond Yes to that question. In the Gallup Poll, only 84 of the 204 infrequent fast food diners surveyed answered Yes.

    b. Is this enough evidence to convince the company to change its mind? Justify your answer.

4. Pro bowling for dollars

Each year, the Hawaiian State Government pays the NFL about $5 million for the rights to host the Pro Bowl[5]. In return, the state gets to showcase its warm weather to about 6 million viewers in the depth of winter. Additionally, about 18,000 mainlanders who come to Hawaii to watch the game help boost the local economy. Assessing the impact of its spending is critical for the government that spends almost 10% of its annual tourism budget on the event. One important question is if these Pro Bowl tourists spend more or less time in the state during their stay than typical mainlanders who spend an average of 10.1 days per visit.

In 2003, the Hawaiian Tourism Authority conducted a poll of 260 Pro Bowl visitors and learned that the average stay was only 8.6 days. The sample standard deviation, s, was 5.7 days. Is this strong evidence that the average Pro Bowl visitor stays fewer than 10.1 days?

---

5. All data from *Survey Adds Up Return on Pro Bowl* in the Honolulu Advertiser, 2/13/03.

PROBLEMS

For problems 1–3, you will need to access the file **bigmovies.xls**[6] that contains data on major films released in 1998.

1. Studios believe that one important predictor of movie revenues is the release date. Since many young people have more free time when school lets out for the summer, more big films might be released during the summer months to take advantage of the surge in demand. Of course, studios might choose to release their movies at other times when there might be less competition. Another good time might be the holidays when more people have time off to go to the movies.

   a. If summer months are more popular for film releases than the rest of the year, then the proportion of films released during the three months of summer should be more than 3/12 or 0.25. Define p_s to be the true proportion of films released during the summer months. Set up a hypothesis test to prove that summer months are more popular as release dates for big movies.

   b. Use the data in the column titled "Summer Release" to carry out the test you set up in part a.

   c. Conventional wisdom states that about 10% of all movies are released during the holidays, but you disagree. Define p_h to be the proportion of films released during the holidays. Set up a hypothesis test to show the conventional wisdom is untrue.

   d. Use the data in the column "Holiday Release" to carry out the test you set up in part d.

2. Another variable to consider is a movie's Motion Picture Association of America (MPAA) rating. An R rating, for instance, might prevent many younger moviegoers from seeing the film, which can reduce its revenue potential.

   a. Use Excel to calculate the sample average Total Domestic Gross (TDG) for each of the four MPAA rating categories (R, PG-13, PG, and G.) To do this, you will want to use Excel's **Data>>Sort** capabilities to sort the movies based on MPAA ratings.

   b. Use Excel to calculate the sample standard deviation of TDG for each MPAA rating category.

   c. Set up hypothesis tests to determine if a statistically significant difference in population average TDG exists between each pair of categories. You will need to set up six separate tests (R vs. PG-13, R vs. PG, R vs. G, etc.).

   d. Use the formulas from Section 2.5 to calculate the test statistic for each of the six tests.

---

6. From Internet Movie Database at http://www.imdb.com.

    e. Use the test statistics from part d to compute p-values for each of the six tests.

    f. Repeat the p-value calculations for each test directly using Excel's TTEST function. Ensure your answers resemble the ones you found in part e. Some rounding in the hand calculations will give you slightly different answers.

3. Another important factor in determining movie revenues is genre. Certain film types such as comedies might have a broader appeal than other types, e.g., horror films.

    a. Use Excel to calculate the sample average Total Domestic Gross (TDG) for the following four types of films: Action, Comedy, Drama, and Horror.

    b. Use Excel to calculate the sample standard deviation of TDG for each of these four genres.

    c. Set up hypothesis tests to determine if a statistically significant difference in population average TDG exists between each pair of categories. You will need to set up six separate tests.

    d. Use the formulas from Section 2.5 to calculate the test statistic for each of the six tests.

    e. Use the test statistics from part d to compute p-values for each of the six tests.

    f. Repeat the p-value calculations for each test directly using Excel's TTEST function. Ensure your answers resemble the ones you found in part e. Some rounding used in the hand calculations will give you slightly different answers.

4. The file **Hawaiipercapita.xls**[7] contains information about the annual per capita income for Hawaii's four county governments. This information, collected by the Hawaii Department of Business Economic Development and Tourism, is used to allocate state funds for many social services.

    a. Use KStat or Excel to calculate the sample mean and standard deviation for each county.

    b. Set up hypothesis tests to determine if a statistically significant difference exists between each pair of counties. You will need to set up six separate tests.

    c. Use the formulas from Section 2.5 to calculate the test statistic for each of the six tests.

    d. Use the test statistics from part c to compute p-values for each of the six tests.

    e. Repeat the p-value calculations for each test directly using Excel's TTEST function. Ensure your answers resemble the ones you found in part d. Some rounding in the hand calculations will give you slightly different answers.

---

7. See http://www2.hawaii.gov/DBEDT/.

5. The file **bank.xls** has data from a mid-sized local bank. The bank has recently begun offering online banking services to its clients and is curious about the level of interest in the new product. The two columns contain data on the number of online banking brochures distributed on a sample of weekdays and Saturdays. Management has claimed that about 330 people are taking brochures about the new service every day.

   a. Use KStat or Excel to calculate the sample mean and standard deviation for each column of data.

   b. Test the management's claim for Weekdays using $\alpha = 0.05$.

   c. Test the management's claim for Saturdays using $\alpha = 0.05$.

   d. Use Excel's TTEST function to test if a difference exists in the number of brochures distributed on weekday and Saturdays using $\alpha = 0.05$. Do these results make sense given your answers to parts b and c?

6. The file **restaurantstocks.xls** contains monthly data on the excess returns of five publicly traded restaurant stocks from 1984–1994. The excess returns measure the difference between the stock's performance and the government T-bill rate. We would like to know if each stock performs significantly better, on average, than the government T-bill rate over time. This would be true if their average excess returns were positive.

   a. Use Excel or KStat to calculate the sample mean and standard deviation of excess returns for each stock.

   b. Calculate the test statistic for each stock appropriate for proving average excess returns are positive.

   c. Test if each restaurant stock performs better on average than the government T-bill rate (i.e., has positive average excess return) using an $\alpha = 0.05$.

   d. Which of the five stocks has performed the best over the 11-year period?

   e. Which stock has the smallest p-value in the tests from Part C?

   f. Given that the sample size is the same for each stock, how can the stock which has the highest average return be different from the one with the smallest p-value?

7. The file **forbeswealth.xls**[8] contains data on the wealthiest 100 Americans in 2001 and 2002 from a list compiled by *Forbes* magazine. Due to the sagging stock market, the wealth of many Americans declined between 2001 and 2002. We would like to know if the decline was experienced by the wealthiest Americans.

   a. Compute the mean and standard deviation of the net worth of the wealthiest Americans in both years.

   b. Did the average value of the net worth of the top 100 Americans decline from 2001 to 2002?

   c. Was the change you observed in part b statistically significant? Use $\alpha = 0.05$.

---

8. From *Forbes*, 10/6/2003, Vol. 172 Issue 7, p136

8. The file **forbeswealth.xls** from problem 7 contains data on the age of the 100 wealthiest Americans. An interesting question is if the average age of the wealthy is increasing, decreasing, or remaining constant. A decrease in the average age tends to correlate with new wealth being created, whereas an increasing age tends to be associated with less turnover and fewer new members on the list.

    a. Compute the mean and standard deviation of the age of the top 100 wealthiest Americans in 2001 and 2002.

    b. Did the mean age increase, decrease, or stay the same?

    c. Was the change you observed in part b statistically significant?

CHAPTER 3

THE AUTORAMA: INTRODUCTION TO REGRESSION THROUGH INVENTORY PLANNING

In this chapter, we will introduce linear regression. The Autorama case presents a situation where a manager is planning how to allocate a limited amount of inventory space in a new car dealership. The manager has access to data from another dealership, which allow us to explore the relationship between car buyers' income and the amount of money they pay for their cars. Since the income levels in the two areas where the dealerships are located are different, the optimal number of each type of car to stock might be different as well. Projecting the relationship between income and price that exists in the first dealership onto the new one using the technique of regression analysis will allow the manager to plan the best mix of inventory. The theory of regression is mostly left to the final subsection of this chapter. The next chapter will elaborate on the technique and extend its applicability.

3.1 Introduction

Imagine that you work for a chain of auto dealerships. Your company is opening a new dealership, and you are in charge of choosing inventory. To do this, you need to predict what product mix is appropriate, i.e., what kinds of cars your customers will buy. The total number of cars you may stock is fixed at 200 (owing to considerations of space), and your job is to decide how to break those 200 cars down by price bracket. You have two kinds of data to help you. One dataset consists of a sample of (accepted) credit applications for financing new car purchases. These data come from another dealership (in the file **autorama.xls**). The credit application tells you the income of the applicant, and the price of the car each is buying. A second set of data shows the neighborhoods served by each dealership; specifically, you have obtained estimates of the income distributions in each neighborhood, i.e., for each neighborhood you know the percentage of people in each income bracket. You also know something about the auto purchase habits of the public. (Specifically, you know the percentage of people in each income bracket who buy a new car in any given year.) The data for the new neighborhood (which is the data relevant to you) are presented in Figure 3.1. The total adult population of the new neighborhood is 10,000 people.

How was this table constructed? We divided the population up into income brackets using known information on the income distribution in the new neighborhood. This information is summarized in the first two table rows. In the third row, we state the historical percentage of people in each income bracket (nationally) who buy new cars in a given year. This enables us to calculate our expected customer base in each income bracket as a proportion of the total population. Recall that this neighborhood has a population of 10,000 adults. For example, since 16.10% of these adults fall into the $15,000–$25,000 income bracket, and each year 3% will buy a car, we arrive at the number 10,000*(16.10/100)*(3/100) = 48.3 customers.

A first approach might be to examine the mix of cars being purchased in the sample from the existing dealership (and shown in the histogram in Figure 3.2) and use that as an estimate of the percentage of cars that will be sold in each price bracket at the new dealership.

Figure 3.1 Income distribution and expected number of customers by income for the new neighborhood.

income bracket ($000's)	<15	15–25	25–35	35–45	45–55	55–65	65–75	75–85
% in income bracket	7.7	16.1	26.25	26.25	16.1	6.05	1.4	0.2
% (per year) who buy new cars	1	3	5	5	5	5	5	5
number of customers	7.7	48.3	131.25	131.25	80.5	30.25	7	1

Figure 3.2 Frequency of purchases by price.

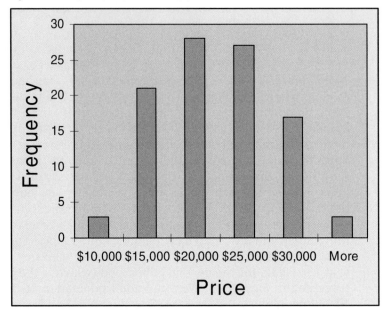

However, this approach has a problem, which is that you know the two neighborhoods have quite different income distributions. Though the average income in the new neighborhood is about $35,000, in the old one it is about $60,000. This suggests that your new customer base will be more interested in less expensive cars, so copying the product mix that is appropriate for the other dealership would be a mistake. You, therefore, decide to do something better: You will use the data from the first dealership to predict the car prices that people in a given income bracket will be interested in. You will combine this with what you know (from Figure 3.1) about the income distribution of your new customer base to get a more accurate prediction of what they will want.

3.2 Regressing Price on Income

The first thing you need to do is understand the relationship between people's income and the amount they will spend on a car. To do this, you will use the technique called regression.

Look at the data (in the **autorama.xls** file). The data consist of 100 data points, i.e., 100 credit applications. The variable income stands for the annual income of each applicant and the variable price stands for the price of the car each is buying. Both variables are measured in dollars.

Figure 3.3 Univariate statistics of income and price.

Univariate statistics		
	income	price
mean	60359	19522
standard deviation	17104.882	5759.35918
standard error of the mean	1710.4882	575.935918
minimum	18900	5100
median	59800	19650
maximum	101300	32500
range	82400	27400
skewness	0.070	0.041
kurtosis	0.081	−0.598
number of observations	100	
t-statistic for computing 95%-confidence intervals	1.9842	

As you can see, the average income of applicants in our sample is $60,359 and the average price of the auto they are buying is $19,522. We get a better sense of what is in the data set by looking at a scatterplot:

Figure 3.4 Scatterplot of price vs. income.

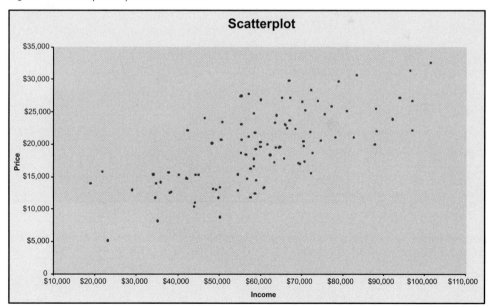

People seem to spend more on cars as their income rises, which is not surprising. More usefully, the relationship seems to be linear, i.e., you could draw a straight line through the scatterplot that would represent the data fairly well. But how should we choose the line, i.e., what line is going to give us the "best fit" to the data? The answer is provided by regression. We will ask KStat to produce the best-fit line by giving the regression command.

[STATISTICS > REGRESSION]

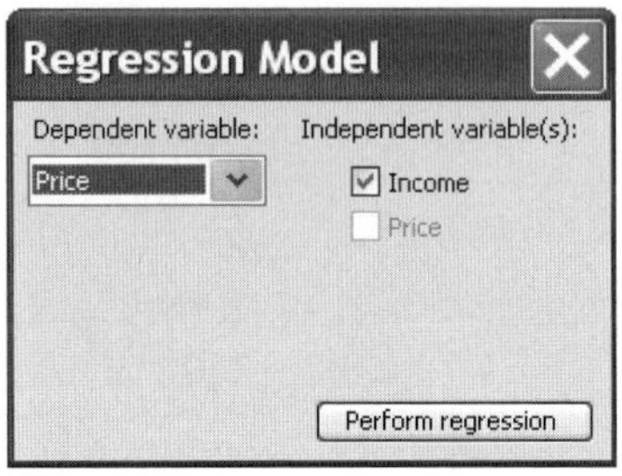

Doing so gives the following output (plus some other stuff we examine later on).

Figure 3.5 Regression of price vs. income.

Regression: Price		
	constant	**income**
coefficient	5787.89988	0.22754022
std error of coef	1572.26135	0.02507093
t-ratio	3.6813	9.0759
p-value	0.0380%	0.0000%
beta-weight		0.6758
standard error of regression		4266.85781
R-squared		45.67%
adjusted R-squared		45.11%
number of observations		100
residual degrees of freedom		98
t-statistic for computing		
95%-confidence intervals		1.9845

What does all this mean? First, we can write the estimated regression equation using the regression output table. In the regression we ran, **Price** is the variable on the left-hand side. On the right-hand side, we have the constant coefficient (5787.9) plus the coefficient on **Income** (0.2275) times **Income**. By equating left-hand side to right-hand side, we obtain the following equation:

$$\text{price} = 5787.9 + 0.2275 * \text{income}$$

This equation represents what Excel has determined to be the best-fit line, as shown in the following diagram.

What it says is that the average amount spent on a new car by people with a given income is equal to, or best estimated by, $5,787.9 plus 0.2275 times their income. So, for someone earning $20,000, this estimate is $(5787.9 + 0.2275*20000) = $10,337.90, and for someone earning $80,000, it comes to $(5787.9 + 0.2275*80000) = $23,987.90.

All we have done is press a few buttons on the computer, so this may seem like magic. Before going on to use this equation, we will attempt to answer the two important questions that will allow us to understand regression better:

1. Where does this equation come from?
2. Why should we believe it provides a good estimate?

Figure 3.6 Scatterplot of price vs. income with regression line.

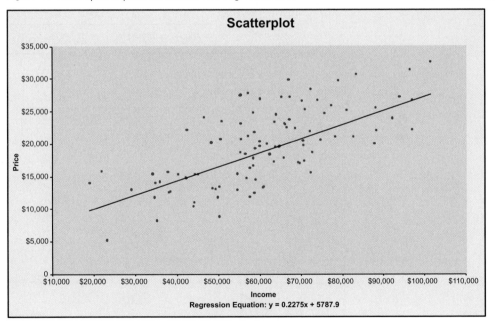

3.3 Method of Least Squares

Given any scatterplot, we would like to draw the best-fit line through the points in the diagram. To do so, we need to have some criterion for measuring what is a good fit. Intuitively, a line is a good fit if it is as close to the points as possible. So start off with a line, and see how far it is from each point. We call this distance the error, and we would like to make the errors as small as possible. We can see these errors more easily on a scatterplot with fewer points, as in Figure 3.7.

In this picture, we have drawn a straight line through a set of five points. The error associated with each point is the vertical distance from the line to that point. (We have marked the first two errors in the picture.) We define the sum of squared errors as the number obtained by calculating each of these distances in turn, squaring each one, and then adding all these squares. Intuitively, the number we get this way will be small if the line is close to the points, and large if it is far from them.

We can use this procedure to compare two different lines for goodness of fit. Do the calculation for each line, and then say that the one with the smaller sum of squared errors is a better fit. This suggests that we define the best-fit line as follows:

The best-fit line is the line that produces the smallest possible sum of squared errors.

Now, we can answer our first question. The equation that KStat spits out from the dataset is the equation of the best-fit line. Examine the following equation of the best-fit line:

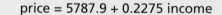

price = 5787.9 + 0.2275 income

Figure 3.7 Generic scatterplot.

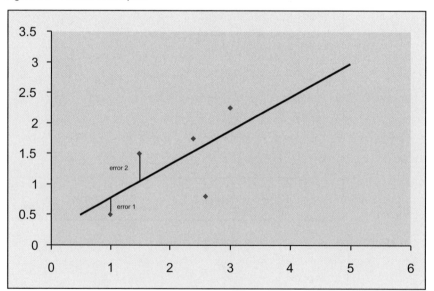

If we take this line, calculate the sum of squared errors, and take any other line at all and repeat the calculation, we will get a bigger number the second time.

How does KStat do this? For our purposes we really do not need to know. That is not to say that we will be using regression in a mindless or mechanical way, but what we need to understand are the underlying statistics and interpretation and not the mechanics of selecting the best-fit line. In practice and in this text, the mechanics of regression are always carried out by computer.

This approach also provides a partial answer to our second question. For example, if you look back at the summary statistics, you will see that the average price of a car ($19,522) is about one third of the average income of the people in our sample ($60,359). So, rather than running a regression, someone might suggest using the simple rule of thumb that people will buy a car whose price is about one third of their annual income. We will need to justify why the regression equation is considered a better way of estimating than this rule. One argument is that the regression equation is better than the one-third rule in the sense that it provides a better fit. We can represent the one-third rule by the following line, depicted as the 'rule of thumb' line in Figure 3.8.

$$\text{price} = 0.333 \text{ income.}$$

Using this line, the sum of squared errors is larger than the sum of squared errors from the regression line. The practical consequence of this is that estimates found using the regression line will be more precise (i.e., have a smaller variance) than estimates from the rule of thumb or any other line.

Now we will examine how to use the regression equation to predict demand for cars at our dealership.

Figure 3.8 Scatterplot of price vs. income with regression and rule of thumb lines.

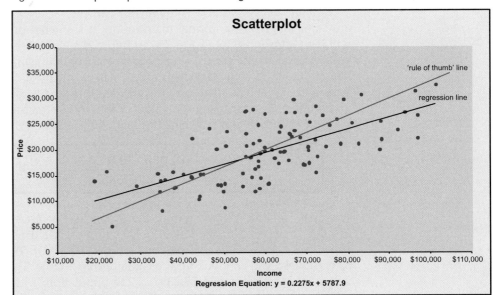

3.4 Predicting Spending from the Regression Equation

Think about the people in our customer base (in statistics jargon, the population) who earn $30,000 a year. Not all of them will want to spend the same amount on a car, so what we would like to find is a distribution of their spending levels. We will make two assumptions about the distribution of spending levels for a given income.

ASSUMPTIONS

1. For each income level, spending on a car purchase is approximately normally distributed.
2. The distribution for different income levels need not have the same mean, but it does have to have the same standard deviation.

Later in this text, we will discuss the second of these assumptions in some detail. For the time being, we will ask you to take their validity on trust. They can both be tested, and in this case, the tests suggest they are reasonably correct.

   Starting with our $30,000 income group, the first assumption implies we only need to know two things about the distribution of spending for this group: its mean and its standard deviation. The regression output gives us estimates of both. The mean is estimated by setting income = $30,000 in the regression equation, so it is $(5,787.9 + 0.2275*30,000) = $12,612.90. You can find an estimate of the standard deviation in the regression output above in the row labeled standard error of regression. It is estimated by s = 4266.86, i.e., it is $4,266.86. So, our best guess is that, among people with annual income of $30,000, spending on a car purchase is normally distributed with a mean of $12,612.90 and a standard deviation of $4,266.86, as shown in the histogram in Figure 3.9. The estimate of the mean depends on these people having an income of $30,000, but the estimate of the standard deviation does not, which fits assumption 2 above.

   What we will do now is divide our cars into a series of price brackets and use our knowledge of the normal distribution to say what proportion of these people will buy autos in each bracket. For example, we know that the proportion of prices paid by this income group, which are below $16,000, is the same as the area to the left of 16,000 in a normal distribution with a mean of 12,612.90 and a standard deviation of 4,266.86. One way to calculate this area is to use the standard normal distribution. Standardizing the value 16,000 by subtracting the mean and dividing by the standard deviation yields the following:

$$z = \frac{16,000 - 12,612.90}{4,266.86} = 0.7938$$

Therefore, for this income group, the proportion of prices paid that are less than $16,000 is the area to the left of 0.7938 in a standard normal distribution. Using Excel, you can calculate this area by typing =**NORMSDIST(0.7938)** in an empty cell. Alternatively, you can look up the value from a z-table. This area is 0.7863. So, this tells us that an estimated 78.63% of the population in the $30,000 income group buys cars priced below $16,000. By a similar analysis, the proportion buying cars priced below $14,000 is 62.74%, so this tells us that (.7863−.6274)*100 = 15.89% of these customers will buy in the $14,000–$16,000 price bracket. We can do the same

Figure 3.9 Price distribution for income level of $30,000.

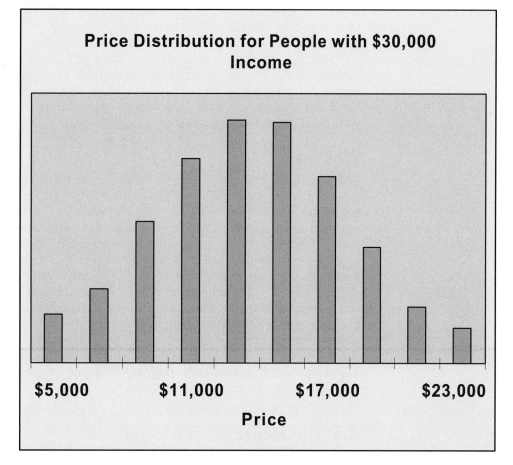

calculations for $10,000–$12,000, $12,000–$14,000, and every other price bracket, giving a complete picture of the demand for customers with an income of $30,000. (For convenience, we have divided car prices into $2,000 price brackets.)

We now know something about the price preferences of the customers with a given income. How do we use this information to get a picture of the overall spending distribution? Well, there are several steps.

For each income bracket in the table giving the income distribution for the new neighborhood, we will assume that all individuals in a bracket behave as if they had the median income for that bracket. The median for this neighborhood happens to be the mid-point of each income range, with the exception of the lowest income bracket, for which the median is $10,000. Also, the median for the highest bracket is $120,000. Now, for each income bracket, we use the regression estimates to calculate the number of customers we expect to fall inside each price bracket.

For example, if we want to predict the number of customers in the $35,000–$45,000 income bracket who will buy a car in the $12,000–14,000 car bracket, we proceed as follows: First, we calculate, using the regression estimates and the median income for the bracket, that purchases of cars by that income bracket are normally distributed with a mean of $(5,787.9 + .2275*40,000) = $14,887.90 and a standard deviation of $4,266.86. Then, we use the normal distribution to find what proportion of that demand lies between $12,000 and $14,000.

You can work this out by the same technique as above. You should get an answer of about 0.1683 (or 16.83%). Then, multiply this proportion by the number of customers in that income bracket (131, from Figure 3.1) to get the number who are expected to buy in that price bracket ((131*0.1683) = 22.05, or about 22 people).

For any particular price bracket, add the number of customers from each income bracket who will want to buy a car in that price bracket. This gives the total number of cars in that bracket that would be sold in a year, given our neighborhood of 10,000 people. This gives you the demand information you need to make your decision on what mix of cars to stock.

WARNING:

This procedure is reasonably good. However, we have made one dubious approximation. For the purposes of our prediction, we are acting as if the estimates of the mean and standard deviations of prices for each income level were exact; they are not. The mean and standard deviations are estimates from our sample and, therefore, subject to sampling error. This could be taken into account by using slightly more sophisticated statistical techniques, which we will learn when we talk about prediction intervals. Meanwhile, you should be aware that we have used this shortcut. Of course, some other approximations are present as well, due to income bracketing. Additionally, you should worry about whether the sampling technique is genuinely unbiased since people who buy cars on credit are not necessarily a representative sample of all car buyers. The problem with income bracketing is not too serious since we can always use smaller brackets to reduce the degree of approximation, but we can do nothing about the sampling problem short of collecting more data from a different source.

3.5 The Regression Model

Remember the basic ideas behind statistical inference: We have a **population** of interest, and this population is characterized by some **population parameters** that we would like to know. We take a **sample** from the population, and **estimate** the parameters. Since any estimate is based on a sample, it will contain some **sampling error**, and we use probability theory to quantify that error, so we are able to produce confidence and prediction intervals and carry out hypothesis tests. For example, our population might be the adults living in Texas, and we may want to know the average amount they spend on dining out each year. The relevant population parameter is, therefore, the population mean, and we would estimate it from a sample by looking at the sample mean. For reasonable sample sizes, we know the sampling error is normally distributed around the true value, with standard deviation equal to

$$\sigma_{\bar{x}} = \frac{\sigma}{\sqrt{n}},$$

where σ is the population standard deviation.

Regression analysis involves the same concepts; however, the population parameters are different, and we must be certain we understand exactly what they are. We will illustrate them using the Autorama example.

DIVIDING THE POPULATION BY INCOME LEVEL

When predicting auto purchases, we divided the population (our customers) into many sub-populations according to income. In other words, we did not think about the distribution of demand for all our customers but about the distribution for all customers with a given annual income.

Each of these sub-populations has different auto purchase patterns. For any given sub-population, a mean price exists that people in that population pay for a car. If we knew these means, we could see how the mean price varies across the different income brackets. A nice way to do so is by drawing a graph of mean price against income.

> **Regression Assumption 1. This graph would be a straight line.**

Of course, this assumption may not be true. Later on, we will talk about how you can check the data to see whether this is a reasonable assumption for any particular dataset, and what you can do if it is not.

Returning to our example, as a consequence of Regression Assumption 1, we may assume there are some constants, β_0 and β_1, such that for any given income level, the average price paid by people in that income level satisfies the following equation:

$$\text{average price} = \beta_0 + \beta_1(\text{income})$$

β_0 is the intercept and β_1 the slope of the graph of average price against income as shown in Figure 3.10 below.

Figure 3.10 Regression line for price and income.

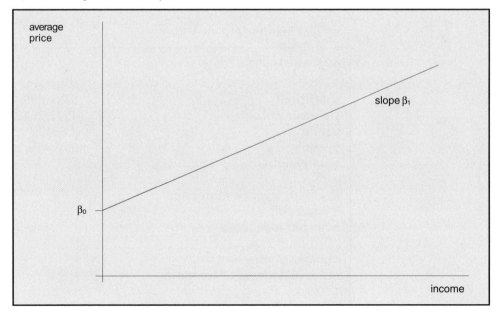

WHAT REGRESSION ESTIMATES

We can now talk about two of the population parameters regression estimates: They are the intercept and slope of this line, i.e., the constants β_0 and β_1. Look at the regression output in Figure 3.11.

What is KStat providing here? Based on our sample, 5787.9 is the best estimate of the intercept β_0, and 0.2275 is the best estimate of the slope β_1. The constants β_0 and β_1 are the population parameters we would like to know, and the regression formulas that KStat implements give us estimates (often written $b_0 = 5787.9$ and $b_1 = 0.2275$) of the parameters. We can use these to estimate the average expenditure for any income group by substituting for income in the regression equation provided by KStat. This estimate is often written $\hat{y}$ and is referred to as a predicted value or a fitted value.

QUANTIFYING THE SAMPLING ERROR

These estimates are based on our sample, and if we had a different sample, we would get different estimates. Remember from Chapter 1, by thinking about the sample mean obtained from each possible sample we may obtain a sampling distribution, i.e., something like a histogram of all the possible sample means one would obtain from different random samples of the population. The same concept applies here, so we can talk about the sampling distributions of b_0 and b_1. We are less often interested in b_0, so we'll focus on b_1 and summarize what we have learned so far.

The idea is that when we compare two different groups of people, one of whom has an average income (say) \$1,000 higher than the other, the difference between the average amount that the higher-income group will spend on an automobile and the average amount that the lower-income group will spend on an automobile is equal to \$1,000 times some constant β_1. (This conclusion follows from the straight-line equation.) We do not know this constant, but we can use our

Figure 3.11 Regression of price vs. income.

Regression: Price		
	constant	income
coefficient	5787.89988	0.22754022
std error of coef	1572.26135	0.02507093
t-ratio	3.6813	9.0759
p-value	0.0380%	0.0000%
beta-weight		0.6758
standard error of regression		4266.85781
R-squared		45.67%
adjusted R-squared		45.11%
number of observations		100
residual degrees of freedom		98
t-statistic for computing		
95%-confidence intervals		1.9845

sample to estimate it, which we do by taking the slope of KStat's best-fit line through our sample points. The estimate this produces is called b_1, and it is a random variable, i.e., the outcome of an experiment. If we repeated the experiment by taking a different sample, we would get a new estimate, and if we did this many times, we would get a distribution of estimates. The important things about this distribution are the following:

> 1. On average, b_1 is right, i.e., $E(b_1) = \beta_1$ (b_1 is called an **unbiased** estimator).
>
> 2. The distribution of b_1 has a standard deviation, written σ_{b_1}, which is estimated by KStat. We call this estimate s_{b_1}, and in this example, $s_{b_1} = 0.02507$. KStat reports this number in the std error of coef row as seen in Figure 3.10.
>
> 3. We can generally assume that the distribution of b_1 is normal.

Regression analysis usually makes a number of other assumptions of varying importance in addition to the straight-line assumption. Later, we will discuss some of these other assumptions and talk about what happens when they are not satisfied. Nothing we have said so far in this section depends on the other assumptions, with one exception, noted below. For the time being, we will mention one of these assumptions, which you have seen in the previous section:

> Regression Assumption 2. The standard deviation of price for each income group has the same value, σ.

Of course, σ is another unknown population parameter. KStat produces an estimate of σ in the regression output, which is denoted by s. KStat prints the value of s in the row labeled standard error of regression (here, s = 4266.86). The units for this estimate are the same as the units for your dependent (y) variable. Here, s = $4266.86. The formula KStat uses to get s_{b_1} (= .02507 here) makes use of this s, so point 2 in the box above does depend on this assumption.

Do not confuse σ, the standard deviation of price for each income group, with σ_{b_1}, the standard deviation of our estimate of β_1. In Chapter 1, we made the same distinction between the population standard deviation, σ, and the standard deviation of the sample mean, $\sigma_{\bar{x}}$.

CONFIDENCE INTERVALS ON THE REGRESSION COEFFICIENTS

We can use our knowledge of the sampling distributions to make statistical inferences, i.e., to form confidence and prediction intervals and carry out hypothesis tests with our regression results.

Since b_1 is distributed normally, we know

$$\frac{b_1 - \beta_1}{\sigma_{b_1}}$$

has the standard normal distribution. So, for example, we can be 95% confident that β_1 is within ± 1.96 standard deviations of b_1. In other words, $b_1 \pm (1.96)\sigma_{b_1}$ forms a 95% confidence interval for β_1. We do not know σ_{b_1}, so we use our estimate s_{b_1}

instead and must use a t-distribution instead of the standard normal. The general formula for a $100(1-\alpha)\%$ confidence interval for β_1 is the following:

$$b_1 \pm t_{\alpha/2,n-2} s_{b_1}$$

$t_{\alpha/2,n-2}$ is the $\alpha/2$ t-value with $n-2$ degrees of freedom (where n is the sample size) (=**TINV**(α, $n - 2$)). Later, you will see that the KStat output tells you how many degrees of freedom to use, so you have one less thing to worry about.

For example, try to produce a 90% confidence interval for β_1. If you look at the last regression output, you will see the sample size was 100, so we have 98 degrees of freedom. (This is given directly in the regression output table as the **residual degrees of freedom.**) The 90% confidence interval is $.2275 \pm t_{.05,98}(.02507) = .2275 \pm \text{TINV}(.1,98)(.02507) = .2275 \pm (1.6606)(.02507) = .2275 \pm .0416 = (.1859, .2691)$. The interpretation is that 90% of the time we take a sample of size 100 and use it to calculate an interval according to the formula, the interval will contain the true slope, β_1. We are therefore 90% confident $(.1859, .2691)$ contains the true slope, β_1.

HYPOTHESIS TESTS ON THE REGRESSION COEFFICIENTS

Suppose the common industry wisdom is people will spend on average an extra $180 on their new auto for every extra $1,000 in income. In terms of our regression model, this says that the true slope, β_1, of the regression line is 0.180. (Make sure you understand why.) Our estimate seems to be higher than this, but is the difference large enough to indicate strong evidence that the true slope is higher than 0.180? If it is, then we might want to re-evaluate the common wisdom. Therefore, we would like to know if our estimate is statistically significantly greater than 0.180. We test this by the following hypothesis test:

$$H_0: \beta_1 \leq .180$$
$$H_a: \beta_1 > .180$$

We will follow the usual hypothesis-testing procedure. Give the benefit of the doubt to the null hypothesis by assuming that $\beta_1 = .180$. Under this assumption, we know our test statistic, t, follows the t-distribution with 98 degrees of freedom:

$$t = \frac{b_1 - .180}{s_{b_1}}$$

Using KStat's numbers, we have $t = (.2275 - .180)/.02507 = 1.895$. To determine the p-value, use Excel's **TDIST** function remembering that we are conducting a one-tailed test and want the area in the upper tail. This function (=**TDIST**(1.895, 98, 1)) yields a p-value of 0.0305. This tells us that if the null hypothesis were true, there would only be about a 3% chance that a sample of size 100 would give an estimated slope as large as ours here. So, unless we want to be particularly careful about making a type I error (i.e., unless we want to set our level of significance, α, at less than .03), we will reject the null and conclude that our results do shed doubt on the conventional wisdom and strongly suggest that for every additional $1,000 of income, people spend more than an additional $180 when they buy a new car.

READING SIGNIFICANCE IN THE REGRESSION OUTPUT

We can now explain the **t-ratio** and **p-value** rows of KStat's regression output. Consider the following (two-tailed) hypothesis test:

$$H_0: \beta_1 = 0$$
$$H_a: \beta_1 \neq 0$$

The relevant test statistic would be

$$t = \frac{b_1 - 0}{s_{b_1}} = .2275 / .02507 = 9.075.$$

This is so large that the corresponding p-value is 0.000. If you look back at the regression output in Figure 3.11, you will see KStat has done this calculation for us: In the "income" column that tells us about b_1, the row labeled **t-ratio** contains the test statistic, and the next row labeled **p-value** contains the p-value. Similarly, if we wanted to test whether or not the true intercept, β_0, is equal to 0, we can look in the constant column to read the p-value for the test where $\beta_0 = 0$ is the null hypothesis (which we reject since p = 0.00038).

Traditionally, people have been especially interested in testing coefficients against zero because they often use regression to test if one variable has any effect on another. In this case, saying that $\beta_1 = 0$ means that income has no effect on the price people pay for cars. Since the test is so commonly used, KStat and any standard statistical package reports it automatically. Typically, we will be able to determine what affects what but we also need to know the effect's size. The example here illustrates that nicely. Rejecting the null in this automatic hyopthesis test allows us to conclude that your income affects how much you spend on a car. This is not very profound. However, we do care that the extent of this effect is larger than the conventional wisdom. In other situations, we may be interested in small non-zero effects. (For example, in finance, tiny effects can provide arbitrage opportunities that are important.)

The usual terminology is to say that the estimate b_1 (or the variable income) is statistically significant at the α level if the two-tailed test of β_1 against zero leads to a rejection of the null hypothesis (at the α level of significance). Remember that all this indicates is that we have evidence that we have a non-zero coefficient. If we want to test against any other value as we did earlier with 0.18, we will have to calculate the test statistic and p-value for ourselves, as in the previous section.

Finally, you may wonder why KStat reports both the t-ratio and the p-value for the test. The answer is that some people like to know the t-ratio. However, the p-value contains all the information you need.

OVERVIEW OF THE REGRESSION OUTPUT TABLE

It may help you to go through part of the regression output again. After running a regression, KStat produces a table. You can see part of this table in Figure 3.12.

We will go through this table now. Recall that the regression estimates the coefficients of a straight line. These coefficients are the intercept β_0, and the coefficient on the income variable, β_1. The column labels tell us which of these coefficients each column concerns. Thus, the **constant** column is concerned with the constant coefficient or intercept, β_0, and the next column is concerned with the coefficient on the income variable, β_1. The **coefficient** row contains the actual estimates of these coefficients ($b_0 = 5787.9$, $b_1 = 0.2275$). The **std error of coef** row is more interesting. Each of the coefficient estimates is subject to sampling error and has a distribution whose standard deviation we can estimate. Those estimates are found in this row. For example, we know that b_1 is normally distributed, its expected value is the true slope β_1, and we can estimate its standard deviation to be $s_{b_1} = .02507$. Similarly, the estimated standard deviation of b_0 is denoted by $s_{b_0} (= 1572.261)$. The next two rows tell us the results of specific hypothesis tests. There is one test for each estimator. The null hypothesis is that the true value of the parameter we want to estimate is zero. The t-ratio row tells us the test statistic value we obtain from this test, and the p-value row tells us the corresponding p-value. The **beta-weight** row tells us the beta weight corresponding to income. The beta weights are coefficients of a regression where, instead of the variables themselves, standardized versions of the variables are used. Looking at the regression output table in Figure 3.11, we see the beta weight on income is 0.6758. This tells us that, on average, for a one standard deviation increase in the income, price will increase by 0.6758 standard deviations of price.

SUMMARY

We looked at how KStat chose the best-fit line through a scatterplot and how to use the equation of that line to make predictions. We applied this to predict the average price of a car bought by customers with a given income.

We assumed that, for any given income level, the amount spent on a car is normally distributed and the standard deviation of that distribution is the same for each income level. The mean of that distribution is the estimate provided by the regression equation, and the regression also provides the estimated standard deviation.

We used this information, together with some demographic data on our customer base, to predict the overall distribution of car purchases. We divided our

Figure 3.12 Partial regression output.

Regression: Price		
	constant	income
coefficient	5787.89988	0.22754022
std error of coef	1572.26135	0.02507093
t-ratio	3.6813	9.0759
p-value	0.0380%	0.0000%
beta-weight		0.6758

customers into income brackets and our cars into price brackets. For each income bracket, we worked out how many of our customers would come from that bracket and how their purchases of cars would fall among the different price brackets. This told us how many cars would be sold in each price bracket by adding up how many cars would be sold in that bracket to people in the lowest income bracket, the second lowest, etc.

We examined the regression model and learned that regression studies how one variable (e.g., auto price) varies across different populations indexed by another variable (e.g., income). It assumes that this relationship is linear on average and estimates the linear relationship. We can use this estimate to make predictions and use statistical theory to perform inferences about those estimates, including confidence intervals and hypothesis tests.

NEW TERMS

Best-fit line The line generated by the least squares method that produces the smallest possible sum of squared errors

Unbiased estimator An estimator whose expected value is equal to the parameter it estimates

Residual degrees of freedom The number of data points in a regression minus the number of coefficients (including the constant). This is used to calculate the proper t-statistic to use in confidence intervals and is used in calculating p-values of hypothesis tests

Standard error of the regression (s) An estimate of σ, the standard deviation of the dependent variable (y) given (or conditional on) a fixed value of the independent variable (x)

NEW FORMULAS

$100(1-\alpha)\%$ confidence interval for β_1: $b_1 \pm \text{TINV}(\alpha, n-2)^* s_{b_1}$

$100(1-\alpha)\%$ confidence interval for β_0: $b_0 \pm \text{TINV}(\alpha, n-2)^* s_{b_0}$

Hypothesis test to see if coefficient k is statistically significant:

$$H_0: \beta_k = 0,$$
$$H_a: \beta_k \neq 0.$$

NEW KSTAT AND EXCEL FUNCTIONS

KStat

Statistics > **Charts** > **Scatterplots**

This command generates a dialog box that offers to plot one variable against another. Select your Y or dependent variable in the box below the word **Plot**. Choose an X or independent variable in the box under the word **against**. If you would like KStat to add a regression line to your scatterplot, select the box that says **Plot regression line**.

Statistics > **Regression**

This command generates a dialog box asking you to select a dependent variable from a list of all variables in the current data worksheet. You are asked to choose one (or more) independent variables from the boxes on the right-hand side of the box. Clicking on the **perform regression** button will produce the regression worksheet.

CASE EXERCISES

1. A little peek at the Autorama

Consider the 80.5 expected car buyers in the $45,000–$55,000 income group from the Autorama case. Using the same assumptions we made in the chapter, determine the expected number of sales in each price bracket from this group. Hint: Use the normal distribution to determine the probability that someone in this group would buy a car in each price bracket. You may wish to do your calculations in a spreadsheet.

2. Autorama: The big picture

Take the entire set of potential car buyers at the Autorama described in Table 3.1 and complete the objectives of the case. That is, using an Excel spreadsheet, determine the number of cars to stock in each price bracket at your new dealership to match demand. You can easily build the spreadsheet in three steps:

a. For each income group, determine the expected number of sales within each price bracket.

b. Sum the expected sales with each price bracket to determine the total expected sales within each price bracket.

c. Multiply the fraction of total expected sales in each price bracket times 200 to determine how many of each type of car to stock in your inventory.

3. Shore Realty

Shore Realty sells real estate in Oklahoma. The company would like to be able to predict the selling price of new homes based on the home's size. It has collected data on size ("sqfoot" in square feet) and selling price ("price" in dollars), which are stored in the file **shore.xls**. Use the data in that file to answer the following questions:

a. Use KStat to construct a scatterplot for these data with size on the horizontal axis.

b. Use KStat to determine the estimated regression equation.

c. Predict the selling price for a home with 2,600 square feet.

PROBLEMS

For problems 1–3, you will need to access the **bschools2002.xls** file, which contains data regarding the top 30 business schools based on the 2002 *Business Week* ratings.

1. Many business school surveys including this one report **mean base salaries** and **median base salaries**. These two statistics tend to be similar. KStat can help us find a relationship between the two for this dataset.

    a. Use KStat to construct a scatterplot with mean base salary on the vertical axis and median base salary on the horizontal axis.

    b. Does this relationship appear linear?

    c. Use KStat to perform a regression of mean base salary vs. median base salary. Write out the estimated regression equation.

    d. Use your regression equation to estimate the mean base salary for a school with a median base salary of $77,000.

    e. Use your regression equation to estimate the mean base salary for a school with a median base salary of $88,000.

2. Students from better schools might command a higher salary. Comparing a school's mean base salary to its rank might help us understand this relationship.

    a. Develop a scatterplot for these variables with mean base salary as the dependent variable.

    b. Does this relationship appear linear?

    c. Use KStat to perform a regression of mean base salary vs. rank. Write the estimated regression equation.

    d. Use your regression equation to estimate the mean base salary for a school ranked eighth.

    e. Use your regression equation to estimate the mean base salary for a school ranked 25th.

    f. Use the coefficient on the rank variable to estimate the expected increase in mean base salary from a one-unit improvement in a school's rank. Provide a 95% confidence interval for your estimate.

    g. How confident are you that the true slope, β_1, is significantly different from zero?

3. Schools with larger enrollments might have more resources, making their students better prepared and more valuable to employers and, subsequently, commanding a higher salary. Of course, smaller schools may give students more personal attention, which develops better skills and could yield a higher salary for smaller schools. Studying the relationship between mean base salary and enrollment might help us understand this relationship better.

    a. Develop a scatterplot for these variables with mean base salary as the dependent variable.

    b. Use KStat to perform a regression of mean base salary vs. enrollment. Write the estimated regression equation.

    c. Use your regression equation to estimate the mean base salary for a school that enrolls 800 students.

    d. Use your regression equation to estimate the mean base salary for a school that enrolls 1,800 students.

    e. Use the coefficient on the enrollment variable to estimate the expected increase in mean base salary as enrollment increases by one. Provide a 95% confidence interval for your estimate.

    f. Is the true slope, β_1, significantly different from zero? Use a 5% level of significance.

    g. Is the true slope, β_1, significantly greater than zero? Use a 5% level of significance.

4. The top-selling beer in the world is Budweiser, which is produced by Anheuser-Busch. The company's annual reports provide the data in the file **budsales.xls**, which presents 12 years of combined sales (in 31-gallon barrels) of all Anheuser-Busch beers. The file also contains information on the U.S. population (US Pop) based on census estimates.

    a. Develop a scatterplot for these data with **barrels sold** as the dependent variable and **US Pop** as the independent variable.

    b. Use KStat to perform a regression of barrels sold vs. US Pop. Write the estimated regression equation.

    c. What does the coefficient of the variable US Pop represent in this regression equation? Be specific and clear in your answer.

5. Access the file **taxfranchise.xls**. The data come from a regional tax preparation company with 19 locations across the Midwest. The first variable measures the Output per Worker in terms of customers' tax forms completed per month, and the second is the annual Computer Budget per employee at that location.

    a. Use KStat to construct a scatterplot of Output per Worker vs. Computer Budget.

    b. Perform a regression of Output per Worker vs. Computer Budget and write the estimated regression equation.

    c. Use the regression equation to estimate the Output per Worker at a location with a Computer Budget of $2,500 per employee.

    d. Use the regression equation to estimate the Output per Worker at a location with a Computer Budget of $3,500 per employee.

    e. Use the coefficient on the Computer Budget variable to estimate the additional number of tax forms completed per month for each one-dollar increase per employee in the Computer Budget.

    f. Provide a 90% confidence interval for your answer to part e.

    g. Using $\alpha = 0.05$, determine if the Computer Budget is significantly related to Output per Worker.

CHAPTER 4

BETAS AND THE NEWSPAPER CASE: USING THE REGRESSION EQUATION

In this chapter, we will learn more about regression and how to use it to make predictions. We will see one of the major applications of regression in finance, the estimation of asset betas, which are numbers measuring the riskiness of different investments. Then, we will explore a new product start-up problem in the newspaper industry. Along the way, we will learn to do statistical inference with regression: In addition to producing estimates, we will be able to say something about the accuracy of our predictions through the use of confidence and prediction intervals and hypothesis tests.

4.1 Capital Budgeting and Risk

How to deal with risk in capital budgeting is one of the central issues in modern finance theory. Some of you may have encountered, at work or in finance classes, many of the concepts covered in this section. We will concentrate on the use of regression to measure asset betas. These numbers measure the riskiness of different assets, forming the basis for the most widely used approach to capital budgeting under uncertainty, the Capital Asset Pricing Model (CAPM). This section should explain enough to enable you to appreciate the importance of asset betas and how to use them in simple examples. You may wish to supplement this section by reading the relevant sections of any standard finance text, such as *Principles of Corporate Finance*, by Brealey and Myers.[1] There, you will learn about some factors we have ignored here, most notably the relation between capital structure and the cost of capital.

CAPITAL BUDGETING AND THE OPPORTUNITY COST OF CAPITAL

Suppose your company has the opportunity to begin a new project. The project will take place over two years. In year 1, you will have to invest $10 million, and in year 2, you expect average returns of $11.5 million, after which the project will end. Should you undertake the project?

The answer is you should undertake the project if it has positive net present value (NPV). If you are unfamiliar with the concept of NPV, Brealey and Myers or any other finance text will cover it in detail. For a given interest rate or cost of capital, r, the net present value is given by the following:

$$-10,000,000 + \frac{11,500,000}{1+r}$$

You can check that the NPV will be positive if r is smaller than 15% (.15) but will be negative otherwise. This means, you should invest if your cost of capital is less than or equal to 15%. This makes intuitive sense: If you make the investment, you will get a return of 15% in exchange for having your capital tied up for one year. The cost of capital refers to how much it costs you to have your capital tied up for one year, which is the rate of return you could achieve with it. Since this investment pays 15%, you should make it if you cannot earn more than 15% elsewhere. Here, "you" means your shareholders, since as a corporate manager it is your job to maximize shareholder value.

Risk and return

However, things are more complicated once we recognize the role of risk. Assume that this investment is somewhat risky, so the return of $11.5 million is uncertain and is merely your best estimate. Your shareholders need to be compensated for bearing that risk. To determine their cost of capital, we need to see how much they could get for bearing the same risk in a different investment. Again, this makes sense: Risky investments pay more on average than safe ones, but that does not mean that you should automatically choose the riskiest investments you can find.

---

1. *Principles of Corporate Finance*, 7/e. Richard A. Brealey and Stewart C. Myers. McGraw-Hill, 2003.

In practice, what it means is that you need to know how high a return your shareholders need to be compensated for bearing the risk your project represents.

The CAPM formula

This brings us to the bottom line of the CAPM: What it says is that the riskiness of a project or asset can be measured by a single number, known as the beta (β), and the required rate of return satisfies the following formula:

$$r - r_f = \beta \left(r_m - r_f \right)$$

Here, r_f is the risk-free interest rate, i.e., the return on a totally safe asset, and r_m is the return on a market portfolio. We usually think of r_f as the return on U.S. Treasury bills (T-bills), which historically have paid about 3.5%, and we often think of r_m as the return on the S&P500 index, which has earned a much higher return (around 12%.) The difference between the return on any asset and the risk-free return is called the excess return, so the formula says that the excess return on any asset should be proportional to the excess return on the market as a whole, with the constant of proportionality equal to β. If we know the beta of our project, we can use this formula to learn the correct cost of capital, r, calculate the NPV, and decide whether to make the investment.

Measuring Risk I: unique vs. market risk

When we think about a project's riskiness, we have to distinguish between two different kinds of risk: unique risk and market risk. Rational investors will hold a well-diversified portfolio of investments, with money in the stocks of many companies. This may be justified by the principle of not putting all your eggs in one basket. On a more technical level, as we saw in Chapter 1, when you take the average of a number of independent random variables, the standard deviation of that average becomes low. For instance, if you have n independent risks, each with the same standard deviation σ, then their average has a standard deviation of $\sigma / \sqrt{n}$. What this means is that investors do not have to worry much about the risk of any single investment, provided that risk is independent of their other investments' risks. For example, one risk facing Hewlett-Packard is if Dell will continue to steal market share away. However, whether or not that happens is mostly independent of anything else that might happen in the world, which suggests that a well-diversified investor should not have to worry about it. That is an example of a unique risk, also known as a specific risk, unsystematic risk, or diversifiable risk.

On the other hand, suppose that the economy slides into a recession. Hewlett-Packard's sales will fall and so will those of most other corporations in the United States. So, the risk of a recession is undiversifiable because any companies in which we invest will face the same risk. The companies' risks are not independent and their eggs are all in the same basket. This kind of risk is called market risk, systematic risk, or undiversifiable risk. Since investors cannot avoid this risk by diversification, they have to be compensated for bearing it. Because some companies face more such risk than others, they must offer a higher return to interest people in investing in them. For example, during recessions, people often put off buying cars, but such economic conditions do not greatly affect their use of the telephone, so auto companies have more market risk associated with them than do telephone companies.

Measuring Risk II: defining beta

Now that we know the kind of risk to measure, what remains is learning how to measure it. We can get at the right measurement by thinking about how the share price of an auto company like Ford will vary with the market as a whole, compared to that of a telecommunications company like AT&T. It turns out that when the market is doing well, Ford's shares do extremely well, but when the market is doing badly its shares do very badly. This is what you would expect: When the economy is booming, the markets are up and many people buy new cars, but when things are slow, few people do. Between 1984 and 1989, Ford's shares went up/down by 1.3% for every 1% change up/down in the market as a whole (on average and after subtracting the risk-free rate). This number (1.3) gives us a measure of how much risk is involved in holding Ford's shares. By comparison, AT&T shares were safer than the stock market as a whole during this time, with a change of only 0.76% for each 1% change in the market. These numbers are what we call the betas of the assets.

> Beta measures the amount the stock price changes for a 1% change in the market as a whole.

In the next section, we will see how regression is used to calculate/estimate betas. What this section has explained is how to use the beta to make investment decisions.

Summary

We reviewed the following procedure for deciding when to make a risky investment.

1. Obtain a numerical measure of the riskiness called its beta. (We defined the beta, but did not explain how to measure it.)
2. Use the CAPM formula, $r - r_f = \beta(r_m - r_f)$, to obtain the appropriate cost of capital figure r.
3. Use that value of r to calculate the NPV.
4. Make the investment if it has positive NPV.

Implementing step 1 will be discussed in the next section.

4.2 Estimating Betas

The firm you work for owns a chain of upscale pizza restaurants in New England. Your CEO believes the lower end of the market has room for expansion and wants to start up a large chain of fast food pizza places to compete in the fast food market. You are asked to make a preliminary study of the advisability of this investment, based on an initial investment of $8 million and projected average annual profits starting at $1 million and increasing to $2 million after the first two years. You write out the NPV formula for these figures (all in $millions):

$$NPV = -8 + \frac{1}{(1+r)} + \frac{1}{(1+r)^2} + \frac{1}{(1+r)^3} + \frac{1}{(1+r)^4} + \frac{1}{(1+r)^5} + \ldots$$

Before you can calculate this sum, you need to know the relevant discount rate, r. The projected profits are estimates since the true profits are uncertain, so this is a risky investment and the discount rate must reflect this riskiness. As you know from the previous section, the correct rate for discounting uncertain cash flows is given by the CAPM formula:

$$r - r_f = \beta\left(r_m - r_f\right)$$

Suppose the current risk-free rate is 4.0%, and the expected excess return of the market is 8.0%; so, $r = .04 + .08\beta$. All you need is a figure for beta, which measures the riskiness of this kind of investment.

ESTIMATING BETA

Fortunately, you have data on the share performance of some other companies, which operate in the fast food market. Since they are in the same business as this project, their riskiness should be a good guide to the proposed investment's riskiness. You decide to use regression to estimate the beta from these data, which consist of the monthly excess returns of (among others) the shares of McDonald's Corporation and of a portfolio representing the market as a whole. These data are contained in the **stocks.xls**[2] file; the data on monthly excess returns are reported in percentages.

How does regression help us here? The definition of the beta tells us how much the share price moves (relative to the risk-free rate), on average, compared with a 1% move (relative to the risk-free rate) in the market as a whole. So, if we draw a scatterplot of the monthly excess returns of McDonald's (stored in the MACS column) against the monthly excess returns of the market portfolio (stored in the column MARKET) and plot a best-fit line, the slope of the line should tell us the beta.[3]

As you can see, the line is fairly steep. The regression equation tells us that the beta is estimated to be about 1.458; so, on average, a 1% change in the market is associated with a change of almost 1.5% in the value of McDonald's shares.[4] We can use this estimate to get the discount rate: $r = .04 + .08(1.458) = .1566$, which is, about 15.7 percent. Substituting this value into the NPV calculation (and doing some algebra), we find this gives a profit of about $3.1 million, so this investment seems to be a good idea. Before jumping to conclusions, we should check the accuracy of our beta estimate since if it is rough we cannot be too confident that the NPV is positive. The true beta might be a lot higher than our estimate, leading to a much higher discount rate, which could tip the project into unprofitability.

---

2. Derived using data from *The Center for Research in Security Prices* at http://gsbwww.uchicago.edu/research/crsp/.

3. We also obtain the intercept of the best-fit line, usually called the asset's alpha. The estimated alpha shows our best estimate of the excess return of the given asset if the market excess return were 0. According to the CAPM equation, the intercept should be 0 (verify this for yourself).

4. The estimated intercept is about .25% monthly, or 3% annually. In practice (finance), the intercept is usually omitted when computing the asset's expected excess return. That is, the estimated beta is plugged into the CAPM formula as if the constant estimate were zero. We do it the same way below.

Figure 4.1 Excess returns of McDonald's vs. the market portfolio.

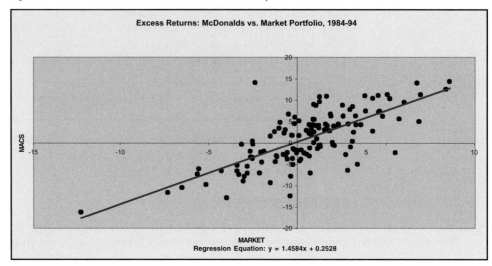

CONFIDENCE INTERVAL FOR BETA

To produce a confidence interval, we need an estimate of the standard deviation of our estimate, which we can find in the regression output from KStat.

The estimated standard deviation of b_1 is 0.1197, and we know that our sample size is 132 (11 years of monthly data). Therefore, a 90% confidence interval is given by $1.4584 \pm (0.1197)t_{0.05,130}$, and $t_{0.05,130}$ is about 1.657 (using $= \textbf{TINV}(0.1, 130)$). This is $1.4584 \pm 0.1984 = (1.26, 1.6568)$. We are interested in using beta to determine the discount rate using the CAPM equation $r = .04 + .08\beta$, so we can turn this into a confidence interval for r. That is, we have a beta between 1.26 and 1.6568 with 90% confidence, so we can say with 90% confidence that r is between $.04 + .08(1.26)$ and $.04 + .08(1.6568)$, i.e., between .1408 and .1725.

Figure 4.2 Regression of MACS vs. market.

Regression: MACS		
	constant	MARKET
coefficient	0.25281975	1.45836977
std error of coef	0.37854964	0.11972467
t-ratio	0.6679	12.1810
p-value	50.5404%	0.0000%
standard error of regression		4.27517041
R-squared		53.30%
adjusted R-squared		52.94%
number of observations		132
residual degrees of freedom		130

We can do a kind of worst-case analysis using this interval as follows. Suppose we have seriously underestimated beta. The true discount rate will be much higher than the 15.7% figure we used above. We can use the confidence interval to produce a sort of upper bound on the true discount rate's size: We do not know the exact value, but we are fairly (95%) confident that it is no more than 17.25%. If we repeat the NPV calculation using $r = 17.25\%$, we will get a figure of $2.1 million, which is still positive by a wide margin. The project will be profitable even under a worst-case assumption where the appropriate discount rate is much higher than the one used. The confidence interval enables us to choose a number we may treat as our worst-case scenario.

You might wonder why we did not do a hypothesis test here. The answer is that we could have done that, but you would have needed to work out the relevant test. Finance theory suggests that the appropriate thing to prove (i.e., the thing you should use as the alternative hypothesis) is whether the true discount rate is less than the internal rate of return (IRR). You could calculate this IRR with Excel or a financial calculator (it turns out to be about 21%) and carry out the hypothesis test.

To prove the true discount rate r is less than 21%, the appropriate hypothesis test is the following:

$$H_0: r \geq 0.21$$
$$H_a: r < 0.21$$

The next step is to use the CAPM formula, $r - r_f = \beta(r_m - r_f)$, to rewrite the hypotheses in terms of beta. Using $r_f = 0.04$ and $r_m = 0.12$, the alternative hypothesis becomes $0.04 + 0.08\beta < 0.21$ or, rearranging, $\beta < 0.17/0.08 = 2.125$. So, the hypothesis test is the following:

$$H_0: \beta \geq 2.125$$
$$H_a: \beta < 2.125$$

Using the results from the regression, we can calculate a test statistic of $t = 1.458 - 2.125)/0.119 = -5.6$. Therefore, the p-value = **TDIST**(5.6, 130, 1) ≈ 0, and we can reject the null hypothesis. We are extremely confident the true discount rate is less than the IRR, meaning this is a profitable project. This is the same conclusion arrived at using confidence intervals above.

Summary
We used regression to estimate the beta of McDonald's from a sample of excess returns on its shares and on the market as a whole. We used this beta to estimate the correct discount rate for a capital budgeting problem. We used a confidence interval approach to get a range of possible values for the beta and did a worst-case analysis to check whether the proposed investment would be profitable under rather pessimistic assumptions about sampling error. We also carried out a similar analysis using hypothesis testing.

4.3 Predicting Circulation

A newspaper in a large metropolitan area is thinking about issuing a Sunday edition. Management estimates that this would involve a start-up cost of $2 million and fixed annual operating costs of $1 million. Once the project is up and running, it figures to make a profit (net of the marginal costs of printing and distribution) of $5 per reader per year. Therefore, if the newspaper gets X thousand readers, it will realize an annual profit of $(5,000X-1,000,000) in perpetuity. The cost of capital for this industry is 15%, so the NPV of this profit stream is the following:[5]

$$\left(5,000X-1,000,000\right)\left(\frac{1}{\left(1+.15\right)}+\frac{1}{\left(1+.15\right)^2}+\frac{1}{\left(1+.15\right)^3}+\ldots\right)$$
$$=\frac{\left(5,000X-1,000,000\right)}{.15}$$
$$=\$\left(33,333X-6,666,667\right)$$

If readership is low, this value will be negative, but even if it is positive, it has to outweigh the initial cost of $2 million. In other words, the project is a good one if the following occurs:

$$33,333X-6,666,667>2,000,000$$

This is true whenever X is greater than 260. So, the break-even figure is a circulation of 260,000.

THE DATA

This projection is useless unless you can forecast what circulation will be. We will use regression to produce such a forecast, based on a dataset called **newspapers.xls**, which consists of the daily and Sunday circulation figures for 35 newspapers in other cities around the country[6]. The daily circulation of the paper is 190,000. We will use these data to forecast Sunday sales and to assess the forecast's accuracy. We begin with a preliminary look at the data, first via descriptive statistics and then graphically on a scatterplot. All figures are in thousands.

Examine the data in the scatterplot shown in Figure 4.4. It looks as if the relationship is close to linear. Now, we will do a regression to see what the estimated relationship is and check to see if a strong relationship exists.

---

5. Using the perpetuities formula, which says that the value of $1 per year in perpetuity is $(1/r).
   If you have not seen this, you can read about it in any standard finance text.
6. Derived from Hedblad, Alan, ed. **Gale** *Directory of Publications and Broadcast Media*, Gale Research, 1992.

Figure 4.3 Univariate statistics for Sunday and daily circulation.

Univariate statistics	Sunday	daily
Mean	609.029461	432.414
standard deviation	385.546763	265.361912
standard error of the mean	65.1692975	44.8543498
Minimum	202.613998	133.238998
Median	440.923004	355.627991
Maximum	1762.01502	1209.22498
Range	1559.40102	1075.98598
Skewness	1.396	1.533
Kurtosis	1.478	2.090
number of observations	35	
t-statistic for computing 95%-confidence intervals	2.0322	

Thus, our estimated regression equation is Sunday = 24.76+1.35 Daily. We may use the regression equation to produce an estimate of Sunday circulation for our newspaper. Substituting the daily circulation of 190 gives the following:

$$\text{Sunday} = 24.76 + 1.35(190) = 281.26$$

Figure 4.4 Scatterplot for Sunday vs. daily.

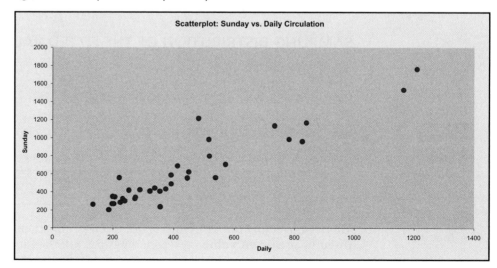

Figure 4.5 Regression of Sunday vs. daily.

[Statistics>Regression] Regression: Sunday	constant	daily
coefficient	24.7631585	1.35117342
std error of coef	46.9866631	0.09297695
t-ratio	0.5270	14.5323
p-value	60.1701%	0.0000%
beta-weight		0.9300
standard error of regression		143.864401
R-squared		86.49%
adjusted R-squared		86.08%
number of observations		35
residual degrees of freedom		33
t-statistic for computing 95%-confidence intervals		2.0345

As the units are in thousands, this equation tells us the estimated Sunday circulation is 281,260. So, it looks as if we are saying that circulation will exceed our break-even figure of 260,000. But we have to be more careful than that. Regression is a statistical procedure: We are estimating the true relationship between Sunday and daily circulation, and the estimate is based on our sample, so it will contain some sampling error. In other words, there is a true line describing that relationship, which we do not know exactly but have estimated. Our best estimates of its intercept and slope are 24.76 and 1.35 respectively, but those are only estimates. We need to take this into account and quantify the sampling error in our estimate of Sunday circulation.

SAMPLING DISTRIBUTION OF THE FITTED VALUE $\hat{y}$

Earlier, we talked about the estimator b_1 and its sampling distribution. Most of what we said about b_1 also applies to the estimator b_0. Now, however, we are interested in a third estimator. The parameter we want to estimate is the average (or expected) Sunday circulation of a paper with a daily circulation of 190,000. If the regression model is right, then this is given (in thousands) by $\beta_0 + \beta_1(190)$, and we estimate this average by using the following:

$$\hat{y}_{190} = b_0 + b_1(190)$$

We need to know the sampling distribution of this quantity, which is called the **fitted** or **predicted value** corresponding to $x = 190$. It makes sense to talk about the sampling distribution as this estimate is the outcome of an experiment. If we repeated the experiment by taking a different sample, we would get a different outcome, i.e., different estimates.

The sampling distribution of this estimator has the following properties:

> The fitted value is normally distributed, with mean equal to the true value, i.e.,
>
> $$E(\hat{y}_{190}) = \beta_0 + \beta_1(190)$$
>
> so it is an **unbiased estimator**. Its standard deviation is written $\sigma_{\hat{y}_{190}}$ and can be estimated from the sample. KStat produces this estimate, called the standard error of estimated mean, which is denoted by $s_{\hat{y}_{190}}$.

CONFIDENCE INTERVALS WITH THE FITTED VALUE

Since we know the distribution of our estimator, we can use it to produce confidence intervals as we have done with every other estimator. By now, you should know what the formula will be. To get a $100(1-\alpha)\%$ confidence interval for $\beta_0 + \beta_1(190)$, use the following:

$$\hat{y}_{190} \pm t_{\alpha/2, n-2} s_{\hat{y}_{190}}$$

Here, $t_{\alpha/2, n-2}$ is the $\alpha/2$ t-value with $n-2$ degrees of freedom, and n is the sample size (i.e., $t_{\alpha/2, n-2} = \text{TINV}(\alpha, n-2)$). Later we will show you where KStat tells you how many degrees of freedom to use and where it displays its estimate $s_{\hat{y}_{190}}$. KStat will even produce the confidence interval for you.

As an example, let's produce a 90% confidence interval for $\beta_0 + \beta_1(190)$. First, run the regression in KStat, and then click **Statistics>Prediction**. You will obtain a worksheet that looks like the one in Figure 4.6.

These particular results were obtained by entering 190 in the **values for prediction** row and 90 in the **confidence level** row. Clicking **Predict** on the worksheet will then produce the information we need. The **predicted value of Sunday** row gives us the actual estimate (the fitted value) $\hat{y}_{190} = 281.486$, the **standard error of estimated mean** row gives us the estimated standard deviation of this estimate $s_{\hat{y}_{190}} = 33.156$, and the **confidence limits for estimated mean** rows give the requested 90% confidence interval. This worksheet also gives output relevant to prediction intervals, which are the subject of the next section. The **standard error of prediction** row gives us the estimated standard deviation we use in calculating prediction intervals. The **confidence limits for prediction** rows give the 90% prediction interval for the fitted value.

Figure 4.6 Prediction of Sunday sales.

Prediction, using most-recent regression			Make multiple predictions
	constant	**Daily**	
coefficients	24.76316	1.351173	
values for prediction		190	
predicted value of Sunday		281.4861	Predict
standard error of prediction		147.6357	
standard error of regression		143.8644	
standard error of estimated mean		33.15637	
confidence level	90.00%		
t-statistic	1.6924		
residual degr. freedom	33		
confidence limits	lower	31.63323	
for prediction	upper	531.339	
confidence limits	lower	225.3736	
for estimated mean	upper	337.5986	

PREDICTION INTERVALS AND THE FITTED VALUE

Prediction intervals are particularly useful tools. A 90% confidence interval gives us a range of values in which we are 90% confident that the mean value falls, i.e., the mean Sunday circulation of all papers with daily circulation of 190,000. In contrast, a 90% prediction interval is a range of values which we are 90% confident would contain the circulation of a particular Sunday paper selected at random from all those with a daily circulation of 190,000.

Below is the formula for prediction intervals. It is similar to the one for confidence intervals except that it uses a different (larger) standard deviation called the standard error of prediction by KStat:

$$\hat{y}_{190} \pm t_{\alpha/2, n-2} \sqrt{s^2 + s_{\hat{y}_{190}}^2}$$

In this formula, s is the **standard error of regression**, $s_{\hat{y}_{190}}$ is the **standard error of estimated mean**, and $\sqrt{s^2 + s_{\hat{y}_{190}}^2}$ is the **standard error of prediction** as reported by KStat. The other symbols are familiar: $\hat{y}_{190}$ is the estimated value of the dependent variable, $t_{\alpha/2, n-2}$ is the $\alpha/2$ t-statistic with $n - 2$ degrees of freedom, and n is the sample size, i.e., $t_{\alpha/2, n-2} = \text{TINV}(\alpha, n - 2)$.

HYPOTHESIS TESTS WITH THE FITTED VALUE

The fitted value, $\hat{y}_{190}$, is our estimator for the population average y when $x = 190$ as well as for an individual value, y_i, when $x = 190$. As we have seen in the previous two sections, we can determine the range around $\hat{y}_{190}$ where the population average should fall (when $x = 190$ with a given confidence) using the standard error of estimated mean, and a similar range where an individual value, y_i, should be using the standard error of prediction. We can use these standard errors to develop hypothesis tests regarding the population average y at $x = 190$ and an individual y_i at $x = 190$.

First, we try to prove the average of the Sunday circulations of all newspapers with a daily circulation of 190,000 is greater than 260,000. The basic steps are the same as in all previous hypothesis tests. The hypotheses are the following:

H_0: at x = 190, population average y $\leq$ 260

H_a : at x = 190, population average y > 260.

We calculate the test statistic that shows by how many standard errors the estimator is greater than 260. The estimator is $\hat{y}_{190}$, and since the hypothesis is about the population average, the correct standard error to use is the standard error of estimated mean (at $x = 190$), which we can find from the Prediction sheet.

$$t = (\hat{y}_{190} - 260) / (\text{SE of estimated mean at } x = 190)$$
$$= (281.49 - 260) / 33.16 = 0.648$$

Now we can proceed to calculate the p-value of the test with the following:

$$\text{p-value} = \text{TDIST}(\text{t-value}, \#\text{degrees of freedom}, \#\text{tails}) = \text{TDIST}(.648, 33, 1) = 0.26.$$

Since p = 26%, we cannot reject the null at a 5% significance level. In other words, we cannot prove at a 5% significance level that the average of the Sunday circulations of newspapers with a daily edition of 190,000 copies is greater than 260,000.

As a manager at your newspaper, you are not necessarily interested in the above result. You are more interested in testing if your own Sunday edition will exceed 260,000 copies per day (you do not directly care about the industry average for papers with your daily circulation); that is, you want to test the following:

$$H_0: \text{at } x = 190, \text{ individual } y_i \leq 260$$

$$H_a: \text{at } x = 190, \text{ individual } y_i > 260.$$

The estimator is the same as before, $\hat{y}_{190}$, but the correct standard error to use in the calculation of the test statistic is now the standard error of prediction at $x = 190$.

$$\text{t-value} = (\hat{y}_{190} - 260) / (\text{SE of prediction at } x = 190)$$
$$= (281.49 - 260) / 147.64 = 0.146$$

The estimator is 0.146 standard errors above 260. We find the t-value in a test for the individual, y_i, is smaller in magnitude than that in the same test for the population average. (Can you tell why?) The p-value of the test is given by the following:

$$\text{p-value} = \text{TDIST(t-value, \#degrees of freedom,}$$
$$\text{\#tails)} = \text{TDIST}(.146, 33, 1) = 0.442.$$

p = 44.2%, which is greater than any reasonable significance level. Therefore, we cannot prove that the Sunday circulation of an individual newspaper with a daily circulation of 190,000 will be greater than 260,000.

THE DECISION

Remember that the break-even point for this project was a circulation of 260,000. The regression gives a point prediction of 281,486, but if we look at the 90% prediction interval (31,633 to 531,339), we see this point prediction is of little use because the margin of error is enormous. The same conclusion arises from our latter hypothesis test, as we cannot prove at any reasonable significance level that our newspaper will have a Sunday circulation in excess of 260,000. In other words, knowing the daily circulation is not informative enough about Sunday circulation.

Was this regression useless? No; however, it suggests we need to collect more information to obtain a prediction accurate enough to make the decision. Newspaper circulation can be predicted much more accurately if we add in some extra variables (various demographics) and perform a multiple regression. We will examine multiple regression techniques in coming chapters.

Though daily circulation on its own is not informative enough to make the kind of prediction we need, it did explain a large fraction of the variation in Sunday circulation. We know this because of something called the R-squared statistic, which you can see in the regression output (R-squared = 86.49%).

THE R-SQUARED STATISTIC

If you have ever studied regression before, you will recognize the R-squared. It is a number that tells you how much variation in the y or dependent variable is explained by the regression equation. In this example, the dependent variable is Sunday circulation, and its total variation is defined this way:

$$\sum \left(y_i - \bar{y}\right)^2$$

$\bar{y}$ is the mean Sunday circulation of all the papers in the sample. This quantity is usually known as the total sum of squares (SST). You can find it by running a regression using KStat, switching to the analysis of variance (ANOVA) worksheet, and looking in the row labeled **total** and column labeled **sum of squares**. Next, we take the estimated regression equation $\hat{y} = b_0 + b_1 x$ and ask how much variation it predicts. Taking each paper in the sample in turn, look at its daily circulation x_i, and calculate the Sunday circulation that the regression equation predicts for that x_i. This number is called the ith fitted value $\hat{y}_i$. This value $\hat{y}_i$ is not equal to the true Sunday circulation of the ith paper because the regression is not totally accurate. But we can ask how much variance there would be if this regression were totally accurate, so that each $\hat{y}_i$ was the true value for its paper. This is given by applying the variation formula to the $\hat{y}_i$'s instead of to the $\hat{y}_i$'s:

$$\sum \left(\hat{y}_i - \bar{y}\right)^2$$

This quantity is known as the sum of squares due to regression (SSR). You can find it on the ANOVA worksheet in the row labeled **regression** and column labeled **sum of squares**. The SSR tells us how much variance there would be in our sample if Sunday circulation were exactly related to daily circulation by the estimated regression equation, i.e., if our best-fit line were a perfect fit. If the best-fit line is close to the data points, the SSR will be close to the SST since in that case the best-fit line is predicting accurately; if the best-fit line is a poor fit, the SSR will be much smaller than the SST.

This intuition leads to the mathematical definition of the R-squared:

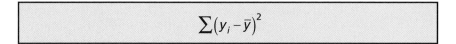

$$R^2 = \frac{SSR}{SST} = \frac{\sum \left(\hat{y}_i - \bar{y}\right)^2}{\sum \left(y_i - \bar{y}\right)^2}$$

In this case, the high R-squared (86.49%) tells us that daily circulation does an impressive job of explaining/predicting the variation in Sunday circulation; however, there is an enormous amount of variation overall. The remaining 13.51% variation that is unexplained represents a thin slice of a very large pie. In this example, the unexplained fraction is too much to make the prediction useful. One moral of this example is you should not overvalue the R-squared. One of the most common mistakes in using regression is thinking that a high R-squared means the regression is automatically useful for prediction. As we have seen, that is not the case. Similarly, a low R-squared does not mean that a regression is useless.

R-SQUARED AND ASSET BETAS

If you look back to our regression of McDonald's excess returns against the market, you will see that the R-squared in that regression is only about 53%. Should we have worried about this? The answer is no. All we were interested in was the accuracy of our beta estimate, and the R-squared is irrelevant to this. What it does tell us is how much of the variance in McDonald's share price is explained by the market's movements as a whole. This has a nice interpretation. Recall that a basic idea behind the beta and the CAPM model is that some risk is specific to each firm, and therefore diversifiable; the rest is due to the movements of the whole market and cannot be avoided by diversification. The R-squared is the ratio of variance (i.e., risk) due to the market and the total variance in McDonald's stock. In other words, it tells you what proportion of the risk in holding McDonald's shares cannot be diversified away. So, in this case, about 47% of McDonald's risk is firm-specific, related to things such as the success or failure of its new ad campaign or new food ideas; the other 53% is systematic risk, related to factors like people spending less at McDonald's in hard times.

SUMMARY

In this chapter, we learned two of the important things that regression can be used for: studying how changes in an independent variable relate to changes in the dependent variable through the coefficient and using a particular value of the independent variable to make predictions of the dependent variable. In both cases, we observed point estimates and interval estimates. In the finance case, we estimated a beta and gave confidence intervals reflecting our uncertainty about the estimate. With our newspaper circulation case, we estimated Sunday sales for a paper with a certain daily sales level and gave a prediction interval to demonstrate the limitations of our estimate.

Between the two cases, we used four different standard errors computed by KStat. Though each of these represents the same basic idea, a measure of the uncertainty of some estimate, you must keep track of which estimates are being assessed by which standard errors.

NEW TERMS

Fitted value The value of the dependent variable (y) predicted by the regression equation for a given value of the independent variable (x). It is a prediction for the average value of y given x and for an individual realization of y given x

Standard error of the coefficient An estimate of the standard deviation of a regression coefficient

Standard error of the estimated mean An estimate of the standard deviation of the fitted value. It is used in constructing confidence intervals for the average value of y given x and in conducting hypothesis tests concerning the average value of y given x

Standard error of prediction An estimate of the standard deviation of our estimate for an individual value of y given x. Calculated by combining the standard error of regression with the standard error of the estimated mean. Used
in constructing prediction intervals for an individual value of y given x and
in conducting hypothesis tests concerning an individual value of y given x

NEW FORMULAS

CAPM formula $\qquad r - r_f = \beta(r_m - r_f)$

Confidence Interval for the average $\qquad \hat{y}_p \pm t_{\alpha/2,n-2}s_{\hat{y}_p}$
value of y given x = p

Prediction Interval for y given x = p $\qquad \hat{y}_p \pm t_{\alpha/2,n-2}\sqrt{s^2 + s_{\hat{y}_p}^2}$

Total Sum of Squares (SST) $\qquad \sum(y_i - \bar{y})^2$

Sum of Squares due to Regression (SSR) $\sum(\hat{y}_i - \bar{y})^2$

R-squared $\qquad R^2 = \dfrac{SSR}{SST}$

NEW KSTAT AND EXCEL FUNCTIONS

KStat

Statistics>**Prediction**

This command creates a spreadsheet to determine fitted or predicted values, the
standard error of the estimated mean, the standard error of prediction as well as
prediction and confidence intervals. Because it uses the output of the most recent
regression, you must run a regression before using this command. Entering values
in the yellow cells beneath the independent variable(s) and clicking on the predict
box will calculate a fitted value, the associated standard errors and each interval.
Typing a value between 0 and 100 into the yellow confidence level cell will create
confidence and prediction intervals with the desired levels of confidence. The
default is 95% confidence. To compare multiple predictions side by side, click the
make multiple predictions box. Each column of yellow cells allows you to enter a
different set of values for the independent variable(s). When you click predict,
results will be calculated for each set of values you have entered.

CASE EXERCISES

1. Estimating betas

Access the **stocks.xls** dataset and use it to estimate betas for the following stocks:
Apple, IBM, and HP. Suppose the excess returns on the stock market (as measured by
the S&P500, stored under **ESP** in the dataset) were to be negative 20% next month.

    a. What would you expect to be the excess return on Apple shares next
month? How about IBM and HP shares? Base your estimate on the estimated beta and the theoretical CAPM equation; that is, discard the estimated constant (alpha), as we did in the chapter.

b. How much money would you expect to lose next month if you had $10,000 invested in Apple shares at the beginning of the month? For the purposes of answering this part of the question only, assume that the risk-free rate next month is 0.25%.

In the example from the chapter, we used the variable **Market** to measure the market excess return. In this problem, we ask you to use an alternative method of measuring the market excess return using the variable ESP. So, for this exercise, use ESP. One problem with the CAPM is that it is not obvious how to measure the market return. Market is a combination of bonds and the S&P 500, and ESP includes only the S&P 500. Finally, all the variables in the dataset are **excess market returns** (i.e., market returns minus the risk-free interest rate).

2. Slippery soap sales

Greenfield, Inc., a manufacturer of a popular bathing soap, tried to find the relation between its product's price and its sales. It supplies over 2,000 retail outlets in the United States. It collected data from 25 of these stores during one week and ran a regression using these data. For each store in the sample, it observed the independent variable **Price** (measured in dollars), and the dependent variable **Sales** (measured in thousands of dollars). The results were as follows:

Regression: Sales ($1000)	constant	Price ($)
Coefficient	5.82919837	-0.29294163
std error of coef	0.42410157	0.061640587
t-ratio	13.7448	-4.7524
p-value	0.0000%	0.0086%

a. If the price of the bathing soap is reduced by $0.50, what is the expected increase in sales per store? Additionally, provide a 95% confidence interval for the expected increase.

b. The product manager claims that if the price is reduced by $0.50, average sales will increase by at least $160 per store. Do the data allow you to reject this claim at a level of significance of 5 percent?

c. The price in all stores next week is going to be $9.99. Predict the total expected sales including all of the 2,000 stores during next week.

3. Shore Realty revisited

Retrieve the **shore.xls** dataset, which we used in Case Exercise 3 in Chapter 3, and run the regression again. Provide a 90% confidence interval for the coefficient on the sqfoot variable, and explain clearly and concisely what this interval means. Predict the selling price for a home with 2,600 square feet, provide the associated 95% confidence and prediction intervals and explain clearly and concisely what each means. Suppose that Shore Realty sells a large number of houses of this size: what proportion of them would you expect to sell for over $383,000?

PROBLEMS

Access the **Retailsales.xls** data file to answer problems 1–3. This data file reports the percentage change in total domestic retail sales and the percentage change in the U.S. GDP over a recent ten-year period. (from A.C. Nielsen's *Facts, Figures and the Future*. Feb. 2003).

1. Use KStat to perform a regression of **%chg in Retail Sales** using **%chg in GDP** as the independent variable.

   a. Write the estimated regression equation.

   b. Use the regression to estimate how much a one percentage point increase in GDP will affect retail sales.

   c. Provide a 95% confidence interval for your estimate in part b.

   d. Provide a 90% confidence interval for your estimate in part b.

   e. Using $\alpha = 0.05$, can you reject the null hypothesis that the true coefficient multiplying %chg in GDP is zero?

2. Use the regression from problem 1.

   a. Predict the **%chg in Retail Sales** in a year where the GDP increases by 3.0%.

   b. Provide a 95% prediction interval for your estimate.

   c. Provide a 98% prediction interval for your estimate.

   d. Using the same prediction, estimate the probability that the **%chg in Retail Sales** will be greater than 8.5.

3. Overall how would you rate the quality of this regression? Justify your answer.

   Access the **Salaries.xls** file to answer problems 4–6. These data represent the salaries of 41 workers at a major corporation based on the number of years employed with the company.

4. Use KStat to perform a regression of **Salary** vs. **Years Experience**.

   a. Write out the estimated regression equation.

   b. Use the regression to estimate the effect of one additional year of work experience at the company on a worker's salary.

   c. Provide a 95% confidence interval for your estimate in part b.

   d. Provide a 99% confidence interval for your estimate in part b.

   e. Using $\alpha = 0.05$, can you reject the null hypothesis that the true coefficient is zero?

5. Use the regression from problem 4.

    a. Predict the salary of a worker with nine years of experience at the company.

    b. Provide a 95% prediction interval for your estimate.

    c. Provide a 75% prediction interval for your estimate.

    d. Provide an interval that you are 90% confident contains the true mean salary of workers with nine years of experience.

    e. How confident can we be that work experience is significantly related to salary?

6. What percentage of salary can be explained using an employee's work experience with the company? Does this number sound reasonable to you?

For problems 7–9, you will need to access the **eurodata.xls** file, which contains information from the *Statistical Annex of the European Economy, 2003*. The dataset consists of 42 years worth of wage rate growth and unemployment rates for 10 countries in Europe. Multinational corporations might be interested in studying how unemployment impacts the growth in wages for some or all of these 10 countries.

7. Use KStat to perform a regression of wage growth vs. unemployment in Belgium (BE) and Denmark (DK).

    a. Write both estimated regression equations.

    b. How does a one percentage point increase in unemployment relate to the growth rate of wages in each country?

    c. Provide a 95% confidence interval for the coefficient multiplying unemployment for each country.

    d. Predict the growth rate in wages for each country in a year that has 3% unemployment.

    e. Provide a 90% confidence interval for each prediction from part d.

8. Use KStat to perform a regression of wage growth vs. unemployment in Germany (DE) and Greece (EL).

    a. Write both estimated regression equations.

    b. How does a one percentage point increase in unemployment relate to the growth rate of wages in each country?

    c. Provide a 95% confidence interval for the coefficient multiplying unemployment for each country.

    d. Predict the growth rate in wages for each country in a year that has 3% unemployment.

    e. Provide a 90% confidence interval for each prediction from part d.

9. Use KStat to perform a regression of wage growth vs. unemployment in Spain (ES) and France (FR).

   a. Write both estimated regression equations.

   b. How does a one percentage point increase in unemployment relate to the growth rate of wages in each country?

   c. Provide a 95% confidence interval for the coefficient multiplying unemployment for each country.

   d. Predict the growth rate in wages for each country in a year that has 3% unemployment.

   e. Provide a 90% confidence interval for each prediction from part d.

CASE INSERT 1   ENERGY COSTS AND REFRIGERATOR PRICING

As a manager in charge of a brand of refrigerators, you are confronted with the following scenario: A representative from your company's research and development team sends you a report announcing a breakthrough in energy-efficient refrigeration technology. Specifically, the team believes that for an additional production cost of $80 per refrigerator, the consumer's annual energy costs to run the refrigerator will drop by $20. Should you incorporate this new technology into your next refrigerator model?

One key issue is how much extra you could charge for a more energy-efficient fridge. To get an estimate of this, you order a study of the relationship between the annual energy costs and price of a refrigerator. The data gathered for this study provide information on 41 popular models of refrigerators[1]. Using these data, a regression of price on annual energy costs is performed. The variables are "Price," which gives the refrigerator price (in $), and "Energy cost," which gives the annual energy cost of running the refrigerator (in $/year).

Regression: Price		
	constant	Energy cost
coefficient	300.156701	17.14956955
std error of coef	290.462959	6.075477932
t-ratio	1.0334	2.8228
p-value	30.7795%	0.7458%
beta-weight		0.4119
standard error of regression		392.6116924
R-squared		16.96%
adjusted R-squared		14.84%
number of observations		41
residual degrees of freedom		39
t-statistic for computing 95%-confidence intervals		2.0227

Case Questions

1. Given this output, what is an estimate for the change in price of a refrigerator model when its annual energy costs decrease by $20?
2. Given this estimate, would you go ahead with the new technology?
3. Does this estimate make sense? Explain.

---

1. You can access this data in the **newfridge.xls** file. Source: *Consumer Reports*, July 2003, Vol. 68, No. 7.

CHAPTER 5

CALIFORNIA STRAWBERRIES: DUMMY AND SLOPE DUMMY VARIABLES

In this chapter, we will learn about using two kinds of dummy variables to capture qualitative features in regression in the California Strawberries and the CEO Seek Cases.

5.1 Dummy Variables

DUMMY VARIABLES: REVISITING THE PACKAGING CASE

A "dummy" or "qualitative" variable is one that only takes on the values 0 and 1. The idea of a dummy variable is it measures not a quantity but a quality. For an example, go back to the consumer packaging example from Chapter 2. The dataset consisted of 72 sales figures, 36 from locations using packaging one and 36 from locations using packaging two. If we number these locations 1 through 72, we can define y_i to be sales at location i (so y_i is a regular, quantitative variable) and x_i to be a dummy variable defined by the following:

$$x_i = \begin{cases} 0 \text{ if location i uses packaging one} \\ 1 \text{ if location i uses packaging two} \end{cases}$$

You will see that dummy variables are one of the most useful techniques available in regression because they enable us to measure the effect of qualitative differences. This section introduces you to dummy variables and how to use them in regression by reproducing the two-sample results we obtained in Chapter 2.

INTERPRETING DUMMY VARIABLES IN THE REGRESSION MODEL

Suppose we regress sales on our packaging dummy. What is the meaning of this regression? Remember the regression model: The assumption is that we may write the following:

$$E(y) = \beta_0 + \beta_1 x$$

That is, the average value of y for a given x is a linear function of x. That seemed to make sense when x was measuring income and y auto price. What does it mean when x is a dummy variable? Suppose $x = 0$; then, the equation says the expected value of y is β_0. So, β_0 is the expected value of y when $x = 0$, i.e., expected sales in districts using packaging one. For $x = 1$, the equation says the expected value of y is $\beta_0 + \beta_1 1$; so, the expected sales in districts using packaging two equals $\beta_0 + \beta_1$. What is the difference in expected sales between districts using packaging two and districts using packaging one? It is $\beta_0 + \beta_1 - \beta_0 = \beta_1$. When we run the regression and estimate β_1, what we are estimating is the difference in expected sales between the two types of packaging, which is what we wanted to estimate in the first place in Chapter 2 because it tells us which packaging we should choose.

THE REGRESSION

Go ahead and run this regression. Our data should consist of two columns. The first (called allpack) is a list of sales figures, one for each district, and the second

Figure 5.1 Allpack regression.

Regression: allpack		
	constant	dummy1
coefficient	290.543889	−27.797222
std error of coef	8.42241331	11.9110911
t-ratio	34.4965	−2.3337
p-value	0.0000%	2.2487%
beta-weight		−0.2687
standard error of regression		50.5344798
R-squared		7.22%
adjusted R-squared		5.89%
number of observations		72
residual degrees of freedom		70
t-statistic for computing 95%-confidence intervals		1.9944

(called dummy1) is 0 for the first 36 entries since the first 36 sales figures come from districts that used packaging one (P1), and 1 for the next 36 since the next 36 sales figures come from districts that used packaging two (P2).

If you look back at the consumer packaging example, you will see that we estimated the difference in average sales with P1 versus P2 to be 27.80 in favor of P1. Here in the regression output we have $b_1 = -27.80$, which says that we estimate that when x goes from 0 to 1, i.e., when we change from P1 to P2, sales go down on average by 27.80. So, the regression has given us the same estimate we had before.

One convenient thing about using the regression is KStat has automatically tested this coefficient for significance: The t-statistic is −2.33, giving a p-value of .02249. Recall that this is the p-value for the following hypothesis test:

$$H_0: \beta_1 = 0,$$
$$H_a: \beta_1 \neq 0.$$

So, the p-value of .02249 tells us we are quite confident (over 97% confident) that $\beta_1 \neq 0$. What does this mean in the context of our example? Since we worked out that $\beta_1 = \mu_2 - \mu_1$, it means that we are quite confident that there is a difference in true average sales between the two types of packaging. Is this what we wanted to know? Not exactly. We wanted to see if the data provided strong evidence that average sales with P1 were above those with P2 using the hypothesis test:

$$H_0: \mu_1 - \mu_2 \leq 0$$
$$H_a: \mu_1 - \mu_2 > 0.$$

Since $\beta_1 = \mu_2 - \mu_1$, this may be rewritten as

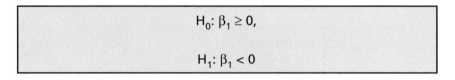

$$H_0: \beta_1 \geq 0,$$

$$H_1: \beta_1 < 0$$

Using the regression output, we calculate the p-value for this test to be p = TDIST(2.3337, 70, 1) = .01124. Thus this data provides very strong evidence that average sales with P1 are higher, supporting a decision to go with packaging 1 rather than continue the marketing experiment.

When we used KStat to conduct the same hypothesis test using the two-sample t-test in Chapter 2, it reported a p-value of .01126 and we reached the same conclusion.

A NOTE ON OUR ASSUMPTIONS

Even though the p-values in the example are similar for the test based on the regression as for the two-sample t-test in Chapter 2.4, the two methods of comparing two population means rely on different assumptions. As you know, regression assumes the y values have the same variances for different x values, which, in this example, is equivalent to assuming the y values have the same variance for each of the two populations. The two sample t-test used in Chapter 2.4 did not use this assumption. Formally, using regression with a single dummy variable yields the same results as using a two-sample t-test assuming equal variances, and these results may differ from those obtained by using a two-sample t-test without assuming equal variances.

SUMMARY

Dummy variables capture qualitative differences rather than quantitative ones. When we have data from two populations, we can define a dummy variable to represent which population each data point comes from, run a regression to estimate differences in the two population means, and test the difference for statistical significance, etc. This is an alternative technique to the two-sample methods we learned earlier and provides a first application of dummy variables.

5.2 California Strawberries

Susan Lee is the chief manager of California Strawberries, Inc. Her firm transports strawberries from local farmers to a chain of grocery stores. The strawberries are packed into the retail boxes in two locations, using two different packaging systems. One is used at the plant in Bakersfield and the other in Monterey. Susan wants to compare the efficiency of the two systems and decide if one of the systems should be abandoned. The personnel and equipment needed for the two systems are basically identical. However, the time taken to pack a box of strawberries in

Figure 5.2 California Strawberries, Inc. data.

	Monterey		Bakersfield	
Row	Time	Boxes	Time	Boxes
1	102	175	95	140
2	69	110	104	153
3	133	225	48	70
4	37	57	108	161
5	28	47	89	128
6	124	217	85	125
7	71	120	90	133
8	36	60	81	122
9	41	65	68	95
10	104	180	98	143
11	126	210	109	161
12	63	106	54	80
13	34	50	85	128
14	38	60	137	205
15	88	150	85	125

Bakersfield and Monterey differs. Susan wants to adopt the quickest system. She asked her assistant to observe the time (measured in minutes) taken to pack different amounts of strawberries (measured in number of boxes) at Bakersfield and Monterey. The data he obtained is in the **california.xls** file and is shown in Figure 5.2.

We can use a regression analysis to study the relationship between the two variables. Time is the dependent variable and Boxes is the independent variable. In this first regression (see Figure 5.3), we use only the data obtained at the Monterey plant.

Figure 5.3 Simple regression for the Monterey system.

Regression: Time		
	constant	Boxes
Coefficient	3.593778	0.567737
std error of coef	1.081558	0.007854
t-ratio	3.3228	72.2871
p-value	0.5501%	0.0000%
beta-weight		0.9988
standard error of regression		2.11901285
R-squared		99.75%
adjusted R-squared		99.73%
number of observations		15
residual degrees of freedom		13
t-statistic for computing 95%-confidence intervals		2.1604

Now, consider a similar regression for the Bakersfield system (see Figure 5.4). In this regression, we use only the data obtained at the Bakersfield plant.

What is the interpretation of these two regressions? The constant term indicates the time needed to start the system (literally, the time to pack 0 boxes). The coefficient on Boxes indicates the time it takes to pack each additional box. The regression analysis suggests it takes a longer time to set up the Monterey system (3.59 min) than the Bakersfield system (2.62 min). However, once the system is ready, the Monterey system (0.57 min per box) is faster than the Bakersfield system (0.66 min per box).

Susan believes the time to set up both systems should be similar, and she decides to maintain this hypothesis unless she discovers strong evidence against it.

Before she examines the regressions, Susan does not have any reason to believe that the time to pack each additional box in Monterey is smaller than in Bakersfield, nor does she have any reason to believe that the time per additional box in Bakersfield is smaller than in Monterey. By looking at the regressions, she feels tempted to abandon the Bakersfield system. However, she decides not to do so unless significant statistical evidence shows the Bakersfield system is slower.

Susan has good reasons to be cautious. Suppose the Bakersfield system is actually faster than the system in Monterey. In this case, if Susan switches to the Monterey system on the basis of the sample data, California Strawberries, Inc. will incur the costs of forcing the workers to adapt themselves to a new (and slower) system. Moreover, she will not be led to correct her mistake in the future because, once the Bakersfield system is abandoned, no more data will be available from it.

If the current sample evidence is not strong enough to prove that one system is faster than the other, it may be wise to obtain more data before making a

Figure 5.4 Simple regression for the Bakersfield system.

Regression: Time	constant	Boxes
Coefficient	2.622385	0.658539
std error of coef	1.489348	0.011015
t-ratio	1.7608	59.7869
p-value	10.1768%	0.0000%
beta-weight		0.9982
standard error of regression		2.79990739
R-squared		99.64%
adjusted R-squared		99.61%
number of observations		15
residual degrees of freedom		13
t-statistic for computing 95%-confidence intervals		2.1604

decision. On the other hand, if the statistical evidence strongly convinces her it takes less time to pack an additional box in the Monterey system than to pack it in the Bakersfield system but there is no strong statistical evidence that shows the time to set up the Bakersfield system is shorter than the time to set up the Monterey system, then Susan can safely decide to abandon the Bakersfield system. How can Susan perform these statistical tests?

A simple and effective solution to this problem is to use dummy and slope dummy variables. A **slope dummy variable** is a variable that takes the value zero in some rows and the value of another independent (i.e., x) variable elsewhere. Such a slope dummy variable may be constructed by multiplying a dummy variable times another x variable.

In simple regressions, we fit the data to a single straight line. However, in this case, the data come from two different sources and may not be well modeled by a single straight line, but may fit two different straight lines. A simple illustration of this possibility is given in Figure 5.5.

If the Bakersfield and Monterey systems are different, then the data may fit naturally in two straight lines. One line is associated with the Monterey system, and another line is associated with the Bakersfield system. A dummy variable allows for differences in the intercepts of these two lines. A slope dummy variable allows for differences in the slopes of these two lines. Next we apply these important dummy variable techniques to Susan's problem.

Consider the dummy and slope dummy variables Plant and Boxplant. Plant equals 1 if the data come from the Bakersfield plant and 0 if the data come from the Monterey plant. Boxplant is equal to the variable Boxes if the data come from the Bakersfield plant and 0 if the data come from the Monterey plant (i.e., Boxplant = Plant*Boxes).

If we put all the data together, we obtain Figure 5.6.

Consider a new regression (see Figure 5.7) making use of all the data. Time is the dependent variable. The independent variables are Boxes and the dummy and slope dummy variables (Plant and Boxplant).

Figure 5.5 Example of data well-modeled by two straight lines.

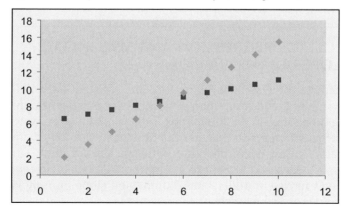

Figure 5.6 Complete dataset for California Strawberries, Inc.

Row	Time	Boxes	Plant	Boxplant
1	102	175	0	0
2	69	110	0	0
3	133	225	0	0
4	37	57	0	0
5	28	47	0	0
6	124	217	0	0
7	71	120	0	0
8	36	60	0	0
9	41	65	0	0
10	104	180	0	0
11	126	210	0	0
12	63	106	0	0
13	34	50	0	0
14	38	60	0	0
15	88	150	0	0
16	95	140	1	140
17	104	153	1	153
18	48	70	1	70
19	108	161	1	161
20	89	128	1	128
21	85	125	1	125
22	90	133	1	133
23	81	122	1	122
24	68	95	1	95
25	98	143	1	143
26	109	161	1	161
27	54	80	1	80
28	85	128	1	128
29	137	205	1	205
30	85	125	1	125

MULTIPLE REGRESSION ANALYSIS INCLUDING A DUMMY AND A SLOPE DUMMY VARIABLE

Examine the results in Figure 5.7. The constant term indicates the time needed to set up the Monterey system. The coefficient on Boxes indicates the additional packing time for each additional box under the Monterey system. The constant plus the coefficient on Plant indicates the time needed to set up the Bakersfield system. The coefficient on Boxes plus the coefficient on Boxplant indicates the additional time to pack each additional box under the Bakersfield system. (This is not obvious. A good exercise to understand dummy and slope dummy variables is to think about the interpretation of these coefficients.)

Figure 5.7 Multiple regression for California Strawberries, Inc.

Regression: Time				
	constant	**Boxes**	**Plant**	**Boxplant**
coefficient	3.59377848	0.56773653	−0.9713931	0.09080294
std error of coef	0.94012944	0.00682691	2.04027485	0.01503162
t-ratio	3.8226	83.1616	−0.4761	6.0408
p-value	0.0741%	0.0000%	63.7973%	0.0002%
beta-weight		0.9349	−0.0158	0.2051
standard error of regression	1.68210603			
R-squared 99.74%				
adjusted R-squared 99.71%				
Number of observations	30			
residual degrees of freedom	26			
t-statistic for computing				
95%-confidence intervals	2.0555			

For the Monterey system, the regression equation simplifies to the following:

Time	= 3.593 + 0. 568 Boxes−0.971 Plant+0.091 Boxplant
	= 3.593 + 0. 568 Boxes−0.971 (0)+0.091 (0)
	= 3.593 + 0. 568 Boxes

For the Bakersfield system, the regression equation simplifies to the following:

Time	= 3.593 + 0. 568 Boxes−0.971 Plant+0.091 Boxplant
	= 3.593 + 0. 568 Boxes−0.971 (1)+0.091 (Boxes)
	= 2.622 + 0. 659 Boxes

These are exactly the same equations as we obtained before using two simple regressions. What is the difference? Our regression equation using dummy and slope dummy variables allows Susan to perform the desired statistical tests, which she could not easily do using two separate regressions.

The key coefficients are the coefficients on the dummy and slope dummy variables. The coefficient on Plant measures difference in the time needed to set up (i.e., the constant term for) the Bakersfield and Monterey systems. The coefficient on Boxplant measures the difference in the time needed to pack each additional box (i.e., the slope term) in the Bakersfield and Monterey systems.

The coefficient on Plant (−0.971) is not significant. The reported p-value is 0.638. Thus, we cannot conclude that the time to set up the Bakersfield system is different than to set up the Monterey system. On the other hand, the coefficient on Boxplant (0.908) is significant. The reported p-value is 0.000002. The p-value for the one-tailed test with alternative hypothesis that the true coefficient on Boxplant is greater than 0 is therefore 0.000001. So, we can conclude that the time to pack each additional box under the Bakersfield system is significantly longer than the time to pack each additional box under the Monterey system.

Our conclusions are as follows:

1. The time to pack each additional box under the Monterey system is significantly shorter than the time to pack each additional box under the Bakersfield system.
2. The time to set up the Monterey system is not significantly different than the time to set up the Bakersfield system.
3. Susan decides to abandon the Bakersfield system.

5.3 Head-hunting Agency

Having finally completed your MBA, you have landed work at a prestigious consulting firm. Your first project is with CEO Seek, a head-hunting agency. CEO Seek looks for CEOs as well as lower-level managers.

To stay ahead of competition, CEO Seek recently came up with a "Within 15 days. Guaranteed!" marketing scheme. The agency wants to guarantee finding a well-suited candidate within 15 days, or the service is free of charge. You are asked to evaluate the scheme and propose possible improvements. Naturally, you have inquired where the number 15 came from. However, the answer you got was, "It's a nice round number and will catch the eye." This did not satisfy you. You decide to investigate further.

You suspect it is harder to find a CEO to manage a bigger company than one to head a small firm. It is, after all, a more responsible job, involving more skills and experience. So, fewer candidates may be suitable for it.

However, the staff at CEO Seek does not agree with your hypothesis. They had the same idea in the past, and they intensified all searches on behalf of larger clients. This method brought no improvement. Thus, they concluded, no relation exists between the size of the firm to manage and the time needed to find a candidate.

But is it true? You decide to check this hypothesis using regression analysis. From the past performance of the agency, you take a random sample of 48 observations from each of the two categories of searches that CEO seek conducts: CEO searches and lower-level searches. Each observation includes the size of the firm to be managed and the time it took to produce a well-suited candidate.

The dataset is in the **headhunting.xls** file. In the variable **SIZE**, the size of the client firm is measured in hundreds of employees. **DAYS** denotes the number of days it took CEO Seek to find a suitable candidate. The first 48 observations are from lower-level searches and the remaining 48 observations are from CEO searches.

You would like to use the data to answer the following questions:
1. Is the size of the firm related to the number of days needed to find a suitable candidate? If it is, describe the relationship.
2. What would you recommend concerning the 15-day guarantee?
3. Is it efficient to treat searches for large firms the same as for small ones? If not, do you have any recommendations for improving the system?

Start with a simple regression. DAYS is the dependent variable, and SIZE is the independent variable (see Figure 5.8).

The estimated slope coefficient is 0.006 with a p-value of 0.769. At first glance, there does not appear to be any relationship between the size of the client firm and the number of days CEO Seek took to find a well-suited candidate. This explains why focusing the search effort more on searches for larger clients did not improve the system.

Nevertheless, the plot of DAYS and SIZE (see Figure 5.9) indicates the size of the firm and the search time are related. However, there appear to be two relationships; a positive one for CEO searches and a negative one for lower-level management searches.

We could proceed in two ways. One is to run separate simple regressions for CEO and lower managerial positions. The other is to run a multiple regression with a dummy and a slope dummy variable. We choose the latter here because it is more convenient and facilitates comparisons. It would have been fine to do this analysis with separate regressions.

Figure 5.8 Simple regression of DAYS on SIZE.

Regression: DAYS		
	constant	SIZE
coefficient	12.8192401	0.00597462
std error of coef	1.10905504	0.02032831
t-ratio	11.5587	0.2939
p-value	0.0000%	76.9477%
beta-weight		0.0303
standard error of regression		5.27796707
R-squared		0.09%
adjusted R-squared		−0.97%
number of observations		96
residual degrees of freedom		94
t-statistic for computing 95%-confidence intervals		1.9855

Figure 5.9 Scatterplot of DAYS vs. SIZE.

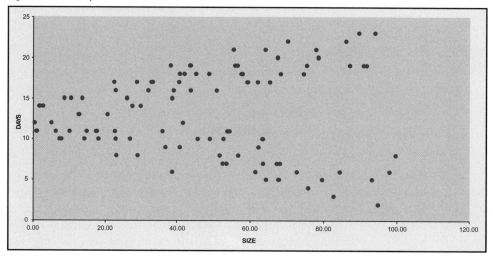

First, we create two new variables. We will call the first one LOWconst. It is equal to 1 if the position is lower-level management and 0 if a CEO is demanded. The second new variable we call LOWslope. It is a slope dummy variable and is the product of LOWconst and SIZE. It is equal to SIZE if the position is lower-level managerial,

Figure 5.10 Regression of DAYS using slope dummy variable.

Regression: DAYS	constant	SIZE	LOWconst	LOWslope
coefficient	13.1745736	0.08873386	−1.0221634	−0.1650824
std error of coef	0.54837761	0.00993329	0.71950776	0.01316637
t-ratio	24.0246	8.9330	−1.4206	−12.5382
p-value	0.0000%	0.0000%	15.8801%	0.0000%
beta-weight		0.4500	−0.0978	−0.9610
standard error of regression	1.68904861			
R-squared	89.99%			
adjusted R-squared	89.66%			
number of observations	96			
residual degrees of freedom	92			
t-statistic for computing 95%-confidence intervals	1.9861			

and it is equal to zero if the position is CEO. Figure 5.10 shows the output from a regression of DAYS on SIZE, LOWconst and LOWslope.

The estimated coefficient on SIZE, 0.0887, is the effect on DAYS of increasing the size of the client firm by 100 employees when looking for a CEO. Testing $H_a: \beta_1 > 0$, we see we are convinced the time to find a suitable CEO candidate increases as the client firm's size grows.

For a lower-level managerial position, the estimated effect on DAYS of increasing the size of a client firm by 100 employees is given by the sum of the coefficients on SIZE and LOWslope or $0.089 + -0.165 = -0.076$.

The basic descriptive statistics for SIZE (for CEO and lower-level management searches) can be seen in Figure 5.11.

The descriptive statistics tell us client firms have between 0.52 and 99.61 hundred employees. The mean is 47.69 and the median is 48.85. Thus, we can consider a firm where SIZE equals 90 as a large firm and where SIZE = 110 as an exceptionally large firm. A client firm with 2,000 employees is relatively small, while 5,000 is typical.

We will use our new regression with the dummy and slope dummy variable to make predictions about the time needed to find suitable candidates of both categories for different sized clients. The 95% confidence and prediction intervals for time to find a well-suited CEO candidate for firms with SIZE = 20, 50, 90, and 110 respectively can be obtained using KStat's prediction function (see Figure 5.12).

For CEO positions, the lower and upper levels of the confidence and prediction intervals increase as the size of the firm increases.

For firms of all sizes, the upper limits of confidence and prediction intervals are greater than 15. Thus, it appears it would be quite costly to attach a 15-day guarantee to CEO-level searches. You would not recommend applying the new guarantee for these searches.

Figure 5.11 Univariate Statistics for SIZE.

Univariate statistics	
	SIZE
mean	47.6894792
standard deviation	26.63812
standard error of the mean	2.71874174
minimum	0.52
median	48.85
maximum	99.61
range	99.09

Figure 5.12 Predictions for CEO position search times.

Predictions, using most-recent regression					
	coefficients	**values for prediction**			
constant	13.1745736				
SIZE	0.08873386	20	50	90	110
LOWconst	−1.0221634	0	0	0	0
LOWslope	−0.1650824	0	0	0	0
predicted value of DAYS		14.94925	17.61127	21.16062	22.9353
standard error of prediction		1.731444	1.706561	1.753443	1.809439
standard error of regression		1.689049	1.689049	1.689049	1.689049
standard error of estimated mean		0.380808	0.243854	0.470824	0.648988
confidence level	95.00%				
t-statistic	1.9861				
residual degr. freedom	92				
confidence limits	**lower**	11.51045	14.22189	17.67813	19.3416
for prediction	**upper**	18.38805	21.00064	24.64311	26.529
confidence limits	**lower**	14.19293	17.12695	20.22552	21.64635
for estimated mean	**upper**	15.70557	18.09558	22.09572	24.22424

The 95% confidence and prediction intervals for lower-level management searches for firms with SIZE = 20, 50, 90, and 110, respectively, are also easily obtained using the prediction function (see Figure 5.13).

For the case of lower-level management, the upper and lower levels of the prediction and confidence intervals for time to find a well-suited candidate decrease as the size of the firm increases.

For all sizes of the client firm, the confidence and prediction intervals are below 14.05. Thus, the 15-day guarantee could be offered at little cost for lower-level managerial positions. Therefore, it would be advisable to apply the new policy only for lower-level managerial searches but not for CEO searches.

Our conclusions can be summarized as follows:

1. The size of the firm and the search time are related but the relationship depends on the category of employee desired. When a CEO is needed, it takes more time to find a suitable candidate for large firms than for small firms. On the other hand, it takes less time to find a suitable lower-level candidate for large firms than for small firms.

2. The 15-day guarantee policy is quite feasible for the case of lower-level positions. This policy would work poorly for the CEO searches. A longer time horizon for the guarantee should be considered for candidates in this category.

3. We might improve the current system (in terms of reducing the lengthiest searches) by allocating more effort to finding CEO candidates for large firms.

Figure 5.13 Predictions for lower-level management search times.

Predictions, using most-recent regression

	coefficients	values for prediction			
constant	13.1745736				
SIZE	0.08873386	20	50	90	110
LOWconst	−1.0221634	1	1	1	1
LOWslope	−0.1650824	20	50	90	110

predicted value of DAYS		10.62544	8.334983	5.281042	3.754071
standard error of prediction		1.7212	1.706915	1.748535	1.794131
standard error of regression		1.689049	1.689049	1.689049	1.689049
standard error of estimated mean		0.331125	0.246319	0.452207	0.604995

confidence level	95.00%
t-statistic	1.9861
residual degr. freedom	92

confidence limits	lower	7.206988	4.944903	1.8083	0.190773
for prediction	upper	14.04389	11.72506	8.753784	7.31737
confidence limits	lower	9.967797	7.845772	4.38292	2.552498
for estimated mean	upper	11.28308	8.824194	6.179164	4.955645

Alternatively, CEO Seek might want to solicit more business from small firms looking for CEOs and large firms looking for lower-level management since it seems to handle these searches more efficiently. Since it takes more time to find a CEO candidate than a candidate for a lower managerial position, a policy recognizing the increased difficulty of finding CEOs would be sensible.

SUMMARY

Dummy and slope dummy variables can be used to test statistical differences between the constant and slope coefficients (respectively) of two regressions.

When we have to decide between adopting different systems, these statistical tests are useful. It may not be easy to tell which system is best and these statistical tests help quantify the strength of our evidence for this question.

A single simple regression may be unsuccessful when the relationship between the independent and dependent variables is changed by a third factor. You need dummy and slope dummy variables to deal with this.

Situations in which slope dummy variables can prove useful can often be detected through graphical analysis. The regression output on its own can be inadequate or misleading as in the simple regression in the head hunting agency case.

NEW TERMS

Dummy variable An artificially constructed variable that takes on the values of zero and one only. Used to quantify non-numerical qualities or categories. When included in a regression, effectively allows the constant to change depending on the value of the dummy variable

Slope dummy variable A variable that takes the value zero in some rows and the value of an independent variable elsewhere. The product of a dummy variable and another variable. When included in a regression, effectively allows the slope on the independent variable used in its construction to change depending on the value of the dummy variable used in its construction

CASE EXERCISES

1. Valuing an MBA for yourself

The purpose of this example is to compare the "value-added" of two different business schools by looking at the incomes of the student body prior to beginning the MBA program, and comparing it to the incomes after completing the program. The data consist of information on 400 students, half from school A and the other half from school B.

'preMBA' = income in year before beginning the program, in thousands of dollars

'postMBA' = income in year after completing the program, in thousands of dollars

'school' = a dummy variable equal to 0 for students attending school A, and 1 for students attending school B

The following regression output was obtained:

Regression: postMBA	constant	preMBA	school
coefficient	24.659	1.83628	1.732
std error of coef	1.868	0.04178	1.136
t-ratio	13.2000	43.9600	1.5200
p-value	0.0000%	0.0000%	12.8000%
standard error of regression		11.26	
R-squared		83.10%	
adjusted R-squared		83.00%	

a. Explain clearly, and as concisely as possible, the interpretation of the coefficient on the school variable.

Suppose we define a new variable as follows:

'school*preMBA' = 'school' multiplied by 'preMBA'.

We redo the regression with this extra variable added as another predictor and obtain the following regression output:

Regression: postMBA				
	constant	preMBA	school	school*preMBA
coefficient	30	1.70426	−7.314	0.23227
std error of coef	2.67	0.06306	3.447	0.08364
t-ratio	11.2300	27.0300	−2.1200	2.7800
p-value	0.0000%	0.0000%	3.4000%	0.6000%
standard error of regression	11.17			
R-squared	83.40%			
adjusted R-squared	83.30%			

Answer the remaining questions, basing your answers on this second regression:

b. Suppose your income this year is $15,000 and you are choosing between the two schools' programs. Assume the two schools have the same fees, similar locations, etc. Which one should you choose? What if your current income is $65,000?

We ask KStat to predict the post-MBA income of someone entering school A with a pre-MBA income of $40,000 and to give 90% confidence and prediction intervals for post-MBA income. This gives the following additional output:

predicted value of		98.171
standard error of estimated mean		0.79
confidence level	90.00%	
confidence limits	lower	79.71
for prediction	upper	116.632
confidence limits	lower	96.868
for estimated mean	upper	99.474

c. What is the predicted post-MBA income of graduates of school A having pre-MBA income of $40,000? If 60 students entering school A this year have pre-MBA incomes of $40,000, about how many of those students do you estimate will make less than $80,000 the year they leave?

d. Explain briefly the meaning of the R-squared statistic in this context (i.e., do not simply say what it means in the abstract, but say what it means for this regression and application).

e. In a few, non-technical words, summarize what the difference seems to be between the two schools.

2. Valuing an MBA for your employer

A well-known consulting company is interested in comparing the performance of the consultants it recruits from MBA programs with that of consultants it recruits from non-traditional backgrounds (such as Ph.D. programs). The accounting department has developed a method of allocating all billing to individuals, so it is possible to say how much revenue any given consultant has produced in the last year. You collect data on 130 consultants. For each person, you get three pieces of information, stored as follows:

experience = the length of time they have been with the company (measured in months)

billing = the revenue they brought in in the last year (in thousands of dollars)

MBA = 1 if they came from an MBA program; 0 for those from non-MBA programs

You define a slope dummy variable as follows:

experience*MBA = experience multiplied by MBA

Then, you run the following regression:

Regression:				
	constant	experience	MBA	experience*MBA
Coefficient	44.13	9.0681	68.43	−1.4317
std error of coef	15.43	0.4516	22.73	0.6167
t-ratio	2.8600	20.0800	3.0100	−2.3200
p-value	0.5000%	0.0000%	0.3000%	2.2000%
Standard error of regression	62			
R-squared		86.30%		
Adjusted R-squared		85.90%		

Answer the following questions.

a. What do you predict to be the average billing of consultants with two years of experience if they came in with an MBA? What if they came in with a PhD?

b. Does the extra value to the company of an MBA as compared to a non-MBA change over the time the MBA is with the company? Test at the 1% level of significance.

c. The sample consists of consultants who have been at the company for up to five years. Suppose you are asked to use your results to predict what the difference in billing (between MBAs and non-MBAs) will be after 10 years. What does the estimated regression equation predict?

d. Use your judgment: What do you think of this last prediction and why?

PROBLEMS

For problems 1–4, you will need to access the **pizzasales.xls** file.

The Waialua Pizza Company is a medium-sized chain of pizzerias located at beaches all over the South Pacific. The chain is known for its delicious pizzas served at all the nice beaches, and it is known for its use of statistical techniques to improve operations.

The company has obtained data reflecting its sales in its 50 beachfront stores. The Waialua Pizza Company feels the income levels of the nearby community and the presence or absence of competition might be major factors in determining sales.

The following variables were tallied:

Sales = $ per day

Income = Average per-capita income in $ per week in the surrounding neighborhood

Competitor = 1 when one or more competing pizzerias are located within ½ mile; 0 when no other pizzerias are located nearby

1. Conduct a regression of Sales vs. Competitor (only use this one independent variable for now) and use the results to answer the following questions:

   a. Estimate the daily sales for a store that has no competition.

   b. Estimate the daily sales for a store that faces competition.

   c. Calculate the difference between your two estimates and comment on the practical and statistical significance of this gap.

   d. Provide a 95% confidence interval for the effect of competition on sales.

   e. What percentage of the variance in sales can be explained using only the Competitor variable?

2. Conduct a regression of Sales vs. Income (only use this one independent variable for now) and use the results to answer the following questions:

   a. Estimate the daily sales for a store whose neighborhood income is $200 per week.

   b. Estimate the daily sales for a store whose neighborhood income is $300 per week.

   c. Estimate the impact of a $100 increase in neighborhood income per week on sales.

   d. Provide a 95% confidence interval for your estimate in part c.

   e. What percentage of the variance in sales can be explained using only the Income variable?

3. Create a scatterplot of Sales vs. Income and have KStat plot the regression line as well. Does the picture reveal any likely opportunities to improve your model?

4. Construct a new variable, Comp*Inc, by multiplying the Competitior and Income variables together. Run a regression to predict sales using all three variables: Competitior, Income, and Comp*Inc.

   a. Is the Competitor variable in this model statistically significant?

   b. Estimate the daily sales for a store without competition whose neighborhood income is $300 per week.

   c. Estimate the daily sales for a store with a competitor whose neighborhood income is $300 per week.

   d. Compare your answers to part b and part c. Reconcile the results of this comparison with your answer to part a.

5. Access the **eurodata2a.xls** dataset, which is a restructured version of the file eurodata.xls used in problems 7–9 in Chapter 4. This file contains information about unemployment and wage growth in Belgium and Denmark. The dummy variable Belgium is set to 1 in Belgium and 0 in Denmark.

Use KStat to perform a regression of Wage Growth vs. Unemployment, Belgium, and BE*Unemployment.

   a. Write out the full estimated regression equation.

   b. Write out the estimated regression equation for Belgium.

   c. Write out the estimated regression equation for Denmark.

   d. Compare the equations from part b and c to your answers from Problem 7, Chapter 4.

   e. How does a one percentage point increase in unemployment relate to the growth rate of wages in Belgium?

   f. How does a one percentage point increase in unemployment relate to the growth rate of wages in Denmark?

   g. Estimate the difference in how unemployment relates to wage growth between the two countries.

   h. Provide a 95% confidence interval for the difference in how unemployment relates to wage growth between the two countries.

   i. Predict the growth rate in wages for each country in a year that has 3% unemployment.

   j. Provide a 90% confidence interval for each prediction from part i.

6. Access the **eurodata2b.xls** dataset, which is a restructured version of the file eurodata.xls used in problems 7–9 in Chapter 4. This file contains information about unemployment and wage growth in Germany and Greece. The dummy variable Germany is set to 1 in Germany and 0 in Greece.

Use KStat to perform a regression of Wage Growth vs. Unemployment, Germany, and DE*Unemployment.

   a. Write out the full estimated regression equation.

   b. Write out the estimated regression equation for Germany.

   c. Write out the estimated regression equation for Greece.

   d. Compare the equations from part b and c to your answers from Problem 8, Chapter 4.

   e. How does a one percentage point increase in unemployment relate to the growth rate of wages in Germany?

   f. How does a one percentage point increase in unemployment relate to the growth rate of wages in Greece?

g. Estimate the difference in how unemployment relates to wage growth between the two countries.

h. Provide a 95% confidence interval for the difference in how unemployment relates to wage growth between the two countries.

i. Predict the growth rate in wages for each country in a year that has 3% unemployment.

j. Provide a 90% confidence interval for each prediction from part i.

7. Access the **eurodata2c.xls** dataset, which is a restructured version of the file eurodata.xls used in problems 7–9 in Chapter 4. This file contains information about unemployment and wage growth in Spain and France. The dummy variable Spain is set to 1 in Spain and 0 in France.

Use KStat to perform a regression of Wage Growth vs. Unemployment, Spain, ES*Unemployment.

a. Write out the full estimated regression equation.

b. Write out the estimated regression equation for Spain.

c. Write out the estimated regression equation for France.

d. Compare the equations from part b and c to your answers from Problem 9, Chapter 4.

e. How does a one percentage point increase in unemployment relate to the growth rate of wages in Spain?

f. How does a one percentage point increase in unemployment relate to the growth rate of wages in France?

g. Estimate the difference in how unemployment relates to wage Growth between the two countries.

h. Provide a 95% confidence interval for the difference in how unemployment relates to wage growth between the two countries.

i. Predict the growth rate in wages for each country in a year that has 3% unemployment.

j. Provide a 90% confidence interval for each prediction from part i.

CHAPTER 6

FORESTIER WINE: GRAPHICAL ANALYSIS, NON-LINEAR REGRESSION AND SPURIOUS CORRELATION

In this chapter, we will learn how to use graphical analysis to supplement regression. We will study residuals and how to use residual plots to supplement our regression analysis. Additionally, we will expand our regression model's domain of applicability by learning how to conduct one type of non-linear regression. Finally, we will explore the notions of outliers, influential observations, and spurious correlation.

6.1 Snowfall, Unemployment, and Spurious Correlation

The following data (see the **unemploy.xls** file[1]) provides the annual inches of snowfall in Amherst, Massachusetts, and the annual U.S. national unemployment (in %) for the years 1973 to 1982 (see Figure 6.1).

In principle, should we expect any relationship between snowfall in Amherst and U.S. unemployment? Look at the plot of these two variables in Figure 6.2.

Figure 6.1 Snowfall data.

Row	Snowfall	Unemployment	Year
1	45	4.9	1973
2	59	5.6	1974
3	82	8.5	1975
4	80	7.7	1976
5	71	7.1	1977
6	60	6.1	1978
7	55	5.8	1979
8	69	7.1	1980
9	79	7.6	1981
10	95	9.7	1982

Figure 6.2 Snowfall vs. unemployment in Amherst.

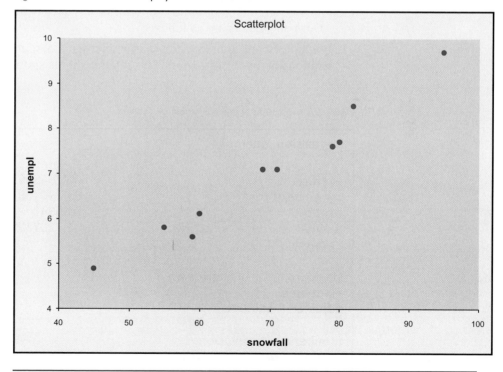

1. From *Statistics for Business and Economics*, by Heinz Kohler, Thomson Learning, 2002.

There is clearly a linear relationship between the two variables in the sample, and a regression will do well here (see Figure 6.3). The R-squared of 96.73% is exceptionally high, which indicates we are explaining most of the variation in U.S. unemployment. Based on our data, should we conclude that there exists a significant relationship between snowfall in Amherst and U.S. unemployment?

To answer this question we can do a hypothesis test on the slope coefficient to find out if it is significant. The t-statistic is 15.385 and the associated p-value is 0; thus, we reject the null hypothesis that the slope is zero and conclude there is a significant relationship.

This example shows that on occasion, clear patterns pop up at random. Since our inferences are based on data, we will make errors. The relationship between unemployment and snowfall is spurious.

Spurious correlation occurs when the data coming from two unrelated variables are apparently linearly related.

The example suggests that if people want to reach a certain conclusion, and they search for data with this in mind, they can often find a dataset that supports the conclusion.

For example, we generated 50 columns of random data with 10 numbers in each column. We know that none of them are related to unemployment or to any other real dataset because the data was generated using Excel's random number generator. However, some of the regressions turned out to fit the unemployment data pretty well with the slope coefficient statistically significant at a standard 5% level of significance. For example, a regression relating unemployment and the 34th randomly generated column turned out this way (see Figure 6.4).

Our conclusions are as follows:

1. Unemployment and snowfall in Amherst have a statistically significant linear relationship over this period. This relationship is spurious.

Figure 6.3 Regression of unemployment on snowfall.

Regression: unempl	constant	snowfall
coefficient	0.37645665	0.09544667
std error of coef	0.44009081	0.00620382
t-ratio	0.8554	15.3851
p-value	41.7207%	0.0000%
beta-weight		0.9835
standard error of regression		0.27886144
R-squared		96.73%
adjusted R-squared		96.32%
number of observations		10
residual degrees of freedom		8
t-statistic for computing 95%-confidence intervals		2.3060

Figure 6.4 Regression of unemployment on random data.

Regression: unempl		
	constant	**C34**
coefficient	8.34562462	−0.2571177
std error of coef	0.56964516	0.08807575
t-ratio	14.6506	−2.9193
p-value	0.0000%	1.9313%
beta-weight		−0.7182
standard error of regression		1.07318381
R-squared		51.58%
Adjusted R-squared		45.53%
number of observations		10
residual degrees of freedom		8
t-statistic for computing 95%-confidence intervals		2.3060

2. It is always possible to find a spurious relation between an independent variable and a dependent variable if you try many different independent variables. This occurs because each relationship you examine has some chance of appearing significant due to luck or sampling error even if there is no underlying relationship. Using a level of significance α when testing a single relationship ensures the probability of finding this type of spurious result is at most α. However, if you examine 100 different possible relationships, the probability that at least one of them appears significant even if none of the relationships are real may be as high as $1-(1-\alpha)^{100}$. So, when $\alpha = 0.05$, this probability is $1-(0.95)^{100} = 0.994$.

3. For this reason, always think hard about what variables are sensible to use in a regression analysis before running the regressions. This helps to limit your risk of obtaining spurious results. Similarly, when presented with others' analyses, make sure to find out the process that led to the reported results. If they were the result of searching through a large number of relationships and reporting only significant results, you should be skeptical.

6.2 Wine and Wealth

In this section, we present some simple (yet deceptive) regression examples. The purpose is to motivate techniques that move beyond an examination of the basic regression output.

Robert Owen is the new chief manager of Forestier, a company that produces, markets, and distributes wine. Forestier produces four brands of wine: Almaden, Bianco, Casarosa, and Delacroix. Almaden and Casarosa are high-quality wines. Bianco is a regular wine. Delacroix is a specialty dessert wine sold only in specific locations.

Robert believes that wine sales are directly related to the average household income of the neighborhoods in which the wine shops are located. Robert is considering expanding the business to rich neighborhoods with $15,000 monthly average income. To learn how the various wines are likely to sell in these neighborhoods, he wants to estimate how average income affects sales of the four Forestier brands.

Robert obtained some data on average monthly household income (measured in units of $1,000) and average monthly wine sales (measured in units of $1,000). He has figures from 11 neighborhoods for each brand. The data are in Figure 6.5 and in the **wineandwealth.xls** file[2].

Robert decides to use regressions to get a feel for the effect of average income on wine sales. He intends to use the regressions to predict wine sales in neighborhoods of $15,000 monthly income.

Consider the Almaden data. Sales A is the dependent variable. Income A is the independent variable (see Figure 6.6).

The regression indicates that monthly sales of Almaden increase, on average, by 50 cents for each extra dollar (equivalently, by $500 for each extra $1,000) in average monthly household income of the neighborhood where the wine shop is located.

The coefficient on Income A (0.50) is statistically significant at our standard 5% level of significance. The t-ratio is 4.242 with a p-value of 0.0022.

The regression estimate and 95% confidence and prediction intervals for Almaden sales when Income A is 15 are 10.501, (8.692, 12.310) and (7.170, 13.833), respectively (as you may calculate using KStat's Statistics>Prediction command). Thus, in any single neighborhood with $15,000 monthly average income, our estimated monthly average sales of Almaden are $10,501, and, with 95% confidence, monthly average sales of Almaden will be between $7,170 and $13,833. Similarly, the average, over the whole population of neighborhoods with $15,000 monthly

Figure 6.5 Forestier data.

Almaden		Bianco		Casarosa		Delacroix	
Income A	Sales A	Income B	Sales B	Income C	Sales C	Income D	Sales D
10	8.04	10	9.14	10	7.46	8	6.58
8	6.95	8	8.14	8	6.77	8	5.76
13	7.58	13	8.74	13	12.74	8	7.71
9	8.81	9	8.77	9	7.11	8	8.84
11	8.33	11	9.26	11	7.81	8	8.47
14	9.96	14	8.1	14	8.84	8	7.04
6	7.24	6	6.13	6	6.08	8	5.25
4	4.26	4	3.1	4	5.39	19	12.5
12	10.84	12	9.13	12	8.15	8	5.56
7	4.82	7	7.26	7	6.42	8	7.91
5	5.68	5	4.74	5	5.73	8	6.89

---

2. Data adapted from Anscombe, F.J., *Graphs in Statistical Analysis*, American Statistican, (27) February 1973, pp17–21.

Figure 6.6 Simple regression analysis using the Almaden data.

Regression: Sales A		
	constant	**Income A**
coefficient	3.00009091	0.50009091
std error of coef	1.12474681	0.1179055
t-ratio	2.6673	4.2415
p-value	2.5734%	0.2170%
beta-weight		0.8164
standard error of regression		1.23660334
R-squared		66.65%
adjusted R-squared		62.95%
number of observations		11
residual degrees of freedom		9
t-statistic for computing 95%-confidence intervals		2.2622

income, of the monthly average sales of Almaden is between $8,692 and $12,310 with 95% confidence.

Plot Almaden sales and average income (see Figure 6.7). That is, plot Sales A versus Income A. There does not seem to be anything unusual or troubling about this plot. The data seem to fit a generally linear pattern with some variance about the line.

Next, Robert analyzes the effects of average income on Bianco sales. In the next regression (see Figure 6.8), Sales B is the dependent variable and Income B is the independent variable.

Figure 6.7 Plot of Almaden Sales vs Income.

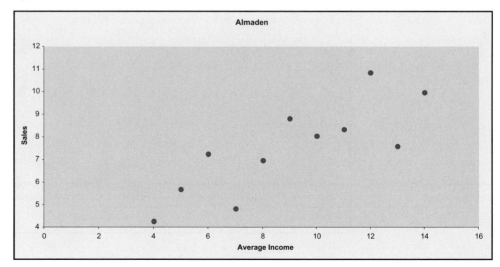

Figure 6.8 Simple regression analysis using the Bianco data.

Regression: Sales B	constant	Income B
coefficient	3.00090905	0.50000002
std error of coef	1.12530254	0.11796376
t-ratio	2.6668	4.2386
p-value	2.5759%	0.2179%
beta-weight		0.8162
standard error of regression		1.23721434
R-squared		66.62%
adjusted R-squared		62.92%
number of observations		11
residual degrees of freedom		9
t-statistic for computing 95%-confidence intervals		2.2622

The regression output when using the Bianco data is almost exactly the same as the regression output when using the Almaden data. Thus, the conclusions we would obtain from this regression are the same as the conclusions we obtained from the regression using the Almaden data. In particular, this regression indicates that Bianco monthly average sales increase, on average, by 50 cents for each extra dollar of average monthly household income. The confidence and prediction intervals for Bianco sales are the same as the ones for Almaden.

Figure 6.9 Plot of Bianco Sales vs. Income.

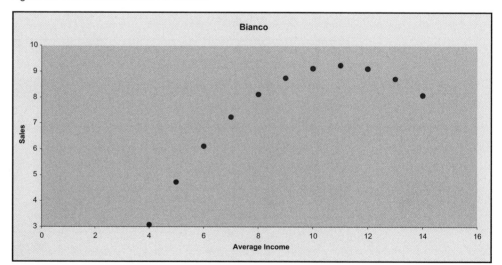

The data on Bianco sales are different from the data on Almaden, but the regressions using the Bianco and the Almaden data are the same. This seems odd. Robert is puzzled. After all, Almaden is a high-quality wine and Bianco is merely ordinary. Many times, a background graphical analysis can help us understand a regression analysis better. Plot Bianco sales and average income (see Figure 6.9). That is, plot Sales B versus Income B.

The plot clearly indicates that the relationship between Bianco sales and average income is not linear. Thus, one of the most fundamental assumptions of regression (linearity) has been violated. The conclusions we obtained concerning Bianco must be revisited.

The regression using the Bianco sales seems, at first glance, to confirm the conclusion obtained from the regression analysis using the Almaden sales. However, this is incorrect. The effects of average income on Almaden sales are not the same as on Bianco sales. The plots indicate that the Almaden sales are higher if the shops are located in richer neighborhoods. The Bianco sales increase if the wine shops are located in richer neighborhoods but only up to a certain point. After this point, the Bianco sales decrease if the wine shops are located in richer neighborhoods. This probably happens because the quality of the Bianco wine is worse than the quality of the Almaden wine. The crucial point, however, is that the relationship between Bianco sales and average income is non-linear, i.e., not a straight-line relationship.

How can we estimate the effects of average income on Bianco sales when this relationship is non-linear?

It may seem that everything we have learned so far only applies to the linear case, and therefore, these techniques are useless if the relationship between the independent and dependent variable is non-linear. Fortunately, this is untrue: We can apply the techniques we have learned to the case of a non-linear relationship between the independent and dependent variable. One useful and important kind of non-linear relationship is a quadratic relationship. Below, we will learn to use regression to estimate such a relationship.

A **quadratic function** is a function of the form $f(x) = a + bx + cx^2$.

If the coefficient on the squared term is negative, i.e., if $c < 0$, then the plot of the function f looks like an inverted U. For example, Figure 6.10 shows the plot of the function $f(x) = 5+10x-x^2$ for values of x between 0 and 8.

On the other hand, if the coefficient on the squared term is positive, i.e., if $c > 0$, then the plot of the function f looks like a U. For example, Figure 6.11 shows the plot of the function $f(x) = 5-10x+x^2$ for values of x between 0 and 8.

Looking at these plots, we can reasonably conjecture that Bianco sales are a quadratic function (with negative coefficient on the squared term) of the average household income of the neighborhoods in which the wine shops are located. That is, we can reasonably conjecture that Bianco sales and average income are related in the following way:

Bianco sales = a+b(Average Income)+c(Average Income)^2+error

Figure 6.10 Quadratic equation with negative coefficient on the squared term.

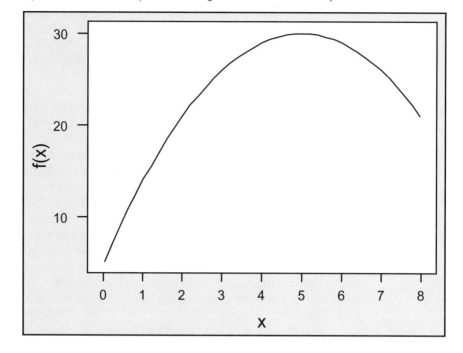

Figure 6.11 Quadratic equation with positive coefficient on the squared term.

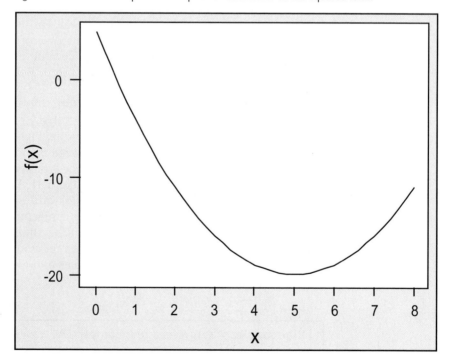

We can estimate the coefficients a, b, and c by running a multiple regression. The dependent variable is Sales B. The independent variables are Income B and Income Bsqr, where Income Bsqr is the square of Income B:

$$\text{Income Bsqr} = (\text{Income B})^2$$

The relevant data for this regression are in Figure 6.12. The regression (see Figure 6.13) appears extremely successful in capturing the relationship. In fact, the R-squared is 100%, indicating a perfect fit. The coefficient on the linear term is positive (2.78) and is significantly greater than zero, and the coefficient on the squared term is negative (−0.127) and is significantly below zero. This makes sense. The estimated coefficient on the linear term in a quadratic regression is the estimated slope of the relationship when x = 0. Here, this tells us that if average monthly income is close to zero, increasing it by a dollar yields an average of $2.78 in extra sales. Thus, for low levels of income the slope relating income to sales is positive and steep.

The estimated coefficient on the squared term in a quadratic regression tells us how quickly the slope of the relationship changes as x increases. The fact that this coefficient is negative in the example tells us that increases in income provide less of a boost in Bianco sales for higher income neighborhoods than for lower income neighborhoods. We expected these signs for the coefficients because we observed (in Figure 6.9) at low levels of income Bianco sales increase as the average income of the wine shops' neighborhoods increases, but gradually this effect lessens, until, eventually, Bianco sales start decreasing as the average income of the wine shops' neighborhoods increases.

What is the meaning of the constant term? It is our estimate of average sales of Bianco when average monthly household income is zero. The estimated constant (−6) is significantly negative. This does not make sense as a prediction. After

Figure 6.12 Bianco data with squared term.

Bianco		
Income B	Income Bsqr	Sales B
10	100	9.14
8	64	8.14
13	169	8.74
9	81	8.77
11	121	9.26
14	196	8.1
6	36	6.13
4	16	3.1
12	144	9.13
7	49	7.26
5	25	4.74

Figure 6.13 Regression analysis of the Bianco data with a quadratic term.

Regression: Sales B			
	constant	Income B	Income Bsqr
coefficient	-5.9957353	2.78083944	-0.1267133
std error of coef	0.00432999	0.00104007	5.7098E-05
t-ratio	-1384.6989	2673.7127	-2219.2142
p-value	0.0000%	0.0000%	0.0000%
beta-weight		4.5396	-3.7680
standard error of regression		0.0016725	
R-squared		100.00%	
adjusted R-squared		100.00%	
number of observations		11	
residual degrees of freedom		8	
t-statistic for computing 95%-confidence intervals		2.3060	

all, we should not expect sales to be negative for the wine shops located in extremely poor neighborhoods. However, an examination of the data indicates no such neighborhoods were in our sample for Bianco. Thus, although the quadratic regression appears be an excellent model for incomes closer to the range of our data, we should exercise caution in using our regression equation to forecast Bianco sales in poor neighborhoods.

Robert wants to predict Bianco sales in wine shops located in neighborhoods with $15,000 monthly average income. Using the quadratic regression, the estimated sales when Income B is 15 (and therefore Income Bsqr is $15^2 = 225$) are $7,206 per month. The corresponding 95% confidence and prediction intervals for Bianco Sales are shown in Figure 6.14.

The confidence and prediction intervals are narrow, indicating little error in our sales estimate. The non-linear regression predicts that the average sales will be $7,206 per month. The linear regression predicted average monthly sales of $10,501. The difference is large (almost 50%). It would have been a big mistake to ignore the non-linearity present in the data.

How do we know if a non-linear model should be used? One way is to plot the dependent against the independent variable and look for distinct curvature. We used this method in the Bianco example. Another method (explained below) involves plotting residuals versus predicted or fitted values and examining this plot for distinct curvature. This method is extremely useful, especially if there is more than one independent variable. The reason is simple. Since a plot can have no more than three dimensions, plotting the dependent versus the independent variables is impossible if more than two independent variables are used. Plotting residuals versus predicted values is always possible because the plot remains two-dimensional no matter how many independent variables are used. Examining such plots to detect non-linearities should become a regular supplement to your basic regression analysis.

Figure 6.14 Confidence and prediction intervals for Bianco sales.

confidence limits	lower	7.200635
for prediction	upper	7.212092
confidence limits	lower	7.202128
for estimated mean	upper	7.210599

According to the simple regression model, every observation, y_i, consists of a part that is linear in x, plus an error term:

$$y_i = \beta_0 + \beta_1 x_i + \varepsilon_i$$

In the case of m independent variables, every observation, y_i, consists of a part that is linear in x_1, x_2, ... x_m, plus an error term:

$$y_i = \beta_0 + \beta_1 x_{1,i} + \beta_2 x_{2,i} + ... + \beta_n x_{m,i} + \varepsilon_i$$

We use regression to estimate the linear part via the fitted (or predicted) value $\hat{y}$:

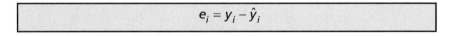

$$\hat{y}_i = b_0 + b_1 x_i$$

In the case of multiple regression, the fitted value $\hat{y}$ is given by the following:

$$\hat{y}_i = b_0 + b_1 x_{1,i} + b_2 x_{2,i} + ... + b_n x_{m,i}$$

The **fitted value** (or **predicted value**), $\hat{y}$, is the value of the dependent variable predicted by the regression model.

The **residual** is the difference between the observed value and the fitted value. That is, the residual for the ith observation in our sample, e_i, is given by the following equation:

$$e_i = y_i - \hat{y}_i$$

Since the residuals depend on our estimates (via the fitted values), it makes sense to talk about their sampling distribution. If the standard assumptions of the regression model are correct, the residuals will be normally distributed with a mean equal to zero, a constant variance, and independent of each other.

For the Almaden and Bianco wines, we can use a plot of the residuals to check our linearity assumption. Consider the Almaden data. To plot residuals against the fitted values, we first have to run the regression for Sales A against Income A again since KStat uses only the most recent regression in calculating the residuals and fitted values. Then, click **Statistics>Charts>Residual plots**, and choose **predicted values** in the dialog box that you obtain and click **OK**. KStat will plot residuals against the fitted values (see Figure 6.15).

Figure 6.15 Residual plot for Almaden sales.

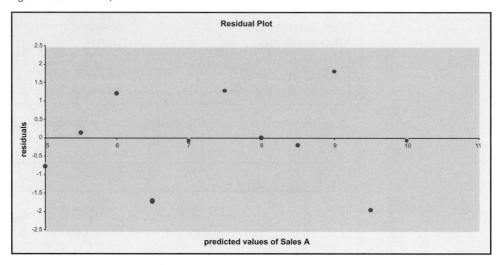

In this plot, the residuals seem to be displayed at random. No distinct curved pattern can be detected as we move from left to right across the plot. This is a good sign, because it indicates that our linearity assumption appears satisfied.

Consider the Bianco data. A plot of the residuals against the fitted values for the regression without the squared income term reveals distinct curvature (see Figure 6.16).

All the residuals are negative when the fitted values are low or high. On the other hand, all the residuals are positive for middle fitted values. This inverted-U pattern indicates a non-linear relationship (in fact, a quadratic relationship in this case) between the dependent and independent variables. In general, distinct curvature in the plot of residuals against fitted values suggests a non-linear relationship between the dependent (y) and independent (x) variables.

Figure 6.16 Residual plot of Bianco sales with linear model.

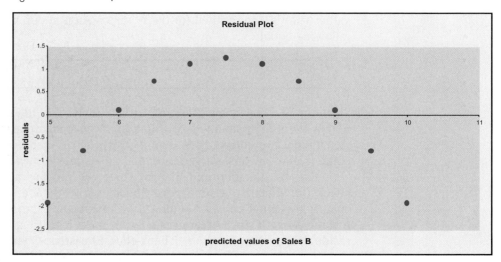

Try running the quadratic regression using the Bianco data and plotting the residuals versus predicted values from that regression. If the quadratic form is successful in capturing the curvature in the relationship, there should no longer be a distinct curved pattern across the residual plot. You will see that is the case. If distinct curvature had remained, that would have suggested that a model other than the quadratic was needed.

It is important to check the linearity assumption whenever you try a regression model. If distinct curvature is ignored, the regression estimates and standard errors will be biased and may be quite misleading. In addition to checking the linearity assumption, residual plots have another use that we will see in Chapter 7 when we learn how to check the assumption of constant variance.

Now, we will move on and analyze the effects of average income on Casarosa sales. As you can see in Figure 6.17, the regression using the Casarosa data is almost identical to the regressions using the Almaden and Bianco (the linear case) data. Thus, a direct interpretation of the regression would indicate that average monthly sales of Casarosa increase, on average, by 50 cents for each extra dollar of average monthly household income for the neighborhood in which the wine shop is located.

The coefficient on income (0.4997) is statistically significant as the t-ratio is 4.239, with a p-value of 0.002176. The 95% confidence and prediction intervals evaluated at income of 15 are (8.690, 12.307) and (7.168, 13.829), respectively, which are almost identical to the intervals we first obtained with the other two wines.

Plot Casarosa sales against average income (see Figure 6.18). That is, plot Sales C and Income C.

Figure 6.17 Simple regression analysis using the Casarosa data.

Regression: Sales C		
	constant	Income C
coefficient	3.00245456	0.49972727
std error of coef	1.12448117	0.11787766
t-ratio	2.6701	4.2394
p-value	2.5619%	0.2176%
beta-weight		0.8163
standard error of regression		1.23631129
R-squared		66.63%
adjusted R-squared		62.92%
number of observations		11
residual degrees of freedom		9
t-statistic for computing 95%-confidence intervals		2.2622

Figure 6.18 Plot of Casarosa Sales vs Income.

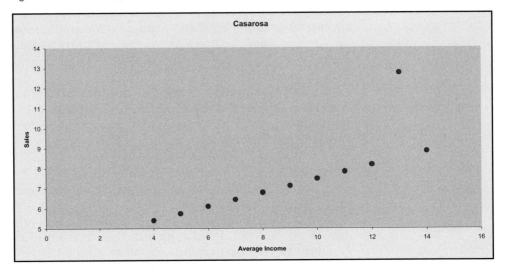

The plot indicates a linear relationship between Casarosa sales and average income, except for one point. In this case, this unusual observation is called an outlier.

An **outlier** is an observation with an unusually large residual. KStat can identify outliers for you. This is especially useful in multiple regressions or large datasets where they may not be visualized as readily. To have KStat do this, run the regression (here Sales C vs. Income C) and then click **Statistics>Model analysis** and examine the **Residuals** worksheet. The **std'ized** column contains the studentized residuals. The studentized residual tells you the number of standard deviations that this residual is from zero, which is the expected value of residuals. The studentized residuals for any outliers will appear in red on your screen. The cutoff for determining if an observation is an outlier is given by the number on top of the **std'ized** label. This number is determined so that if the residuals are normally distributed, approximately 5% of the observations would typically be classified as outliers.

When you encounter outliers (especially if they are large, as in Figure 6.18), you should initially check whether they are due to a mistake such as a data entry error or a measurement error. If that is not the case, it may be worthwhile to try to find out what led to the unusually high or low value: for example, if these are financial data, an outlier might be linked to a stock market crash. In this example, the outlier could be related to a single buyer who is particularly fond of Casarosa wine.

You should not remove outliers from your dataset unless they are due to a mistake: Weird things happen, and it is foolish to pretend otherwise.

On the other hand, if you have a data entry error or a measurement error, then the data should be corrected or removed. In the case of an error, we would have to run a new regression with the corrected data. The results would probably indicate that average Casarosa sales increase by less than 50 cents for each extra dollar on the average income of the wine shops' neighborhood. We can see this in the slope of the line formed by the remaining points being smaller than 0.5.

Finally, we will analyze the effects of average income on Delacroix sales (see Figure 6.19). In this regression, Sales D is the dependent variable and Income D is the independent variable. The regression using the Delacroix data is essentially identical to the regression using the Almaden data, the Bianco data (the linear case), and the Casarosa data. A direct interpretation of this regression would lead to the same conclusions as before. However, we have seen that before deriving conclusions from the regression analysis, it is useful to look further.

Again, click **Statistics>Model analysis**. One of the values in the **leverage** column is displayed in red. This is the way KStat indicates an observation has high leverage. The corresponding entry in the **Cook's D** column is also in red. This indicates an observation has a disproportionately large influence on the regression results.

Plot Delacroix sales against average income (see Figure 6.20). That is, plot Sales D versus Income D. The plot clearly indicates that the regression is entirely driven by a single observation. The estimated regression coefficients would be drastically different if the sales number for just the one influential observation were changed.

An **influential observation** is a data point that has a disproportionately large effect on the regression results.

An influential observation can be an outlier. In this example, however, the influential observation is not an outlier. In fact, the residual associated with the influential observation is zero, i.e., the estimated regression line goes through this point. An influential observation can happen because the point has an unusual x value, i.e., one far above or below the average of the x values (these are called **high leverage points**). This is the case here.

As with outliers, you should check that the influential observation is not due to some data error. If it is not due to error, then you should keep it.

Figure 6.19 Simple regression analysis on the Delacroix data.

Regression: Sales D		
	constant	Income D
coefficient	3.00172731	0.49990909
std error of coef	1.1239211	0.11781895
t-ratio	2.6708	4.2430
p-value	2.5590%	0.2165%
beta-weight		0.8165
standard error of regression		1.23569552
R-squared		66.67%
adjusted R-squared		62.97%
number of observations		11
residual degrees of freedom		9
t-statistic for computing 95%-confidence intervals		2.2622

It is often a good idea to run the regression with and without an influential observation, and report both. This is a way to explicitly see the influence on the regression estimates. In this example, however, it makes no sense to run the regression without the influential observation. (Can you answer why not?)

Robert should be hesitant to rely on the results from the Delacroix regression. The results are all driven by a single observation. More data are necessary for a reliable analysis. In particular, data from more income levels are needed.

We have shown four different datasets generating the same regression output. These examples demonstrate we have to be careful when analyzing data to guarantee we do not mistakenly miss any of these problems. In addition, since these problems do occur with some regularity in real applications, we must have a "toolbox" of fixes at our disposal.

Our conclusions are as follows:

1. The initial regression output for the Almaden, Bianco, Casarosa, and Delacroix data is the same.
2. The regression using the Almaden data seems to work fine. The analysis predicts average Almaden sales of $10,501 in a neighborhood with average household income of $15,000 a month.
3. The simple regression using the Bianco data is unreliable because the relationship between Bianco sales and average income is curved. Curvature may be detected by examining the plot of residuals versus predicted values. Once a quadratic term is introduced, the regression analysis predicts that Bianco sales should be on average $7,200 in a neighborhood with the average income of $15,000 a month. A further residual plot confirms that the quadratic regression has captured the curvature in the relationship.
4. The regression using the Casarosa data contains an outlier. If there is no error associated with this observation, the regression analysis is identical to the analysis of the regression on the Almaden data.
5. The regression using the Delacroix data is driven entirely by one influential observation. More data on Delacroix sales are necessary for reliable conclusions.

Figure 6.20 Plot of Delacroix Sales vs Income.

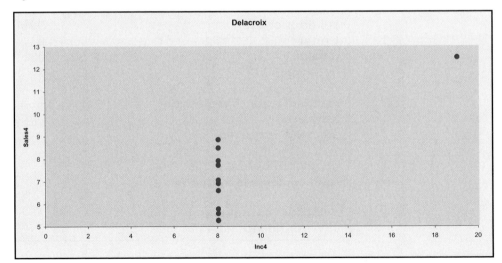

SUMMARY

Spurious correlation occurs when the data indicate a linear relationship that is a statistical artifact (i.e., is due to luck of the draw.) Examples of spurious correlation can be constructed deliberately by generating data at random or (sometimes accidentally) by looking at many different independent variables. This highlights the importance of judgment in constructing and interpreting regressions.

A regression must not be interpreted mechanically. Checking if the underlying assumptions are satisfied is important. If the relationship between dependent and independent variables is non-linear, then we must introduce non-linear terms in our regression. We should also check if outliers and influential observations are associated with some error. These observations should not be modified or deleted unless we find a measurement error or data entry error. Results driven primarily by a few influential observations should be used with care.

NEW TERMS

Spurious correlation The appearance of a significant relationship between unrelated variables

Quadratic function A function of the form $f(x) = a + bx + cx^2$

Fitted value The value of the dependent variable predicted by the regression model

Residual The difference between the observed value and the fitted value

Outlier A data point that is atypically distant from the regression line. Identified by an unusually large residual

Leverage A measure of how different from the norm the values of the independent variables are for a particular observation

High leverage point An observation whose leverage is more than twice the average for the dataset

Influential observation A data point that has a disproportionately large effect on the regression results

Cook's D A measure of the influence a data point has on the regression results

NEW KSTAT AND EXCEL FUNCTIONS

KStat

Statistics>Charts>Residual plots
This command generates a dialog box that asks which variable you would like to plot the residuals against. Select the first option labeled **predicted values**, and click on the OK box.

Statistics>Model analysis
This command creates a new spreadsheet titled **residuals**. The column headed **std'ized** alerts you to outliers by highlighting them in red. Observations that are not outliers appear in black. The column headed **leverage** alerts you to high leverage points by highlighting them in red. The column headed **Cook's D** alerts you to influential observations by highlighting them in red.

CASE EXERCISES

1. The Denny Motors Case

A group of consultants has suggested to Denny Motors that it can predict sales using a forecasting model based on the S&P500. Specifically, as many people view a "Denny" as a luxury good, surges in the stock market may result in subsequent purchases from Denny Motors. After evaluating numerous potential lag times (how long before someone cashes their windfalls into luxury goods is unknown), the consultants have determined that a 30-month lag yields an accurate forecasting model. Specifically, they tried every possible lag time from 0 to 40 months and the highest R-Squared value was found when using a 30-month delay.

Access the data in the **dennymotors.xls** file and run the regression of Denny Motors Quarterly Sales vs. S&P 500 Lagged 30 Months. Knowing that the average value of the S&P during the quarter ending 30 months ago was 1337, construct a 95% prediction interval for next quarter's sales and evaluate its precision. Is it a wide interval or does it seem pretty tight?

Do you agree with the consultants' conclusions?

2. Baseball

A professional baseball team wants to estimate attendance at their ballpark to help make decisions regarding concessions and turnstile revenues. One factor they suspect has an impact on the attendance is weather. The **baseball.xls** data file has data for the first half of the season including both temperature and attendance figures.

Use KStat to estimate the effect of temperature on attendance. Explore the residuals using KStat's model analysis feature. Are there any obvious explanations for the influential observations? Would removing any outliers improve your model? Can you suggest a way to improve the model without removing any outliers?

3. Television for life

The World Almanac and Book of Facts, 1993, reports the following data on televisions and life expectancy in 38 countries. Access the **tvforlife.xls** file, and conduct a regression predicting life expectancy using TVs per person. Are you surprised by the output from KStat? Suggest a possible explanation for these results.

4. Show me the money

Running an agency that represents many professional athletes, you are often forced into serious contract negotiations. One of the baseball players who you represent has had a decent career but has been known to strike out a lot. The team is not offering him a great contract due to his propensity to strike out more than the other players. To improve your negotiating leverage and to add force to your arguments, you have gathered data to conduct a preliminary analysis of ballplayers' salaries and the number of times they strike out. Your assistant, who has analyzed the data, tells you that every strikeout adds about $14,800 to a player's salary; thus, the assistant suggests encouraging your top players to strike out as often as possible.

The **strikeout.xls** file[3] contains the data on 337 professional baseball players. Use these data to conduct a regression of salary vs. number of strikeouts to replicate the assistant's results. Should you go along with the assistant's suggestion?

PROBLEMS

1. Take the dataset from Case Exercise 4 called **strikeout.xls** and run the regression of salary vs. number of strikeouts. Use KStat's model analysis menu to construct a listing of the studentized residuals.

   a. What do the red numbers in the **std'ized** residuals column tell you about those observations?

   b. How many large **std'ized** residuals should you expect for a dataset of this size?

2. Access the data in the **burglary.xls** file[4], which contains information about burglary arrests and employment levels in 90 counties in the United States. Conduct a regression of Burglary Arrests vs. Employed (which contains the number of employed people in the civilian workforce in that county.)

   a. What do these results suggest?

   b. Are these results surprising to you?

   c. Identify any counties that are outliers or highly leveraged or influential observations

   d. What is the probability that a normal random variable will be over 5.6065 standard deviations from the mean (as the LA County residual is)?

3. Access the **beerdata.xls** dataset[5], which contains data on beer consumption and income levels per capita for 19 European countries. Conduct a regression of beer consumption vs. income levels per capita.

   a. On average, as income increases by $1,000 per capita, how much does beer consumption increase?

   b. Does this relationship make sense?

   c. Identify any outliers in this dataset.

   d. How would your answer to part a change if the outliers were removed from the data? (This is generally not a good idea, but we are using the removal of outliers to see how strongly they impact some of our results.)

4. A Midwestern hotel chain has noticed much variation in its electricity costs and would like to be able to explain these changes for planning and budgeting reasons. It has collected samples from random hotels during random months

3. Source: "Pay for Play: Are Baseball Salaries Based on Performance?" by Mitchell R. Watnik, *The Journal of Statistics Education*, Volume 6, Number 2 (July 1998).

4. Source: U.S. Department of Justice, Bureau of Justice Satistics at http://www.ojp.usdoj.gov/bjs/dtdata.htm#crime.

5. Source: http://www.brewersofeurope.org.

during the past year. The variables include the hotels' electricity costs per room and the average temperature that month. These data are available in the **electricitycosts.xls** file. Use KStat to conduct a regression of electricity costs per room vs. average temperature.

a. Does the relationship seem significant?

b. Plot residuals versus predicted values for this regression. Does this graph give you any thoughts on improving the model?

c. Use the tools discussed in this chapter to build an improved model.

CHAPTER 7

THE HOT DOG CASE: MULTIPLE REGRESSION, MULTICOLLINEARITY AND THE GENERALIZED F-TEST

In this chapter, we will further our understanding of multiple regression analysis. One new topic is multicollinearity, i.e., strong linear relationships between independent variables in a regression. Specifically, we will learn to use variance inflation factors to detect multicollinearity and use F-tests to test joint significance of regression coefficients. Other topics emphasized include omitted variable bias, hidden extrapolation, and conducting hypothesis tests concerning linear combinations of regression coefficients. Most of this is done in the context of a case involving the analysis of supermarket price data for several varieties of hot dogs.

7.1 The Hot Dog Case

You have just been hired by Dubuque[1], a hot dog manufacturer that produces Dubuque brand hot dogs for the retail market. On your first day at work, you receive a disturbing memo indicating that Ball Park[2], a competing brand, may substantially reduce the price of its hot dog. Dubuque is concerned about the negative impact this might have on its market share.

At the last staff meeting, some of your colleagues argued that Oscar Mayer[3] is Dubuque's leading competitor and that Ball Park's new campaign will not substantially reduce Dubuque's market share. Others, however, disagreed and no consensus was obtained on the strategy that Dubuque should take to protect its market share.

Ball Park produces two kinds of hot dogs. One is a regular hot dog, and the other is a special, all-beef hot dog. The current prices are $1.79 and $1.89 per package, respectively. Dubuque's current price is $1.49 and Oscar Mayer's current price is $1.69.

According to the memo, Ball Park intends to reduce the price of the regular hot dog to $1.45. Two rumors concern the price of Ball Park's special hot dog. One is that Ball Park will slightly increase the price of the special hot dog to $1.95, and the other is that Ball Park will set the price of the special hot dog to $1.55.

You want to predict Dubuque's market share under these different scenarios. Some data are available from a scanner study conducted at grocery stores located in the western suburbs of Chicago (see the **hotdog.xls** file). The data were compiled at a weekly level and consist of information on Dubuque's market share (MKTDUB) along with its price (pdub), as well as Oscar Mayer's prices (poscar) and Ball Park's prices (pbpreg and pbpbeef) where pbpreg stands for the price of Ball Park's regular hot dog, and pbpbeef stands for Ball Park's special hot dog. Prices are given in cents (i.e., 135 = $1.35) and market share is given in decimal form (i.e., 0.04 = 4%). There are 113 weeks of data.

Questions:

1. How does Dubuque's price affect its market share?
2. Does Oscar Mayer's price affect Dubuque's market share? If so, how?
3. Does Ball Park's price affect Dubuque's market share? If so, how?
4. Is Ball Park or Oscar Mayer Dubuque's leading competitor? Why?
5. Assume that Dubuque does not respond to Ball Park's new campaign. How much market share is Dubuque expected to lose? In what range is Dubuque's market share expected to be?
6. How much should Dubuque charge for its hot dog to maintain its current market share?

7.2 Hot Dog Case: Solutions, Multicollinearity, Hidden Extrapolation and Tests of Joint Significance

We begin by pointing out an interesting issue present in this data. Examine the correlation between Dubuque's market share and the various prices (see Figure 7.1). Calculating the correlation between two variables is a quick-and-dirty way of estimating the extent of the linear relationship between them. The correlation between

---

1. Dubuque is a trademark of Hormel Foods Corporation.
2. Ball Park is a brand of Sara Lee Corporation.
3. Oscar Mayer is a trademark of Kraft Foods Corporation.

Figure 7.1 Correlations.

Correlations	MKTDUB	pdub	poscar	pbpreg	pbpbeef
MKTDUB	1.00000	−0.43293	0.16952	0.35174	0.36947
pdub	−0.43293	1.00000	0.48443	0.35928	0.32257
poscar	0.16952	0.48443	1.00000	0.54881	0.53368
pbpreg	0.35174	0.35928	0.54881	1.00000	0.97938
pbpbeef	0.36947	0.32257	0.53368	0.97938	1.00000

Y and X may be found by regressing Y on X, taking the square root of the R-squared (expressed as a decimal), and making it positive or negative depending on the sign of the estimated coefficient multiplying X. Thus, correlations lie between −1 and 1 with correlations further from 0 corresponding to higher R-squared of the regression relating the two variables. The KStat command **Statistics>Correlations** calculates the correlations between each pair of variables in your data and reports them in a table.

What signs would we expect the correlations between MKTDUB and the various prices to have? Do we see what we expect?

Note the high correlation between pbpreg and pbpbeef (0.979). In this situation, estimating the separate effects from these two variables is likely to be difficult. When one goes up or down, so does the other: hence, it is difficult to tell if the resulting change in market share is due to pbpbeef or pbpreg. This will play a role in our analysis below.

Multicollinearity is the term used to describe the presence of linear relationships among the independent variables. A multicollinearity problem occurs when these relationships are strong. We describe it as a problem because it can make it difficult to accurately assess the separate contributions of the strongly related variables to a regression analysis. Specifically, multicollinearity increases the size of the standard errors of the estimated coefficients multiplying the related independent variables. However, we want to emphasize that multicollinearity does not cause any of the basic regression assumptions to be violated. In this sense, it is a less serious problem than the curvature issue discussed in Chapter 6. Multicollinearity simply decreases the precision with which we can estimate some of the regression coefficients.

In this example, we do have a problem of multicollinearity because pbpreg and pbpbeef are highly correlated. In the case of these two variables, the correlation is so strong that it can be seen by looking at the plot between them (see Figure 7.2).

These two prices move in almost a perfect one-to-one fashion, and so it will be essentially impossible to separate the impact of pbpreg from that of pbpbeef on Dubuque's market share. This is a graphical depiction of the multicollinearity problem we noted above.

Now begin the main analysis by running a regression of mktdub on the price variables (see Figure 7.3).

The 95% confidence and prediction intervals for market share evaluated at Dubuque's price of $1.49, Oscar Mayer's price of $1.69, Ball Park's (regular) price of $1.45, and Ball Park's (special) price of $1.95 are (0.01636, 0.067146) and (0.009533, 0.073973), respectively.

The 95% confidence and prediction intervals for market share evaluated at Dubuque's price of $1.49, Oscar Mayer's price of $1.69, Ball Park's (regular) price of $1.45, and Ball Park's (special) price of $1.55 are (0.032809, 0.042497) and (0.017238, 0.058069), respectively.

Figure 7.2 Scatterplot of Ball Park's prices.

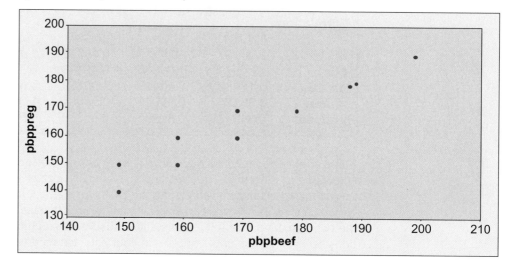

Consider the 95% confidence and prediction intervals for market share evaluated at Dubuque's prices of $1.49, Oscar Mayer's price of $1.69, Ball Park's (regular) price of $1.45, and Ball Park's (special) price of $1.95. The prediction we tried to do

Figure 7.3 Multiple regression analysis of Dubuque's market share.

Regression: MKTDUB					
	constant	pdub	poscar	pbpreg	pbpbeef
coefficient	0.04030263	−0.0007598	0.00026223	0.00034727	0.00010249
std error					
of coef	0.01412257	8.0916E−05	8.427E−05	0.00033161	0.00029376
t-ratio	2.8538	−9.3896	3.1117	1.0472	0.3489
p-value	0.5180%	0.0000%	0.2380%	29.7336%	72.7844%
beta-weight		−0.7258	0.2653	0.3534	0.1159

standard error of regression	0.01000545
R-squared	52.63%
adjusted R-squared	50.88%
number of observations	113
residual degrees of freedom	108
t-statistic for computing 95%-confidence intervals	1.9822

is far from typical. This is true, though the values we picked are within the range of the values we have in the data. (You can check this by examining the univariate statistics for the data.) In particular, while pbpreg has been near 145 and pbpbeef has been near 195, they have never been near these values simultaneously. This is an example of a problem called hidden extrapolation.

Extrapolation occurs when the values of the independent variables used for a prediction are far from those in the sample data. **Hidden extrapolation** occurs when these values, as a group, are far from the values in the sample data, even though for each independent variable individually the data seem reasonable enough.

The effect of extrapolation, hidden or not, is to increase $s_{\hat{y}}$, the standard error of the estimated mean, when we predict for such values. This will make our prediction and confidence intervals larger. In this example, quite large. The lower bound of the confidence interval (0.016) is four times smaller than the upper bound of the confidence interval (0.067). Predicting that Dubuque's average market share is expected to be between 1.6% and 6.7% seems not helpful. After all, with few exceptions, Dubuque's market share is in this range throughout the data.

Consider the 95% confidence and prediction intervals for market share evaluated at Dubuque's prices of $1.49, Oscar Mayer's price of $1.69, Ball Park's (regular) price of $1.45, and Ball Park's (special) price of $1.55. In this scenario, the prediction and confidence intervals are much narrower (see page 151). The reason is we do not have a hidden extrapolation problem in this case. The values we are using for prediction are more typical of those in our data.

The lesson to take from this discussion of hidden extrapolation is that predictions using values of the independent variables far from those in the data will be less accurate than those for values more typical of the data. The "hidden" part of hidden extrapolation emphasizes that values for a group of independent variables may be far from those in the data even if the value for each variable individually is close to those in the data.

Now turn to the estimated effects of each price on Dubuque's market share, controlling for, or holding fixed, the other prices. The coefficients of the independent variables have the expected signs. They are positive for the competitors' prices and negative for Dubuque's price. In particular, the coefficient on Dubuque's price is −0.000759. The coefficient on Oscar Mayer's price is 0.000262. The coefficients on Ball Park's prices (regular and special) are 0.000347 and 0.202, respectively.

Examining the p-values for the coefficient estimates, we see that the coefficient on the constant, Dubuques's price, and Oscar Mayer's price are significantly different from zero. However, the coefficients on the Ball Park prices do not seem to be significant. This is rather curious. The estimated coefficient on Ball Park's regular hot dog price is higher than the estimated coefficient on Oscar Mayer's price. This may indicate Ball Park is Dubuque's main competitor. On the other hand, the coefficient estimates on Ball Park's prices are not significant. This may indicate the opposite. That is, this may indicate our data do not show that Ball Park's prices have any effect on Dubuque's market share.

By looking at the t-ratios and associated p-values for Ball Park's prices, you might think from this first regression that we have little evidence that Ball Park's prices are related to Dubuque's market share. This conclusion seems to support the idea of not reacting to the Ball Park campaign though the estimated coefficient on Ball Park regular hot dog price is higher than the estimated coefficient on Oscar Mayer's price.

However, to decide this issue, we must test if both Ball Park's price coefficients taken together, or jointly, are statistically different from zero. This is particularly important in light of the strong multicollinearity between the Ball Park prices. As observed above, the effect of this multicollinearity is to make it hard to separate the effects of the two Ball Park prices. This appears as an increase in the standard errors of our Ball Park coefficient estimates. The larger standard errors, in turn, result in larger p-values for those coefficients, making them less statistically significant. By giving up on separating the effects of the two Ball Park prices and examining their joint effect on market share, we can sidestep the multicollinearity in the data and, hopefully, arrive at a more precise estimate of the joint effect.

When we want to test whether at least one of a group of coefficients is different from zero, we must consider a hypothesis test called an F-test on the group of coefficients rather than the individual t-tests on each coefficient. As we will see, when x variables are strongly related, the F-test (so-called because the test statistic for this test follows an F distribution if the null hypothesis is true) can give a different answer from the t-tests.

Let's see how we can conduct such a test of joint significance using KStat. Specifically, we will test whether Ball Park's price coefficients taken together, are statistically different from zero. The null and alternative hypotheses are as follows:

$$H_o: \beta_{bpreg} = \beta_{bpbeef} = 0$$
$$H_a: \text{At least one of } \beta_{bpreg} \text{ or } \beta_{bpbeef} \text{ is not equal to zero}$$

To perform this test, click **Statistics>Analysis of variance**. You will obtain the dialog box in Figure 7.4.

Figure 7.4 ANOVA dialog box.

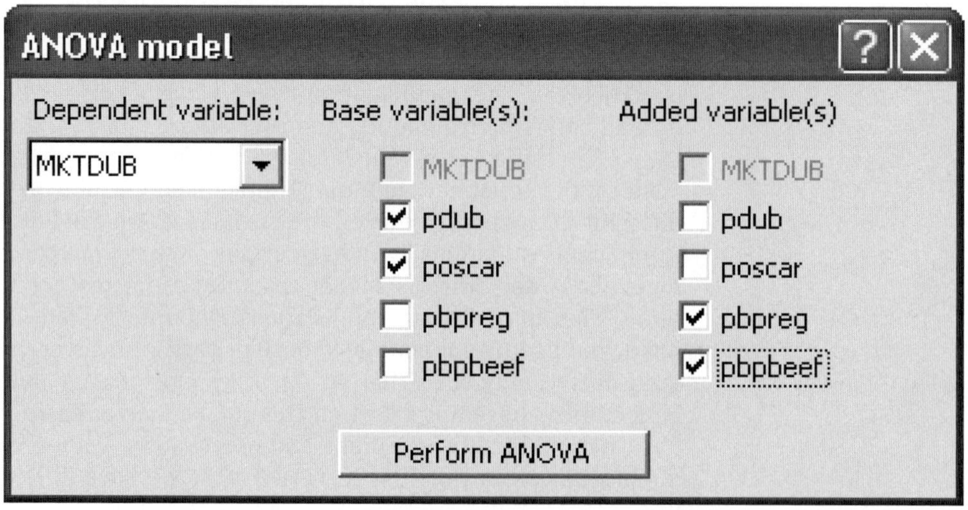

Choose **pdub** and **poscar** as your **base variables** and choose **pbpreg** and **pbpbeef** as your **added variables**. When you click **perform ANOVA**, KStat will run an F-test where the null hypothesis is that coefficients of the added variables (**pbpreg** and **pbpbeef**) are equal to zero, and the alternative hypothesis is that at least one of the coefficients of the added variables is not equal to zero. KStat output for this test is shown in Figure 7.5. This **Analysis of variance** (ANOVA) table provides us all the information that we need about the F-test. Most importantly, it tells us the p-value (0.0000003) associated with this test in the **p-value** row of the **difference** column. Since the p-value is almost zero, we reject the null hypothesis:

$$H_o: \beta_{bpreg} = \beta_{bpbeef} = 0$$

Therefore, we can conclude that, holding Oscar Mayer's and Dubuque's prices fixed, at least one of the Ball Park prices has an effect on Dubuque's market share.

To understand the example above, we need to have a technical discussion on the use of F-tests. Consider a regression with p independent variables. The data consist of n observations of all the variables.

The regression equation is the following:

$$y = \beta_0 + \beta_1 x_1 + \ldots + \beta_q x_q + \beta_{q+1} x_{q+1} + \beta_{q+2} x_{q+2} + \ldots + \beta_p x_p + \varepsilon$$

We want to test if the coefficients $\beta_{q+1}, \ldots, \beta_p$ are jointly significant. The null and alternative hypothesis can be stated as follows:

$$H_0: \beta_{q+1} = 0, \beta_{q+2} = 0, \ldots, \beta_p = 0$$

H_a: One or more of the coefficients (betas) in the null hypothesis is not equal to zero.

Figure 7.5 ANOVA results.

Analysis of variance						
	base model sum of		**extended model** sum of		**difference** sum of	
	squares	**df**	**squares**	**df**	**squares**	**df**
regression	0.008567881	2	0.012013954	4	0.003446072	2
residual	0.014257856	110	0.010811783	108	0.010811783	108
total	0.022825737	112	0.022825737	112	0.014257856	110
F-ratio	33.0508		30.0022		17.2116	
degrees of freedom	(2, 110)		(4, 108)		(2, 108)	
p-value	0.00000%		0.00000%		0.00003%	

Let $SSE(x_1,..., x_q, x_{q+1},..., x_p)$ be the error (or residual) sum of squares of the regression equation using all independent variables (the "extended" model).

Let $SSE(x_1,..., x_q)$ be the error (or residual) sum of squares of the regression equation using only the first q independent variables (the "base" model).

The following F statistic provides the basis for testing whether the additional p-q variables are jointly statistically significant.

$$F = ((SSE(x_1,...,x_q)/SSE(x_1,..., x_q, x_{q+1},..., x_p))-1)*((n-p-1)/(p-q))$$

In general, p is the number of variables in the extended model, and q is the number of variables in the base model; thus, p-q is the number of variables being tested.

We have seen that when we run an F-test, KStat gives us the associated p-value for the test. Sometimes, you may only have access to someone else's output where only the F statistic is reported. In this case, you can use Excel's **FDIST** function to find the p-value corresponding to the F statistic. In the hotdog example, the F statistic was 17.2116 (see the difference column of Figure 7.5). To find the corresponding p-value, click **Insert>Function...**, and choose **Statistical** as the **Function category** and **FDIST** as the **Function name**. Enter the F statistic next to **X**, enter p-q (i.e., the number of variables being tested (= 2 in this example)) next to **Deg_freedom1**, and enter n-p-1 (i.e., the degrees of freedom for the extended model regression with all the variables included (= 108 in this example)) next to **Deg_freedom2**. With the **Formula result**, Excel will give you the p-value. You can also directly type =**FDIST(X, p − q, n − p − 1)** into an empty cell and press **Enter**.

Observe that in our case, q = 2, p = 4, and n = 113. Thus, p − q = 2, and, n − p − 1 = 108. In the **Analysis of variance** table, you can find (p − q, n − p − 1) in the **degrees of freedom** row of the **difference** column. You can find the SSE for the extended model in the **residual** row of the **extended model** column and the SSE for the base model in the **residual** row of the **base model** column.

This analysis provides an excellent example of the danger of relying too heavily on significance tests of individual coefficients in a multiple regression context. Here, individual t-tests from the original regression would have led us to the incorrect conclusion that neither Ball Park price was significant. The test of joint significance showed that at least one of the Ball Park price coefficients is significant. The joint test does not try to distinguish the effects of the two prices while the individual tests do. The multicollinearity between the two prices explains why the joint test was able to succeed even though the individual tests failed: multicollinearity makes it harder to separate the effects of the two prices.

To carry this discussion a little further, watch what would happen if we run a new regression with only one of the Ball Park prices included, as in Figure 7.6. This is for illustration purposes only. Do not take this to mean that the proper response to multicollinearity is to drop one of the variables. This is not generally correct and, as in this case, may lead to regressions that will be interpreted incorrectly if the multicollinearity present in the original set of variables is not explicitly acknowledged.

Figure 7.6 Multiple regression analysis without pbpbeef.

Regression: MKTDUB				
	constant	pdub	poscar	pbpreg
coefficient	0.04006985	−0.0007642	0.00026333	0.00045968
std error of coef	0.01404985	7.9573E–05	8.387E–05	7.817E–05
t-ratio	2.8520	−9.6042	3.1398	5.8805
p-value	0.5199%	0.0000%	0.2176%	0.0000%
beta-weight		−0.7301	0.2665	0.4678
standard error of regression	0.00996506			
R-squared	52.58%			
adjusted R-squared	51.27%			
number of observations	113			
residual degrees of freedom	109			
t-statistic for computing 95%-confidence intervals	1.9820			

As you can see from this output, there is almost no qualitative difference in the overall fit of this regression equation. Once we have removed pbpbeef from the regression equation, pbpreg becomes highly significant (p-value = 0). As noted above, it would have been a mistake to have concluded from the results of the first regression that neither variable matters. It follows from the results of the earlier F-test that at least one of the two Ball Park prices does matter, but because of the multicollinearity problem described above, we cannot tell which does matter in the first regression. The coefficient on pbpreg in the regression in Figure 7.6 is approximately the sum of the two Ball Park coefficients in the first regression. You should not conclude from the regression in Figure 7.6 that the effect of Ball Park's regular price on Dubuque's market share is significant. Rather, its coefficient is an estimate of the combined effect of pbpreg and pbpbeef, and we cannot determine which part belongs where.

You should not conclude from this exercise that there was something special about the choice of pbpreg. We could have easily chosen pbpbeef to leave in the regression. If you do this, the results will be quite similar. This exercise supports the results of our F-test: That the Ball Park prices do matter in determining Dubuque's market share. In the regression with both Ball Park prices, we must remember that the t-ratios should be interpreted recognizing a high degree of multicollinearity.

We can see, from adding together the two Ball Park coefficients in the original regression, that the estimated effect of changing both Ball Park prices by one cent (0.00045) is larger than the estimated effect of changing Oscar Mayer's price by one cent (0.00026). This suggests that Ball Park seems to be Dubuque's main competitor. Of course, to know if we should be confident in this conclusion, we need to know if the difference between the two estimates is statistically significant. The section entitled "Analyzing sums and differences of regression coefficients" explains how this can be done.

Our responses to the case questions are as follows:

1. Dubuque's market share falls by an estimated 0.076% for each cent of increase in its hot dog price, holding fixed the Ball Park and Oscar Mayer prices.
2. Dubuque's market share falls by an estimated 0.026% for each cent of decrease in Oscar Mayer's price, holding fixed the Dubuque and Ball Park prices.
3. Dubuque's market share falls by an estimated 0.045% for each cent of decrease in both of Ball Park's prices, holding fixed the Dubuque and Oscar Mayer prices.
4. Ball Park seems to be Dubuque's main competitor.
5. Assume that Dubuque does not react to Ball Park's campaign. Also, assume that Ball Park's regular hot dog price goes to $1.45, and Ball Park's special hot dog price goes to $1.55. Dubuque's average market share is expected to fall by 1.529%. In this case, we are 95% confident that Dubuque's average weekly market share lies between 3.28% and 4.25%. We are 95% confident that its market share for any given week at these prices will lie between 1.724% and 5.81%.
6. If Dubuque wants to reduce its price to keep its market share, then the correct price reduction will depend upon Oscar Mayer's reaction to Ball Park's campaign. For example, suppose that Oscar Mayer does not change its price. Then, if Ball Park prices are at $1.45 and $1.55, Dubuque must reduce its price by approximately 20 cents (≈ market share to make up/market share gained per cent decrease = 1.529%/0.076%).

We can take away two additional lessons from this case:

Ball Park's prices are highly correlated. This creates a multicollinearity problem. As a result, we cannot accurately estimate separate effects for the two Ball Park prices using these data.

Predicting Dubuque's market share is difficult where Ball Park's regular hot dog price is $1.45 and Ball Park's special hot dog is $1.95 because of the hidden extrapolation problem. In our sample, these two prices are almost always only 10 cents apart.

7.3 Analyzing Sums and Differences of Regression Coefficients

In the case, we asked: "Who is Dubuque's leading competitor, Ball Park or Oscar Mayer? Why?" Since the sum of the estimated coefficients on Ball Park's two prices was larger than the estimated coefficient on Oscar Mayer's price, it appeared that Ball Park was Dubuque's leading competitor. Because these coefficients are estimates, being able to use statistics to say how confident we are in our conclusion that the effect of a Ball Park price change is larger is important. As usual, we will use a hypothesis test (and the resulting p-value) to evaluate the strength of our evidence. The only twist will be that we will have to use KStat's prediction sheet in a new way to calculate the standard deviation we will need for our test statistic.

Since we would like to know if we have strong evidence that a change in Ball Park's prices has a larger effect on Dubuque's market share than an identical change in Oscar Mayer's price, we should make that the alternative hypothesis.

Therefore, using the regression with the four prices as in Figure 7.3, our null and alternative hypotheses are the following:

$$H_0: \beta_3 + \beta_4 - \beta_2 \leq 0$$

$$H_a: \beta_3 + \beta_4 - \beta_2 > 0.$$

Unfortunately, the p-value for such a test is not part of the standard regression output on KStat or any other regression program. However, KStat does make it easy to gather all the information we need to find the p-value. As usual, the next step after writing the hypotheses is to calculate the test statistic. The test statistic is similar to those for the hypothesis tests concerning individual coefficients:

$$t = \frac{\text{estimator} - \text{value in the null hypothesis}}{\text{standard deviation of the estimator}} = \frac{b_3 + b_4 - b_2 - 0}{s_{b_3 + b_4 - b_2}}$$

If the null hypothesis is true, this will have a t-distribution with degrees of freedom equal to the residual degrees of freedom reported by KStat (= n–# of regression coefficients). So, the only problem is, where can we get the value of $s_{b_3 + b_4 - b_2}$?

To do this, run the regression and click **Statistics>Prediction**. Now, instead of plugging in values for the X variables only, we will plug in a value for the constant term as well. Specifically, plug in 0 for the constant, 0 for pdub, −1 for poscar, 1 for pbpreg, and 1 for pbpbeef. Then, click on the Predict button. The resulting prediction worksheet should look like Figure 7.7.

Figure 7.7 Prediction to determine standard error of $s_{b_3 + b_4 - b_2}$.

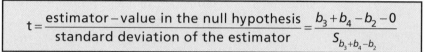

	constant	pdub	poscar	pbpreg	pbpbeef
coefficients	0.040303	-0.00076	0.000262	0.000347	0.000102
values for prediction	0	0	-1	1	1

Prediction, using most-recent regression   Make multiple predictions

predicted value of MKTDUB	0.000188
standard error of prediction	0.010006
standard error of regression	0.010005
standard error of estimated mean	0.000141

Predict

confidence level	95.00%
t-statistic	1.9822
residual degr. freedom	108

confidence limits	**lower**	-0.01965
for prediction	**upper**	0.020022

confidence limits	**lower**	-9.2E-05
for estimated mean	**upper**	0.000468

First, the **predicted value of MKTDUB** (0.000188) is exactly $b_3+b_4-b_2$ (our estimator). Second, the **standard error of estimated mean** (0.000141) is exactly $s_{b_3+b_4-b_2}$, the standard error (or estimated standard deviation) of our estimator. Therefore, the test statistic for our hypothesis test is $0.000188/0.000141 = 1.32749$. We can calculate the p-value = TDIST(1.32749, 108, 1) = 0.093573 or 9.36%. It looks as if we have fairly strong (though maybe not as strong as we hoped) evidence that Ball Park is our leading competitor.

The method presented here is general and will work for any hypotheses comparing a linear combination of regression coefficients to a number. For example, suppose you wanted to estimate if the effect on our market share would be bigger from a 10-cent drop in the Oscar Mayer price or a reduction in the Ball Park prices of 15 cents on the regular brand and 9 cents on the special hot dog. You would want to compare $-10*\beta_2$ with $-15*\beta_3-9*\beta_4$. Therefore, if you were doing a two-tailed test, the alternative hypothesis would be the following:

$$H_a: -10*\beta_2+15*\beta_3+9*\beta_4 \neq 0.$$

If you wanted to see if the effect of the Ball Park changes was at least 0.001 larger than the effect of the Oscar Mayer changes, the alternative would be the following:

$$H_a: -10*\beta_2+15*\beta_3+9*\beta_4 < -0.001.$$

In either case, you would plug in 15 for pbpreg, 9 for pbpbeef, -10 for poscar and 0 for everything else including the constant. Then the prediction output would give you the needed estimated standard deviation (as well as the estimator). The reason we have to plug in 0 for the constant in all these examples is that otherwise KStat includes the estimated constant, b_0, in the calculation. Normally, when we are doing a prediction that is exactly what we want. However, in examples like the ones here, we may not be interested in all terms in regression but only in some combination of specific regression coefficients, and that combination may not include the constant.

7.4 Detecting Multicollinearity

In the hot dog example, the presence of a multicollinearity problem was clear from looking at the correlation between pbpreg and pbpbeef. However, in general, it may be not so clear if a multicollinearity problem is present. For example, suppose you found the correlation between two independent variables is 0.65 or 0.75. Is there a multicollinearity problem? How can we quantify this? More importantly, looking at the correlation between pairs of variables often may miss important interactions among three or more variables. These can cause multicollinearity problems as well.

Is there an indicator of a multicollinearity problem that may overcome these shortcomings of simple correlations? The answer to this question is the variance inflation factor.

Variance inflation factors measure how much the variance of the estimated regression coefficients are enlarged compared to when the independent variables are not linearly related. For example, suppose the variance of a coefficient is 6, and the variance inflation factor is 2. In this case, the variance of this coefficient should be 3 (6 divided by 2) in the absence of multicollinearity. Clearly, the larger the variance inflation factors, the more severe are the multicollinearity problems (i.e., the more that multicollinearity is contributing to the lack of precision in our estimates).

For example, assume the t-ratio of a coefficient estimate is 0.5. In this case, the coefficient might appear to be insignificant. On the other hand, assume the variance inflation factor is 36. This means that the standard deviation of this coefficient is six times (because the square root of 36 is 6) larger than the standard deviation of this coefficient would be in the absence of multicollinearity. The t-ratio is the estimated coefficient divided by its standard deviation. Thus, the t-ratio (0.5) is six times smaller than it would be in the absence of a multicollinearity problem. In conclusion, in the absence of a multicollinearity problem, the t-ratio of this coefficient would be 3 (= 0.5*6) and the coefficient estimate would have been significant. Of course, since multicollinearity is present in our data, we cannot conclude we have significant evidence of an effect. We can say, however, that multicollinearity was severe enough to have led to the insignificance in the t-test.

Consider the same example as before, but now assume the variance inflation factor is 4. In this case, the t-ratio of the coefficient would be only 1 in the absence of multicollinearity.

A threshold often used for the variance inflation factor is 10. That is, if the variance inflation factor is above 10, then a serious multicollinearity problem exists in the data.

To obtain the variance inflation factors using KStat, run a regression and then click **Statistics>Model analysis**. Variance inflation factors will be displayed in the cell just above the name of each variable. To illustrate how to check the variance inflation factors, we will reexamine the hot dog regression.

Consider the regression with all the prices (see Figure 7.3). MKTDUB is the dependent variable. The independent variables are all four of the price variables. The variance inflation factors may be found in Figure 7.8. The variance inflation factors of the two Ball Park prices are 25.96 and 25.14. These are well above 10. Therefore, as we determined before, a multicollinearity problem exists in this regression and the two Ball Park prices are the multicollinear variables.

Figure 7.8 Variance inflation factors for the Hot Dog case.

Predicted values and residuals

	15.6803	0.008%	Breusch-Pagan heteroskedasticity test						
	57.6285	0.000%	Jarque-Bera non-normality test						
	1.7770		Durbin-Watson statistic			variance			
						inflation			
			1.9822	0.0442	0.8445	1.3624372	1.6578026	25.968328	25.147855
MKTDUB	predicted	residual	std'ized	leverage	Cook's D	pdub	poscar	pbpreg	pbpbeef
0.0454565	0.0484474	-0.002991	-0.3033	0.0284	0.0005	149	169	169	179
0.0930145	0.0653094	0.0277051	2.9361	0.1106	0.2143	149	199	189	199

Consider another regression. MKTDUB is once more the dependent variable. The independent variables are all the price variables except the Ball Park prices. The variance inflation factors are the following:

pdub	poscar
1.3066269	1.3066269

The variance inflation factors of Dubuque's price and Oscar Mayer's price are 1.3; therefore, both the variance inflation factors are below 10. This indicates we do not have a serious multicollinearity problem in this regression.

7.5 Omitted Variable Bias

Multicollinearity can make it difficult to obtain precise estimates of the coefficients of strongly related variables in the regression equation. A different and often more serious problem can occur if we leave out one or more related independent variables from a regression. This is called an **omitted variable bias** and we've seen it at work in the refrigerator case and some of the case exercises in Chapter 6.

Examine Case Exercise 4 from Chapter 6 called **Show me the money**. In that case, we were surprised to see that the more often a baseball player strikes out, the higher his salary tends to be. This outcome is neither spurious nor phony but is the result of an omitted variable bias. That is, players who strike out a lot actually do make more money then those who do not, but they also hit a lot of home runs. (For instance, Sammy Sosa is, as of this writing, third in the all-time career strike-out list behind

Figure 7.9 Salary vs. strike outs.

Regression: Salary	constant	Strike outs
coefficient	405.669708	14.86359541
std error of coef	120.832425	1.830670864
t-ratio	3.3573	8.1192
p-value	0.0878%	0.0000%
beta-weight		0.4055
standard error of regression		1135.184104
R-squared		16.44%
adjusted R-squared		16.19%
number of observations		337
residual degrees of freedom		335
t-statistic for computing 95%-confidence intervals		1.9671

Figure 7.10 Salary vs. home runs and strike outs.

Regression: Salary			
	constant	**Home runs**	**Strike outs**
coefficient	629.045034	87.15261736	−3.058299395
std error of coef	108.99232	8.872895953	2.436641557
t-ratio	5.7715	9.8223	−1.2551
p-value	0.0000%	0.0000%	21.0309%
beta-weight		0.6529	−0.0834
standard error of regression		1001.412533	
R-squared		35.17%	
adjusted R-squared		34.78%	
number of observations		337	
residual degrees of freedom		334	
t-statistic for computing 95%-confidence intervals		1.9671	

Reggie Jackson and Andres Galarraga, and all three are in the top-40 career home run list.) The **strikeouts2.xls** dataset extends the dataset used in the case exercise.

The original regression using just strike outs is shown in Figure 7.9. Watch what happens when we add the home runs variable to our model. We will see a major change in the coefficient on strike outs (see Figure 7.10).

The coefficient on strike outs has dropped from 14.86 to -3.06. What's happening here? Which one is the "right" coefficient? Well, they're both right, but the proper number depends on the question you ask:

i. On average, how much does salary increase for every strike out?

ii. On average, for a player with a certain number of home runs, how much does salary increase for every strike out?

The answer to the first question is about $14,860, and the answer to the second is about −$3,060.

The direct effect of one more strike out is negative; that is, holding home runs constant, the owners would pay players less if they had more strike outs. What's important here is the existence of an indirect effect. Hitting a lot of home runs will make the owners happy enough to pay the player a higher salary, but trying to hit a home run will often lead to a strike out. So, more strike outs is associated with more home runs, which is associated with a greater salary. When the regression only includes the strike-out variable, the coefficient has to carry the weight of the direct effect (which is negative) and the indirect effect (which is overwhelmingly positive) on salary. In other words, omitting the home-run variable from the regression biases the coefficient of the strike out variable. We will see this effect whenever related independent variables each have a measurable impact on the dependent variable.

Figure 7.11 Influence diagram.

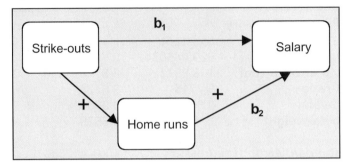

CALCULATING THE EXTENT OF THE BIAS

Compare two estimated regression equations, where we omit one of the variables in the second one:

$$y = b_0 + b_1 x_1 + b_2 x_2$$
$$y = b_0' + b_1' x_1$$

The **bias** on the coefficient of x_1 is defined to be $b_1' - b_1$. It turns out that this bias is given by the following:

$$b_1' - b_1 = (\text{effect of } x_1 \text{ on } x_2)*(\text{effect of } x_2 \text{ on } y)$$

The effect of x_2 on y is given by b_2, and the effect of x_1 on x_2 is given by regressing x_2 on x_1:

$$x_2 = c_0 + c_1 x_1$$

So, the exact formula is the following:

$$b_1' - b_1 = c_1 b_2$$

This formula remains valid if we have more than two x variables, provided we drop only one of them between the two regressions. The only thing that changes is that now the c_1 is the coefficient on x_1 in the **multiple** regression of the omitted variable on all the non-omitted variables.

As an illustration, we can determine the bias in the strike-outs case by using the previous regressions plus the one in Figure 7.12. This new regression tells us that every additional strike out yields an average of 0.2056 home runs. The rule for determining the bias on the coefficient of strike outs from omitting home runs tells us to multiply the effect of strike outs on home runs times the effect of home runs on salary holding strike outs fixed (the coefficient on home runs from the regression in figure 7.10) or 0.2056*87.1526 = 17.92. We can verify that this is the same as the change in the value of the strike-out coefficient when we go from the multiple regression with both variables to the simple regression with just strike outs: 14.86 − (−3.06) = 17.92.

Sign of the Bias

The omitted variable bias in this example was positive (omitting home runs caused an increase in the coefficient on strike outs) but that is not always the case. The influence diagram in Figure 7.11 gives us an idea how to generalize these results. In terms of the figure, the omitted variable bias on the coefficient of the variable in the upper-left box from omitting the variable in the lower box is given by the product of the two lower legs of the triangle.

If the signs of the relationships depicted by both lower legs are positive, then the bias will be positive as we saw in the strike-out example. Similarly, if both relationships have a negative sign, then the bias will be positive. For instance, consider a simple regression of the value of a house in Hawaii on its age. You might be surprised to find a positive coefficient here since newer houses are usually more valuable. However, this result is easily explained by taking into account omitted variable bias and the local real estate market. There is not much land in Hawaii, so the earliest houses were built in the best places like the beachfront. The omitted variable of "Distance to the beach" will have a negative relationship with the house's age and with its value. Though the direct impact of age is negative on the

Figure 7.12 Regression of home runs vs strike-outs.

Regression: Home runs		
	constant	**Strike outs**
coefficient	−2.5630363	0.205638056
std error of coef	0.65636048	0.009944185
t-ratio	−3.9049	20.6792
p-value	0.0114%	0.0000%
beta-weight		0.7488
standard error of regression		6.166308234
R-squared		56.07%
adjusted R-squared		55.94%
number of observations		337
residual degrees of freedom		335
t-statistic for computing 95%-confidence intervals		1.9671

Figure 7.13 Influence diagram of real estate value.

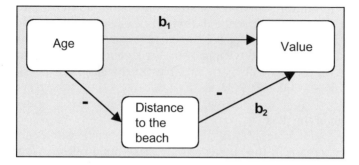

value of a house, the addition of the positive omitted variable bias can create an overall positive coefficient.

What if one sign is positive, and the other one is negative? For instance, consider a regression of the number of priests in a city on the air quality, which has a negative coefficient. What might cause that result? Does dirty air cause people to become more religious? The omission of the variable **population size** would explain it. A city with dirty air is usually big (a negative relationship), and a city with many people living in it will usually need more clergy (a positive relationship). The product of these two effects creates a negative omitted variable bias on the coefficient of air quality. If this indirect effect is stronger than the direct effect of air quality on the number of priests, which in this case is probably near zero, then the coefficient in the simple regression will be negative.

SUMMARY

It is often useful to conduct hypothesis tests concerning sums and differences or general linear combinations of regression coefficients. KStat's Prediction Sheet is helpful in calculating the relevant standard errors for use in such tests. In the context of the Hot Dog case we used such a test to compare the combined effect of Ball Park's prices to the effect of Oscar Mayer's price on Dubuque's market share.

A multicollinearity problem arises when two or more independent variables are strongly related. In the Hot Dog case, the relationship was between two highly correlated price variables; however, correlation is a limited pair-wise concept, and the problem of multicollinearity is more general than this. Observing a lack of high correlation coefficients does not ensure a freedom from multicollinearity problems; therefore, variance inflation factors need to be used to detect multicollinearity problems accurately.

If a multicollinearity problem exists, then significant variables may have low t-ratios and high p-values. An F-test for joint significance must be conducted on the group of multicollinear variables to properly evaluate their significance if one or more independent variables appear insignificant according to the tests on the individual coefficients and some of these seemingly insignificant variables are involved in the multicollinearity. Nothing can be done to get rid of multicollinearity short of gathering new data where the strong linear relationships among independent variables are lacking.

The estimated regression coefficient on an independent variable may be biased by the omission of another independent variable that is related both to it and to the dependent variable. In many practical situations, you may suspect that such a variable may have been omitted from the analysis, but no data is available to allow you to include it. In such cases, being able to reason about the likely sign of the bias using the influence diagram can be helpful in understanding the potential impact and importance of the omission.

NEW TERMS

Multicollinearity The term used to describe the presence of linear relationships among the independent variables

Hidden extrapolation Making a prediction using values of the independent variables that are collectively far from the sample data though each x variable is individually within the sample data's range

ANOVA Short for *analysis of variance*

Base variables The variables in your regression you are not testing for joint significance

Added variables The variables in your regression you wish to test for joint significance

Variance inflation factor (VIF) A measure of how much the variance of the estimated regression coefficients are enlarged as compared to when the independent variables are not linearly related. Used to detect multicollinearity. A common rule is a VIF above 10 indicates strong multicollinearity involving that variable

Omitted variable bias The effect on a regression coefficient caused by omitting an important correlated variable from the model

NEW FORMULAS

$$F \text{ statistic, } F = ((SSE(x_1, ..., x_q)/SSE(x_1, ..., x_q, x_{q+1}, ..., x_p))-1)*((n-p-1)/(p-q))$$

p is the number of variables in the extended model, q is the number of variables in the base model, and p–q is the number of variables being tested.

The omitted variable bias on the coefficient of x_1 from omitting x_2 is $b_1'-b_1 = c_1 b_2$ where each of these values come from the following estimated regression equations:

- $y = b_0 + b_1 x_1 + b_2 x_2$
- $y = b_0' + b_1' x_1$
- $x_2 = c_0 + c_1 x_1$

NEW KSTAT AND EXCEL FUNCTIONS

KStat

Statistics>Analysis of variance

This command opens a dialog box that asks the user to input the dependent variable and some **base** and **added** independent variables. Clicking on the **Perform ANOVA** box will provide the results of an F-test, which we used to determine joint significance of the added variables in a regression with the base and added variables as the independent variables.

Statistics>Correlations

This command produces a worksheet containing a table with the estimated correlations between each pair of variables on the data sheet.

Statistics>Model analysis

This command computes an assortment of information regarding the most recent regression performed by KStat. In this chapter, we used the variance inflation factors reported above each variable on the right-hand side of the worksheet to detect multicollinearity.

EXCEL

FDIST

Typing =**FDIST(X, p–q, n–p–1)** into an empty cell returns the p-value associated with a given F statistic, X. p is the number of variables in the extended model, q is the number in the base model, and n is the sample size.

CASE EXERCISES

1. Show me even more money

Running an agency that represents many professional athletes, you are often forced into serious contract negotiations. Having recently fired your assistant, you have decided to evaluate the data collected to support your argument that the player whose contract you are negotiating is currently underpaid. The data in the **strikeouts3.xls**[1] file extends the previous dataset to include much more information.

Start by conducting a regression using all of the data provided to predict salary. Do the signs of all of the coefficients make sense?

Next, remove each of the variables that are insignificant based on $\alpha = 0.05$. Are the variables that you removed jointly significant? How can you tell?

2. Video sales

Your company has the rights to distribute home videos of previously released movies. Your goal is to estimate the volume of DVDs you can expect to sell based on box office totals of the original movies. Data are available for 30 movies that indicate the box office gross (**Gross**, in millions of dollars) and the number of DVDs sold (**Videos**, in thousands).

---

1. From "Pay for Play: Are Baseball Salaries Based on Performance?" by Mitchell R. Watnik. The Journal of Statistics Education, Volume 6, Number 2 (July 1998)

```
Regression: Videos
                        constant        Gross
coefficient             26.5351424      8.083109
std error of coef       11.8318417      0.50084349
t-ratio                 2.24269         16.13899
p-value                 3.3016%         0.0000%
beta-weight                             0.8531

Standard error of regression            47.8667885
R-squared                               72.78%
Adjusted R-squared                      71.80%

number of observations                  30
Residual degrees of freedom             28

t-statistic for computing
95%-confidence intervals                2.0484
```

You are planning for the video release of *Matchstick Men* that grossed $36 million. In the Prediction sheet, you plug in 36 for **Gross** and get the following:

```
Prediction, using most-recent regression
                        constant        Gross
coefficients            26.53514        8.083109
values for prediction                   36

predicted value of Videos               317.53
Standard error of prediction            49.84182
Standard error of regression            47.86679
Standard error of estimated mean 13.89164
```

   a. Predict the DVD sales for *Matchstick Men*.

   b. Construct a 95% prediction interval for the video sales of *Matchstick Men*.

   c. Your firm has a truckload of films that were huge flops and grossed $0 each. What would you expect average video sales to be for these films known as the "flops"?

   d. Based on your regression, can you prove at a 5% significance level that the average DVD sales of the flops will be greater than 10,000 copies per film?

3. **B-school costs**

The **bschools2002.xls**[2] dataset contains information on the top business schools according to a 2002 *Business Week* magazine survey. Use all four numerical variables to develop a model that explains the "estimated total costs" of attending the program. Does the coefficient of "base salary: median" make sense? What might be causing this unusual result?

4. Video libraries

A group of independently owned video stores in the south has formed a trade group to help support their survival in the face of competition from dominant national chains. The group of 29 store owners have collected data in the **videostores.xls** file, which contains the average monthly sales, neighborhood population (in thousands,) annual advertising expenses, and the number of DVD and VHS films in the libraries (films that have been available for over one year) of each store. A big problem facing these small stores is if they should update their collections of older films by adding DVD versions to their current library. Though they usually buy the new movies in both formats, the lower sales volumes at these small stores make the expense of an older DVD hard to justify. The typical store can break even if the DVD brings in more than 1 dollar per month.

Using all of the variables provided to you by the trade group:

    a. Which of the four variables given seem to be significant predictors of sales?

    b. On average, how much does one DVD add to the monthly sales of one of the stores?

    c. Provide a 95% confidence interval for your estimate.

    d. Should the stores upgrade their DVD libraries?

---

2. Merritt, Jennifer. *Business Week*, 10/21/2002 Issue 3804, p84

CASE INSERT 2   COLONIAL BROADCASTING

In this case, we will use our regression skills to help run a broadcasting company. The Colonial Broadcasting Company case describes the problem of Barbara Warrington, vice president of Programming at Colonial Broadcasting Company, who has to decide which television movies to broadcast and when to schedule them.

The assignment is to answer all questions in part A of the case except question 7a and all questions in part B except question 12.

In the regression output in the case, some numbers appear within parentheses indicating a negative number. That is, (8) means – 8. All questions can be answered without running any additional regressions. However, you are free to do any supplementary analysis using the data contained in **colonial.xls**.

In answering question 11, you will think you need to know the standard error of prediction, and you will be right. However, the regression output in the case only provides the standard error of regression. So, for convenience only, you may use the standard error of regression to approximate the standard error of prediction in your answer.

The Colonial Broadcasting Company case (parts A and B)[1] is located in the packet of cases bundled to the back of this text.

---

1. Colonial Broadcasting Co., Harvard Business School Case, Product #9-894-011.

CHAPTER 8

THE ADVERTISING CASE: HETEROSKEDASTICITY AND LOGARITHMS

This chapter presents a brief overview of natural logarithms and demonstrates their use as a technique to model curvature in regression and as a method for removing heteroskedasticity or non-constant variance. Special concerns when making predictions while using regressions with logarithmic dependent variables are discussed. An example relating advertising expenditures to sales is explored. The detection and implications of heteroskedasticity are explained. Case Exercise 1 re-examines the hot dog case from Chapter 7 with these new tools and issues in mind.

8.1 A Primer on Logarithms in Regression

Logarithms are used extensively in statistics. In particular, log-linear regression models are a useful alternative to the standard linear form. They work well in various applications where some of the assumptions of the standard linear regression are not satisfied. Moreover, the coefficients of the independent variables in a logarithmic regression are easy to interpret, and the whole equation is easy to use for prediction.

Log forms of regression are used at least as much, if not more often, than the linear form. So, we need to have a good understanding of what they mean and how they work. To achieve this goal, we describe the **main properties** of the logarithm function (the so-called natural logarithm, or LN in Excel), and show how the logarithmic transformation of variables can be used in regressions. We will talk about different log regression forms (log-log and semi-log), and the **interpretation of coefficients** in these regressions. Then we will highlight the differences between linear and logarithmic regressions as far as **prediction** with these regressions is concerned. Finally, we will introduce an important practical motivation for using log-regressions: logs often "cure" heteroskedasticity. A more in-depth analysis of heteroskedasticity including detection, effects, and fixes is the final subject of the chapter.

PROPERTIES OF THE NATURAL LOGARITHM FUNCTION (LN)

LN(x) is a function that can be evaluated for any positive x value. We show the graph of the function below (Figure 8.1, generated in Excel). To get the graph, we created a column of different x-values (ranging from .0018 to 20), generated their logs (by typing =LN(A2) in cell B2, etc.), and generated the graph with the chart-wizard.

The function is increasing everywhere, LN(1) = 0, and, as x approaches 0, LN(x) tends to negative infinity. The logarithm is a concave function in that it increases more slowly as x increases (i.e., the slope decreases as x increases).

Figure 8.1 Graph of LN(x) vs. x.

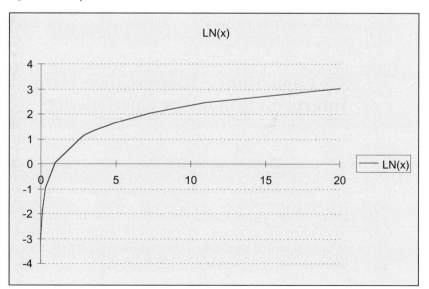

An interesting property of the logarithm function is that if you keep multiplying x by a constant (for example, if you double it starting from one, i.e., 1, 2, 4, 8, 16), then the logarithm will increase by a constant increment. In the example, $LN(1) = 0$, $LN(2) = 0.693$, $LN(4) = 1.386$, $LN(8) = 2.079$, $LN(16) = 2.773$; the increment is about 0.693 or the log of the multiplier, $0.693 = LN(2)$.

In general, if you increase a number by a fixed proportion (say, by 15%, i.e., you multiply it by 1.15), then the logarithm of the number will increase by the logarithm of the multiplier (in the example, by $0.1398 = LN(1.15)$).

The logarithm function transforms the **proportional increments** ("doubling" or "increasing by 15%") into **additive increments** ("adding $LN(2) = 0.693$" or "adding $LN(1.15) = 0.1398$"). In other words, the logarithm function transforms **growth rates** into (additive) **growth**.

Perhaps more interesting, the following rule of thumb can be used for translating small percentage changes in x into absolute changes in $LN(x)$.

> Every 1% change in x corresponds to (approximately) a 0.01 change in $LN(x)$.

That is, a k% change in x corresponds to a $0.01*k$ change in $LN(x)$, for any k not too large. For example, a 5% increase from 20 results in 21; if you take logs, the difference between LN(21) and LN(20) is equal to $LN(21)-LN(20) = 3.04-2.99 = 0.05$.

The LN function has many other interesting and related properties. For example, the logarithm of a product, $LN(2*3)$, is equal to the sum of the logarithms of the two factors, $LN(2)+LN(3)$. Also, $LN(x^a) = a*LN(x)$, and $LN(1/x) = -LN(x)$.

Many examples show where logarithms play an important role in the world. In music, the position of a key on the keyboard is a logarithmic function of its pitch's frequency. Our senses, in general, measure things in logs (this is called Fechner's law): "As stimuli are increased by multiplication, sensation increases by addition." Logs come up in financial computations, too. Suppose that you put $1 in the bank, and a year later receive $1.20 (quite a good deal). What interest rate does this gain correspond to if interest is compounded continuously? The answer is $r = LN(1.2) = 0.1823$, or 18.23%.

The inverse of the natural logarithm function is the **exponential function**, EXP. If you have the value for the logarithm of a variable, then, to get the variable's value, you "exponentiate" it. That is, $EXP(LN(x)) = x$ for any positive number x.

8.2 Logarithmic Regressions: Forms And Interpretation of the Coefficients

Recall that in the standard linear regression setting we assume the following:

> (L) $Y = \beta_0+\beta_1X+\text{error term.}$

Here, we are saying that a one-unit increase in X causes Y to increase by β_1 units, on average. For example, if X is price in dollars and Y is sales of wheat in thousands of tons, β_1 is the number of thousands of tons that average wheat sales change by when the price is increased by one dollar.

We examine two logarithmic regression forms when you have a single independent variable. One is called the **semi-log** specification, and the other the **log-log** specification. In the semi-log specification, you create a new variable, $\ln Y = LN(Y)$, and regress it against X. In the log-log specification, you regress $\ln Y$ against $\ln X = LN(X)$.

That is, the semi-log regression model can be written as follows:

(SL)	$\ln Y = \beta_0 + \beta_1 X + \text{error term.}$

Here, the interpretation of the coefficient β_1 is that when X increases by 1 unit, $\ln Y$ changes by β_1 units, on average. Because of the interpretation of logs given above, we can say that a one-unit increase in X is associated with approximately a $(\beta_1 * 100)\%$ change in Y.

For example, let the equation be $\ln Y = 1 - 0.03 * X$. Each unit increase in X leads to a 0.03 decrease in $\ln Y$, which corresponds to a 3% decrease in Y. (We had to multiply 0.03 by one hundred to get 3, and then we added "percent".)

The log-log regression model with a single X variable is as follows:

(LL)	$\ln Y = \beta_0 + \beta_1 \ln X + \text{error term.}$

Some X variables cannot appear in a log-log regression because they take non-positive values. A good example is when X is a dummy: You cannot take the log of a dummy because it sometimes equals 0.

The interpretation of the coefficient in (LL) is interesting: A 1% increase in X will imply a $\beta_1\%$ change in Y. Why? A 1% increase in X corresponds to (approximately) a 0.01 increase in $\ln X = LN(X)$. According to (LL), a 0.01 increase in $\ln X$ will lead to a $\beta_1 * 0.01$ change in $\ln Y$. This change, in turn, corresponds to (approximately) a $\beta_1\%$ change in Y.

For example, let the equation be $\ln Y = 1 - 3 * \ln X$. Then a 1% increase in X leads to a 0.01 increase in $\ln X$, which implies a 0.03 decrease in $\ln Y$. This corresponds to a 3% decrease in Y. Therefore, a 1% increase in X leads to a 3% decrease in Y. Here, we do not multiply the coefficient by 100 in contrast to what we had to do in the semi-log case.

The natural interpretation of the coefficient of X in the (LL) regression is that it relates a percentage increase in X to a percentage change in Y. Contrast this with the interpretation of the coefficient in a linear regression (L), which relates a unit increase in X to a unit change in Y.

You might recall from microeconomics that the percentage response in a quantity to a percentage change in another quantity is called the **elasticity**. Thus, in equation (LL), we are assuming the elasticity of Y with respect to X is β_1. Examples include where Y is sales, X is price, and β_1 is the price elasticity of demand; where Y is sales, and X is income, and β_1 is the income elasticity of demand; and where Y is cost, and X is output, and β_1 is the output elasticity of cost. For this reason, the form (LL) is widely used and of practical importance.

In a multiple regression, you may have some X variables in logs and some others in their original linear "measurement units:"

$\ln Y = \beta_0 + \beta_1 \ln X_1 + \beta_2 X_2 + \ldots + \text{error term.}$

Such a mixed semi-log/log-log regression form may be necessary to accommodate dummy variables in a log-log regression, for example. Remember, you cannot take LN of a dummy or other variable that sometimes has zero or negative values. The interpretation of the coefficients follows just as above. Holding the other included variables fixed, a 1% increase in X_1 will change Y by $\beta_1\%$. Holding the other included variables fixed, a unit increase in X_2 will change Y by approximately $(\beta_2*100)\%$.

8.3 Prediction With Logarithmic Regressions

When you transform some variables using logs and run a logarithmic regression, remember you are no longer working with the original X,Y data. This affects how you do forecasting in two ways.

First, when you are using a log-log model, lnX is the independent variable. This means that if you want to predict when X = 100, you do not put 100 in the KStat **Prediction** worksheet. Rather, the X in the regression is LN(X). Thus, you must remember to type in the formula =LN(100) in the appropriate cell in the **Prediction** worksheet.

The second important thing is that if you are using lnY as the dependent variable (e.g., in the SL model or the LL model), what the **predict** command will give you is a prediction, a confidence interval, and a prediction interval for lnY and not for Y. Since this is not typically what you want, you must reconstruct the prediction for Y, the CI, and the PI. To do this, you must exponentiate KStat's output so you are getting Y and not lnY. This must be done for the fitted value (i.e., the prediction) and the ends of the confidence and prediction intervals. In addition to this, it turns out that exponentiating introduces a downward bias in the CI and in the estimate for the **average** value of Y (but not for the estimate of an individual value of Y). Typically, this bias is small in practice, but it can be large and you should get in the habit for correcting for it. The way you do this is to multiply through by EXP($s^2/2$) after exponentiating, where s is the **standard error of the regression** which is found in both the Regression worksheet and the Prediction worksheet. The expression EXP($s^2/2$) is called the correction factor. This bias is absent from the PI or when estimating an individual value of Y. Therefore, you must not use the correction factor in calculating the PI or your estimated individual value of Y.

8.4 Ad Sales: Using Logarithmic Regressions

We will study an interesting application of logs in the Ad Sales case that uses the data in the file **adsales.xls**. This dataset contains observations for the sales of a product (variable **sales**) and advertising expenditures for the same product (variable **exp**). Each are measured in thousands of dollars. Should we anticipate a linear relationship between sales and advertising or do diminishing returns exist? In other words, is it likely that each additional dollar spent on advertising may not have as much of an impact as the previous dollar? The scatterplot in Figure 8.2 suggests diminishing returns from advertising.

A log-log model might be appropriate. To see this, you may use the residual plot techniques introduced in Chapter 6 to diagnose curvature problems. If you regress sales against exp and then plot the residuals versus the predicted values, you will see distinct curvature in that plot. This means that the linear model is inadequate.

Figure 8.2 Scatterplot of sales vs exp.

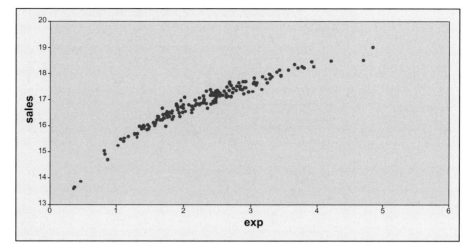

We have seen three types of non-linear models thus far: quadratic, semi-log, and log-log. In order to implement them, create three new columns that contain the natural logarithms of variables **exp** and **sales** and the square of **exp** respectively. Label them as **lnexp**, **lnsales** and **expsquared**. By trying each of the three non-linear models and examining the plots of residuals versus predicted values, you may verify that the log-log model appears to be the one that best captures the curvature in the relationship (and so removes the curvature from the residual plot).

Run the regression for **lnsales** against **lnexp**, and click **Statistics>Prediction**. Suppose we want to obtain the predicted individual and average values of sales and confidence and prediction intervals using a 95% confidence level when spending $2,000 on advertising (exp = 2). First type **=LN(2)** in cell D5 and press **Enter**. Then click **Predict**. KStat will give you the predicted value and confidence and prediction intervals with 95% confidence level for lnsales when lnexp = ln 2 = 0.693147. To get the predicted average value for **sales** when exp = 2, type **=EXP(D7)*EXP((D9^2)/2)** in cell D11 (i.e., exponentiate the prediction for lnsales and then multiply by the correction factor). When you press **Enter**, you will obtain the predicted average sales when ad spending (exp) = 2 in cell D11. The resulting number should be 16.71939 or $16,719.39. To get the predicted individual value for sales when exp = 2, type **=EXP(D7)** in cell E11. The resulting number should be 16.71864 or $16,718.64.

To obtain the corrected confidence interval, type **=EXP(D19)*EXP((D9^2)/2)** in cell E19 and type **=EXP(D20)*EXP((D9^2)/2)** in cell E20. You will obtain the 95% confidence interval for average sales when exp = 2 as (16.69529, 16.74352) or ($16,695.29, $16,743.52).

To obtain the correct prediction interval, type **=EXP(D16)** in cell E16 and type **=EXP(D17)** in cell E17. You will obtain the 95% prediction interval for sales when exp = 2 as (16.40878, 17.03435) or ($16,408.78, $17,034.35). Notice that we did not use the correction factor in calculating the prediction interval.

When you are done, the prediction worksheet will look like one in Figure 8.3. If you want to see the confidence and prediction intervals for any other confidence level, type the confidence level that you want in the **confidence level** cell and the numbers will automatically adjust. Similarly, you may type in other values of lnexp and get the appropriately transformed prediction, CI and PI.

Figure 8.3 Prediction for sales with exp = 2.

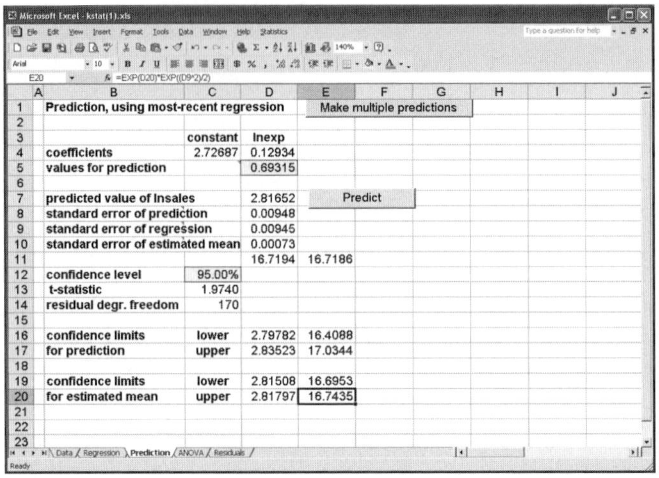

	B	C	D	E
1	Prediction, using most-recent regression			Make multiple predictions
2				
3		constant	lnexp	
4	coefficients	2.72687	0.12934	
5	values for prediction		0.69315	
6				
7	predicted value of lnsales		2.81652	Predict
8	standard error of prediction		0.00948	
9	standard error of regression		0.00945	
10	standard error of estimated mean		0.00073	
11			16.7194	16.7186
12	confidence level	95.00%		
13	t-statistic	1.9740		
14	residual degr. freedom	170		
15				
16	confidence limits	lower	2.79782	16.4088
17	for prediction	upper	2.83523	17.0344
18				
19	confidence limits	lower	2.81508	16.6953
20	for estimated mean	upper	2.81797	16.7435

8.5 Introduction to Heteroskedasticity

Finally, we should talk about an important reason why log-regressions are useful that is separate from their use in modeling curvature as in the Ad Sales application. A key reason for using logarithmic regressions is simple: by taking the logarithm of Y and regressing it on the X variables, which may be in linear units or in logs, we are often able to reduce heteroskedasticity (non-constant error variance).

Why? Suppose the relationship between Y and X is such that average $Y = \beta_0+\beta_1X$; however, an individual observation's deviation from the average (the "error term") is proportional to Y. For simplicity, imagine the individual Y_1 (at any given level of X_i) is within $\pm 2\%$ of the average Y at X_i. This structure is heteroskedastic. The standard error of the regression is not constant but instead increases proportionally with Y.

Now see what happens when we create lnY = LN(Y), and regress this variable against X or lnX. That is, we can use a semi-log or a log-log specification. A $\pm 2\%$ error in Y will become a ± 0.02 error in lnY. The new error term is not increasing with Y anymore; the error has become homoskedastic.

This example exhibits what often happens in practice: a heteroskedastic regression, where the error term is approximately proportional to Y, can be transformed into a homoskedastic regression by transforming the dependent variable into logarithms. (We need not transform X for this purpose.) To further illustrate the effect of logs on a regression, we show three versions of the same data using three different scatterplots (with a fitted line): the first plot shows Y against X (the relation is visibly heteroskedastic); the second one is lnY against X, and the third one is lnY against lnX.

In Figure 8.4, Y against X appears to be linear but heteroskedastic. The errors are getting larger as Y increases, Note the "cone-shaped" cloud of data points.

In the second scatterplot (see Figure 8.5), the variance of the error term seems to be roughly stable, and so the heteroskedasticity is gone, but there is possibly some curvature. This is not surprising: If Y is indeed linear in X, then lnY will be non-linear in X. (The logarithmic transformation of Y introduces curvature.)

Figure 8.4 Y vs. X.

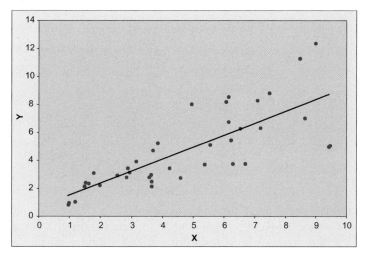

The third plot (see Figure 8.6) shows that the heteroskedasticity is gone, and the curvature introduced by the semi-log model is gone, too, in this log-log model. This is beautiful.

The situation illustrated in these three scatterplots is not always the case when we find heteroskedasticity in the linear specification, but it is fairly typical. A log-transformation of the dependent variable often resolves heteroskedasticity, and at least one of the possible log-regressions (LL or SL) often works in terms of linearity. In the scatterplots, the SL specification exhibited curvature, and the LL specification did not. However, there are many examples in which the reverse is true and LL exhibits curvature. In other examples, both models effectively capture the curvature in the data.

In Section 8.7, we will explore heteroskedasticity, its detection, effects, and possible fixes, in more depth.

Figure 8.5 lnY vs. X.

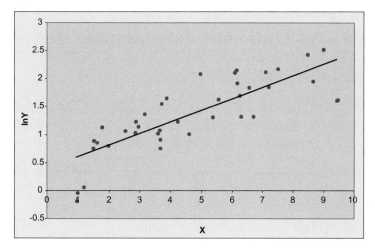

Figure 8.6 lnY vs. lnX.

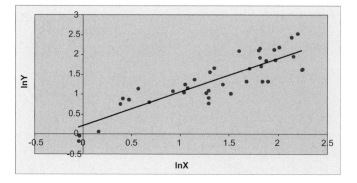

Summary for logarithms in regression

As we stated earlier, a k% change in (any variable) X corresponds to approximately a $k*0.01$ change in its logarithm, lnX, for any k not too large. This property of the logarithm is useful in guiding the interpretation of coefficients in a log regression. It also allows us to eliminate heteroskedasticity when the error term is approximately proportional to the dependent variable: we take the logarithm of Y and regress it against X or lnX.

The two forms of logarithmic regression we examined are semi-log (lnY against X) and log-log (lnY against lnX). In the semi-log case, we multiply the coefficient on X by 100 to get the percentage change in Y as a result of a unit increase in X, holding all other included variables constant. In the log-log case, the coefficient is the elasticity of Y with respect to X (the percentage change in Y for a 1% increase in X), holding all other included variables constant. If a variable takes on zero or negative values, then we cannot take its logarithm.

When using a logarithmic regression for prediction, we must exponentiate the fitted lnY to get the prediction for an individual Y (and the same applies to the prediction interval). For the estimated mean of Y (predicting an average), we have to exponentiate the predicted lnY and multiply it by the **correction factor**, $EXP(s^2/2)$, where s is the standard error of regression. The same applies to the calculation of a confidence interval for average Y: exponentiate the two limits and multiply them by the correction factor.

8.6 An Optional Mathematical Digression

Two comments for the more mathematically inclined:

1. Another look at the change in lnX for a change in X using derivatives:

Those of you who took calculus may remember that the derivative of the natural logarithm function is $dln(x)/dx = 1/x$. In other words, the slope of the (natural) logarithm curve is $1/x$ at x.

What does this mean? The slope tells us that for a small Δx increase in x, the function $ln(x)$ will increase by $\Delta ln(x) \approx (1/x)*\Delta x = \Delta x/x$. In other words, the absolute change in the logarithm of x is approximately the percentage change in x (the approximation works best for small Δx changes).

2. Another look at the logarithmic form:

The inverse of the LN function, the EXP function, can be written as $EXP(x) = e^x$, where $e = 2.7183...$ is a famous constant known as the basis of the natural logarithm, or Euler's number. Exponentiating both sides of the equations SL and LL, we get the following equations:

(SL')	$Y = e^{\beta_0 + \beta_1 X}$
(LL')	$Y = e^{\beta_0} X^{\beta_1}$

We have omitted the error term from these expressions for simplicity. (The error term would be multiplicative: there would be a factor e^{error} multiplying the right hand sides of SL' and LL'.) You can see the relationship between Y and X is non-linear in either model. Moreover, these regression forms make precise the meaning of the coefficient on the X variable in the SL and LL specifications.

Consider the SL specification and increase X by one. For concreteness, suppose X increases from 0 to 1. As a result, Y will change by a factor of e^{β_1}; in the example, it goes from e^{β_0} to $e^{\beta_0 + \beta_1}$. So, the percentage change in Y is $100*(e^{\beta_0 + \beta_1} - e^{\beta_0})/e^{\beta_0} = ((e^{\beta_1} - 1)*100)$, which, for small β_1, approximately equals a $(\beta_1 * 100)\%$ change. (You can check: $e^{\beta_1} \approx 1 + \beta_1$ for small β_1.)

The interpretation given earlier for the coefficient in the LL specification is exact: In the LL regression, β_1 is the elasticity of Y with respect to X.

8.7 Heteroskedasticity: Detecting, Effect on Results, Possible Fixes

Four basic assumptions are needed for the regression model to give us the best estimates: linearity, constant error variance, independent errors, and normal errors. The second of these assumptions is the assumption that the error term has the same variance for all observations:

Regression Assumption: $Var(\varepsilon_i) = \sigma^2$ for all i. (homoskedasticity).

The purpose of this section is to show you two methods for checking whether this assumption is satisfied in any particular application, to tell you what goes wrong when this assumption is violated, and to suggest possible ways of fixing violations.

Detecting a Violation: There are at least two useful ways to detect variations (heteroskedasticity) in the error variances. The first technique is to run the regression and examine a plot of the residuals versus the predicted values. What should we expect to see on this graph? If our regression assumptions are satisfied and the error term for each observation has the same variance, then the predicted value we look at should not affect the vertical spread (a way of visualizing variance) of the residuals. Thus, the vertical spread in points on the graph should remain approximately the same all the way across.

In contrast, if the graph of residuals versus predicted values is cone-shaped or otherwise varies in a systematic way in the vertical spread of the residuals, this indicates a violation of our constant variance assumption. Below is an example of a plot of residuals versus predicted values that displays a spread in the residuals that increases as the predicted value increases (see Figure 8.7). This pattern is often seen when analyzing data on income levels, prices, or asset values.

Though examining the graph of the residuals versus the predicted values can be useful, it can be difficult to see if clear evidence of non-constant variance exists through graphical methods. To avoid some of these problems, more quantitative techniques are

Figure 8.7 residual plot with heteroskedasticity.

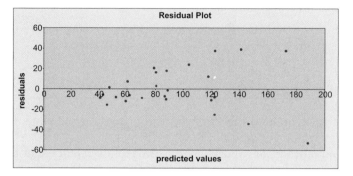

available for detecting non-constant error variance. One of the easiest to implement is a version of the Breusch-Pagan Test (named after its inventors). This consists of a hypothesis test where the null hypothesis is that $Var(\varepsilon_i)$ is constant (homoskedastic) and the alternative hypothesis is that $Var(\varepsilon_i)$ varies with the predicted values (y-hat's) in a linear way. KStat performs this test and produces the p-value for us. To do this, run a regression, click **Statistics>Model Analysis**, and switch to the **Residuals** worksheet. The p-value for this test will be in the cell to the left of where it says **Breusch-Pagan heteroskedasticity test** in the **Residuals** worksheet. A low p-value suggests rejecting the null and a high p-value suggests not rejecting it. Therefore, a small p-value (usually below .1 or .05) is strong evidence of heteroskedasticity.

Effect of a Violation: Suppose we discover the constant error variance assumption has been violated. What are the consequences? The estimates of our regression coefficients remain unbiased, but the calculated standard deviations and interval estimates are no longer good estimates. Thus, we will no longer have a good measure of the accuracy of our estimates and predictions. Without a good measure of accuracy, we will not know how much to rely on our estimates in making decisions, we will not be able to judge if we need to gather more data, and we will not be able to conduct correct hypothesis tests to measure the strength of our findings. What can be done to remedy this?

Possible Fixes: Transforming the variables using logarithms (in semi-log or log-log form) if variance increases in the fitted values often helps. To see if it does, transform the variables, run the transformed regression, examine the residuals versus predicted values, and run the Breusch-Pagan Test again. Transformation using logarithms has worked if a serious indication of non-constant variance no longer occurs. More advanced techniques than we will cover, such as Weighted Least Squares, may help in situations where data transformations do not. (An advanced reference describing this procedure is Chapter 10.1 in *Applied Linear Regression Models, 4th ed.* by Neter, Kutner, Nachtsheim, and Wasserman.) Other advanced methods include procedures for calculating standard errors (and the associated interval estimates and hypothesis tests) that are robust to heteroskedasticity.

NEW TERMS

Elasticity The percentage response in one quantity to a percentage change in another

Semi-Log (SL) Model A regression model in which the dependent variable is transformed using the natural logarithm function LN and the independent variable(s) are not

Log-Log (LL) Model A regression model in which the dependent and independent variables are transformed using the natural logarithm function LN

Correction factor The value, $EXP(s^2/2)$, used to correct for a downward bias in regression estimates of average Y (including confidence intervals for average Y) induced by using LN(Y) as the dependent variable

Heteroskedasticty Non-constant variance. This violates the assumptions of the regression model

Breusch-Pagan Test A statistical test used to detect heteroskedasticity in a regression. Low p-values of this test indicate heteroskedasticty is present.

NEW FORMULAS

Properties of Logarithms

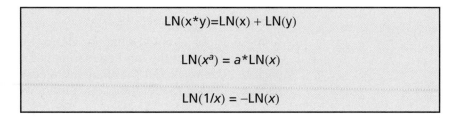

$$LN(x*y)=LN(x) + LN(y)$$

$$LN(x^a) = a*LN(x)$$

$$LN(1/x) = -LN(x)$$

Correction Factor $= EXP(s^2/2)$ where s is the standard error of regression

NEW KSTAT AND EXCEL FUNCTIONS

KStat

Statistics>Model analysis

This command computes an assortment of information regarding the most recent regression performed by KStat. In this chapter, we used the Breusch–Pagan Test p-value reported near the top of the worksheet to detect heteroskedasticty.

EXCEL

LN

Typing $= \mathbf{LN(X)}$ into an empty cell returns the natural logarithm of the number X as long as X is positive. Typing $= \mathbf{LN(A2)}$ into an empty cell returns the natural logarithm of the number contained in cell A2.

EXP

Typing $= EXP(X)$ into an empty cell exponentiates the number X. Typing $= EXP(A2)$ into an empty cell exponentiates the number in cell A2. Exponentiating is the mathematical opposite or inverse of the natural log function. $EXP(X) = e^X$ where e is a special mathematical constant having the property that $LN(e) = 1$.

CASE EXERCISES

1. Hot Dog revisited

We return to the market for supermarket hot dog dominance. Previously, we investigated some weekly scanner data from grocery stores on Dubuque's market share and price and the prices of two competitors: Oscar Mayer and Ball Park. We used these data to investigate how Dubuque's market share depends on these prices. We saw how multicollinearity affected our findings. Now we are prepared to be on the lookout for heteroskedasticity (non-constant variance).

Keeping this in mind, we would like to use the data in the **hotdog.xls** file to help Dubuque answer some further questions:

  a. If Dubuque prices at $1.65, Oscar Mayer prices at $1.75, and Ball Park prices at $1.50 for regular and $1.60 for beef franks, what is Dubuque's expected market share?

  b. If, at these prices, we observe Dubuque with a 1.5% market share, would this give us reason to think the market had changed? What if Dubuque had a 4% market share?

  c. At these prices, should Dubuque raise or lower its price? You may assume the size of the hot dog market is roughly fixed at 12,000 hot dog packages per week and Dubuque has a cost per unit produced of $1.30/ package. Does it matter how competitors would react to this change?

2. Office networks

A tech support company, Net Geeks, is bidding on a major contract to provide networking support to a firm that owns a chain of tax preparation consultancies across the country. In preparing its bid, Net Geeks has acquired the data contained in the **email.xls** file, which lists the average number of daily internal emails and the number of computers for a sample of 24 of the tax firm's offices. One key question in determining their bid involves the expected number of internal emails in an office with 20 computers; specifically, Net Geeks needs to know the probability that any particular office with 20 computers will have an average daily internal email volume below 200. Your job is to develop the best regression model to answer this question and use it to respond to the following questions:

  a. What is the best estimate for the average daily internal email volume for an office with 20 computers?

  b. Provide a 95% prediction interval for this estimate.

  c. Estimate the probability that the average daily internal emails at a particular office with 20 computers will be under 200.

  d. What can you say about the validity of the estimate in part c?

  e. Estimate the probability that the mean number of average daily internal emails for offices with 20 computers will be under 200.

3. Super staffing

Your company is currently building a new factory, which will employ 1,200 workers. You are confronted with the question of how many supervisors (supers) to hire for this plant to supervise the workers and to ensure a well-organized production process. You have employee data (**Factory.xls**) from your other factories, namely the number of supervisors and workers at these facilities.

Construct a linear regression of supers vs. workers.

    a. Mathematically, what does the coefficient on workers tell us about our staffing needs?

    b. Estimate the number of supers needed for our new factory and provide a 95% prediction interval for your estimate.

    c. Are there any problems in using this regression to answer part b?

Construct a regression of ln(supers) vs. workers.

    d. Mathematically, what does the coefficient on workers tell us about our staffing needs?

    e. Estimate the number of supers needed for our new factory and provide a 95% prediction interval for your estimate.

    f. Are there any problems in using this regression to answer part e?

Construct a regression of ln(supers) vs. ln(workers).

    g. Mathematically, what does the coefficient on workers tell us about our staffing needs?

    h. Estimate the number of supers needed for our new factory and provide a 95% prediction interval for your estimate.

    i. Are there any problems in using this regression to answer part h?

    j. Which of the three regressions above is the best one to use for this scenario? Explain.

4. Big movies revisited

Movie studios spend a great deal of energy determining which films will be successful. A major hit or flop can have a measurable effect on the bottom line of companies as big and diverse as Disney and Time Warner. The **bigmovies.xls**[1] file contains information on the major films of 1998 that we briefly examined in Chapter 2. Use this information to develop a model that predicts total domestic gross for a film based on the following independent variables:

Best Actor	The number of actors or actresses in the movie who were listed in Entertainment Weekly's list of the 25 Best Actors and the 25 Best Actresses of the 1990s
Top Dollar Actors	The number of actors or actresses appearing in the movie who were among the top 20 actors and top 20 actresses in average box office gross per movie in their careers at the beginning of 1998 and had appeared in at least 10 movies at that time

---

1. Source: The Internet Movie Database, http://www.imdb.com

Summer   A dummy variable indicating if the movie was released during the summer season (May 31 to Sept 5 inclusive) (= 1 if released during summer, = 0 otherwise)

Holiday   A dummy variable indicating if the movie was released on a holiday weekend (President's Day, Memorial Day, Independence Day, Labor Day, Thanksgiving, Christmas Day, New Year's Day) (= 1 if released on a holiday weekend, = 0 otherwise)

Christmas   A dummy variable indicating if the movie was released during the Christmas season (December 18th – 31st) (= 1 if released during the Christmas season, = 0 otherwise)

Opening   The number of movie screens the film was shown on during the
Screens   film's first weekend of general release

a. Construct a linear model using total domestic gross as the dependent variable.

b. Use the model analysis function of KStat to check the assumptions of the regression model.

Now add a new column of data titled ln(total gross) that contains the natural logarithm of the total domestic gross.

c. Construct a semi-log model using ln(total gross) as the dependent variable.

d. Use the model analysis function of KStat to check the assumptions of the regression model.

e. Choose the better model from the two above and use it to predict the total gross of a movie opening on 2,600 screens with no big or top–dollar actors on a non-holiday weekend during the summer. Provide a 90% prediction interval for your estimate.

CHAPTER 9

SODA SALES AND HARMON FOODS: DEALING WITH TIME AND SEASONALITY

We will use two forecasting cases in this chapter to demonstrate different techniques for modeling seasonality. Quarterly data in the soda case display a seasonal pattern as summer sales outpace winter sales. We use multiple dummy variables to additively model and measure the seasonal impact on sales. Next, the longer Harmon Foods HBS case uses a multiplicative seasonality model to forecast sales of its breakfast cereal. The case introduces the technique of lagging independent variables to model lingering effects. Finally, we will explore different techniques for analyzing time series data including the Cochrane-Orcutt method and the Auto Regressive Integrated Moving Average (ARIMA) model.

9.1 Soda Sales

INTRODUCTION

You have been asked by Cesca, Inc., to forecast future sales of Dada Soda. The data are in the **soda.xls** file. It consists of quarterly Dada Soda sales figures for the last four years (see Figure 9.1). Quarter 1 is the beginning of a year and is, therefore, a winter quarter.

Two things are apparent from the graph: Sales are growing over time, and a strong seasonal factor exists. Suppose we ignore the seasonality and regress sales against the quarter variable, i.e., draw a best-fit line through the graph (see Figure 9.2).

Figure 9.1 Quarterly sales for Dada Soda.

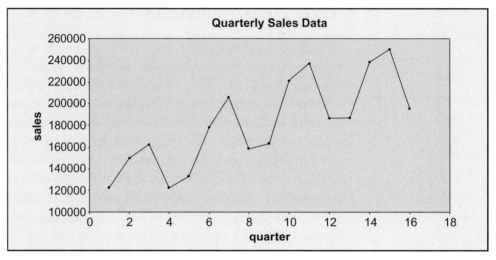

Figure 9.2 Quarterly sales for Dada Soda with regression line.

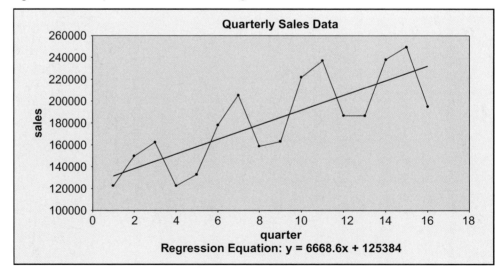

This procedure enables us to estimate future sales growth by extrapolation since the coefficient on the X variable represents average sales growth per quarter in the last four years, so predicted sales growth is $4 \times 6669 = 26{,}676$ units per year. However, there are two problems: One is practical and the other is technical, but still important. The practical problem is that it would be useful to have an estimate of the seasonal effects as well as of the average sales growth. At the moment, the regression is predicting sales will increase every quarter, and that is not the case: From year to year, sales are going up, but, for example, they consistently decrease from summer to fall in a given year. Solving this practical problem takes care of the technical one, so we will go through the solution first and explain what the technical problem is at the end.

INTRODUCING SEASONAL DUMMIES

We need to introduce dummy variables to take account of the effect of the different seasons. To cope with the four seasons, we will need three dummy variables because one season will function as a benchmark to which we will compare the other three. We choose to include one for each of winter, spring, and summer, so our extended dataset looks like Figure 9.3.

Now we will run the new regression and discuss what the coefficients tell us (see Figure 9.4).

INTERPRETING THE DUMMY COEFFICIENTS

As always when dealing with dummy variables, we work out what the equation means by going through the different qualitative states, i.e., the different seasons, one at a time. For example, in fall, we know that all three dummies equal zero and the regression equation from Figure 9.4 reads as follows:

$$\text{sales} = 98817 + 6708 \text{ quarter}$$

Figure 9.3 Dada Soda data.

quarter	sales	winter	spring	summer
1	122520	1	0	0
2	149931	0	1	0
3	162481	0	0	1
4	122630	0	0	0
5	132818	1	0	0
6	178325	0	1	0
Etc...				

Figure 9.4 Regression of Dada Soda with seasonal dummy variables.

Regression: sales					
	constant	quarter	winter	spring	summer
coefficient	98817.4375	6708.05625	5612.16875	44590.3625	54721.0563
std error of coef	6670.51532	497.190856	6463.48113	6367.14965	6308.64473
t-ratio	14.8141	13.4919	0.8683	7.0032	8.6740
p-value	0.0000%	0.0000%	40.3782%	0.0023%	0.0003%
beta-weight		0.7817	0.0614	0.4881	0.5990
standard error of regression	8894.02042				
R-squared	96.52%				
adjusted R-squared	95.26%				
number of observations	16				
residual degrees of freedom	11				
t-statistic for computing					
95%-confidence intervals	2.2010				

If we compare fall of one year to fall of the next year, this equation will apply to both, but the quarter variable has increased by four, so it predicts that fall quarter sales should increase by $4 \times 6708 = 26{,}832$ units per year. If we look at summer instead, we know that the summer dummy equals 1 and both of the others equal 0, so the regression equation from Figure 9.4 reads as follows:

$$\text{sales} = 98817 + 6708 \text{ quarter} + 54{,}721(1)$$
$$= 153{,}538 + 6708 \text{ quarter}$$

Again, this tells us that if we compare yearly summer quarter sales, we should expect an increase in sales of $4 \times 6708 = 26{,}832$ units per year. The same will apply if we look at spring and winter, so the first conclusion is that once we have controlled for seasonality, the predicted annual increase in sales is 26,832 units. In addition, we can predict how sales will change quarterly. Suppose we move from summer to fall. The quarter variable increases in value by 1, giving an extra 6,708 units, but the summer dummy changes from 1 to 0 so we lose 54,721 units, a net decrease of 48,013 units. Things are a little more difficult when (for example) we move from winter to spring. The quarter variable goes up by 1 as before, the winter dummy goes from 1 to 0, and the spring dummy goes from 0 to 1, so the net effect is $+6{,}708 - 5{,}612 + 44{,}590 = 45{,}686$ units.

We have, therefore, managed to resolve the changes into a quarterly seasonal effect, and a yearly growth trend. The R-squared has increased from around 60% to over 95%, which suggests this multiple regression fits the data better than the regression without the seasonal terms did. However, R-squared is not the appropriate way to compare the fit of two regressions that have the same dependent (Y) variable but different numbers of independent (X) variables. A better measure for such a comparison is something called the **adjusted R-squared**. It is reported on the KStat output directly below the R-squared. The purpose of the adjusted R-squared is to adjust the measure of a regression's fit to account for the extra degrees of freedom that adding additional X variables absorbs. In this example, even after this adjustment there is a large improvement in variation explained by the regression with the seasonal dummy variables as demonstrated by the large increase in the adjusted R-squared. Finally, we will discuss the technical problem mentioned earlier.

SEASONALITY AND AUTOCORRELATION

The regression model makes a number of assumptions about the distribution of the error terms (i.e., the distribution of Y around its average given the values of the independent (X) variables). One of these is the rather mysterious sounding assumption that "the errors are independent." Look again at Figure 9.2. For any particular quarter, the estimated error term is the distance from the fitted line to that quarter's data point.[1] "Independence" means that knowing the size of one quarter's error does not say anything about the next quarter's error. But that isn't true here. If you tell me this quarter's sales were "well above average," i.e., well above the fitted line, then I can guess this quarter is summer, next quarter will be fall, and the fall quarter's sales will likely be well below the fitted line because of the seasonality in soda sales. This phenomenon of the failure of independence is known as autocorrelation and, much like the heteroskedasticity studied in Chapter 8, interferes with the statistical inference we do using regression. When it is present, our estimated coefficients are still unbiased estimates, but the estimated standard deviations are not, so we cannot use confidence intervals or hypothesis tests unless we correct this problem, which we did here by adding the seasonal dummy variables. We discuss autocorrelation more generally in Section 9.4, including a method for detecting it and removing it.

SUMMARY

We saw how seasonal dummies may be used to "de-trend" time series data, enabling us to estimate a yearly growth trend and seasonal effects. This also solved the problem of autocorrelation in the data.

9.2 Seasonality: Using Seasonal Indices in Forecasting

The Dada Soda case shows us one way to account for seasonal variations in our data. In that case, the sales seemed to vary consistently over the four quarters or seasons. We captured this variation in our estimated regression prediction by including dummy variables for the different seasons. By using these intercept dummy variables to capture the seasonal effects, we were implicitly assuming the seasonal effect was **additive**. In other words, we only allowed the season to move the regression line up or down by a constant, and we did not allow the season to change the slope of the line. In practical terms, we assumed that the summer, winter, spring, and fall effects were each of a fixed size. The effects would be identical if we were selling 1 million cases or if we were selling 100 million cases.

---

1. It is an estimated error term because it is calculated using the estimated regression line. The true error term is how far the data point lies from the true regression line.

Sometimes, we may want to use a different model of seasonal effects, one where the effect of the season is expressed as a percentage of the number of sales. In other words, the summer effect might be to increase sales by 10%. With this model, the effect of summer at the 1-million-case level is to add about 100,000 cases; at the 100-million-case level, it would add 10 million cases. This percentage-based model is known as a **multiplicative** model of seasonality in contrast to the additive model. Why multiplicative? Because we can express each season's effect (month's effect, day-of-the-week's effect, etc.) by a **seasonal index**, which is a number multiplied by our regression results to get a prediction.

For example, in the Harmon Foods, Inc. case (see Section 9.3), the seasonal index for January shipments is 113. This number should be interpreted as saying that, all else equal, shipments in January will be 113% (or 1.13 times) the average of all months' shipments. We say all else equal because we know other factors such as a time trend or advertising affect shipments.

So, how can you use these seasonal indices in combination with regression to make forecasts?

Step 1: Deseasonalize the Y variable by dividing each observation by its corresponding seasonal index (converted from percentages if necessary). In the Harmon Foods, Inc. case, this means dividing January shipments by 1.13, February shipments by 0.98, etc.

Step 2: Build a regression model as usual (ignoring seasons) with the deseasonalized data as your Y variable.

Step 3: Use your estimated regression model to get a predicted deseasonalized value for the time period of interest.

Step 4: Multiply this predicted value by the appropriate seasonal index to get a prediction. You should multiply any interval estimates by the seasonal index as well.

That's all there is to it. If the seasonal effect works in percentage terms, the multiplicative model and seasonal indices will be appropriate; if the seasonal effects are of a fixed absolute size, the additive model will be a better choice.

Seasonally adjusted data are data that have been deseasonalized. For example, many economic statistics such as unemployment, retail sales, and housing starts are usually reported in a deseasonalized form. How are seasonal indices estimated? Some statistics packages can do this procedure for you. In fact there are many ways, some quite complicated, to estimate seasonal effects. For a taste of how part of the U.S. government does it, go to the Bureau of Labor Statistics web site at http://stats.bls.gov/, search for the term "seasonal adjustment," and explore some of the links.

Often, as in the Harmon Foods, Inc. case, seasonal indices previously estimated by others (in this case, an industry group) using a large set of historical and industry-wide or country-wide data are provided; thus, these indices do not need to be estimated from your data. You need only use them in your analysis.

9.3 The Harmon Foods, Inc. Case

The Harmon Foods, Inc. case is located in the packet of cases bundled to the back of this text.

QUESTIONS TO PREPARE:

1. Using only the data giving monthly shipments of Treat (and possibly a time trend, but no variables that allow for seasonal or monthly cycles), provide a forecast for shipments of Treat in January 1988. Give a 95% prediction interval for this forecast. This forecast shows what one can do without the rest of the data in the dataset and without seasonal information.
2. Develop and estimate a model you think makes the most sense to use for forecasting monthly shipments of Treat cereal. How did you arrive at this model?
3. Use the model you developed above to forecast shipments for January 1988, assuming that 200,000 consumer packs are shipped in that month and $120,000 in dealer allowances are provided. Give a 95% prediction interval for your forecast.
4. Use your estimated model to comment on the impact and effectiveness of consumer promotions and dealer promotions.
5. What improvements, if any, would you recommend to the product manager in terms of the timing and amounts of dealer promotions and consumer promotions in the future?

9.4 Regression Analysis of Time Series Data

Most of the datasets that we have encountered in previous chapters are so-called **cross-sectional samples**: We have some data on a population (e.g., car buyers, newspaper subscribers) at a fixed point in time, and analyze the relationship among various variables in the sample (e.g., price and income, Sunday and daily circulations). Time plays no role in these analyses. In other datasets, notably in the Harmon Foods and Dada Soda cases, we have consecutive observations of several variables (sales of the product and marketing efforts). These data are called **time series data.**

When we work with a time series dataset and build a regression model to explain a dependent variable, we should immediately consider including two types of variables among the explanatory variables: a **time index** (a variable that increases by one every period, representing a linear trend) and **seasonal dummies** (variables that allow us to represent seasonal variations in the dependent variable). Another lesson that we learned in the Harmon Foods case is that, in the regression, we can easily incorporate the idea that our current actions matter for the future by using **lagged explanatory variables**.

We mentioned earlier a new problem that may arise when we run a regression using a time series dataset. We may encounter the problem of **autocorrelated residuals**: The error terms that represent the difference between the actual observations of the Y variable and the theoretical regression line may not be independent (completely random) over time. This is the case, for example, if the shocks that affect the dependent variable are persistent over time.

Suppose the Y variable represents the sales of our product. If sales this week were higher than expected due to a random event (e.g., good weather, a favorable review in the local paper), it is likely that we will be "lucky" next week as well since weather tends to persist, information about the review will diffuse among our potential customers, etc.

Autocorrelation of the residuals has the same consequences as heteroskedasticity: The standard errors (of the coefficients, the estimated mean, the regression and the prediction) become unreliable. In particular, in the most common forms of autocorrelation, the standard errors on the coefficients will be underestimated, resulting in p-values for the coefficients that appear to be lower than they are in reality. As a result, we may conclude that a coefficient is significant when in reality it is not. In a time series regression, one must be exceptionally wary of this possibility.

Another issue in time series regressions is if we can include the lagged dependent variable among the regressors. If residuals are autocorrelated, then the inclusion of lagged Y among the X variables will cause bias in the coefficients and must be avoided.

To see this, consider the following example. Suppose (as in the Harmon Foods case) we have a time series dataset, where our dependent variable is **Sales** and the explanatory variables measure marketing efforts (e.g., number of **Coupons** issued, cash **Incentives** provided to dealers). It is reasonable to believe that promotions have different immediate and delayed effects (e.g., consumers stock up on the product when there is a discount). Moreover, **Sales** in previous periods may affect our current sales, e.g., satisfied customers tend to become repeat customers. You may think a variable like **Sales_1** (**Sales** lagged one period) could successfully represent the effects of our past actions (promotions and the resulting sales) on our current sales.

However, it may be wrong to regress **Sales** on **Coupons**, **Incentives**, a **time index**, **seasonal dummies**, and **Sales_1**. Why? **Sales_1** may be correlated with the error term in this regression because **Sales_1** contains last period's error term and errors may be autocorrelated. For example, the error term may reflect the effects of a newspaper review on **Sales**, and that effect is likely to be persistent. The error term essentially stands for all variables omitted from the regression, and we know coefficients become biased when an included variable (**Sales_1**) is correlated with omitted variables. Therefore, if error terms are autocorrelated then including **Sales_1** leads to biased coefficients. Instead of including the lagged dependent variable (**Sales_1**), you should include **lagged explanatory variables** to represent the idea that our past actions (marketing efforts) matter for current **Sales**.

Several simple and intuitive tests exist to detect specific forms of autocorrelation in the residuals. For example, after having run the regression of the dependent variable on the appropriate explanatory variables, you can regress the residuals (the difference between the actual and the fitted values of Y for each observation) on past values of the residuals (lagged residuals) and see if the coefficient on the lagged residuals is significant.

In KStat, you can find the residuals in the Model Analysis worksheet. Copy the entire column of residuals back into the dataset, create its lag, and perform this simple regression (residuals on lagged residuals). If the slope coefficient is significant, this indicates first-order autocorrelation. This procedure is called the Cochrane-Orcutt test.

A cure for this autocorrelation is relatively simple using the Cochrane-Orcutt method. Suppose you find autocorrelation in the Cochrane-Orcutt test: The coefficient on lagged residuals in the regression of residuals, call it ρ, is significant. Transform each observation (the Y and X variables) as follows. For each observation, at t = 2,3,..., create $Y^*_t = Y_t - \rho Y_{t-1}$; similarly, create $X^*_t = X_t - \rho X_{t-1}$. (The first observation is dropped because no observation occurs before it.) Now regress Y^* on the transformed explanatory variable(s), X^*. This new regression usually does not exhibit autocorrelated residuals; if it does, then the procedure of transforming the variables can be repeated. The coefficients on all the X^* variables will be the same as the coefficients on the corresponding original X variables. However, the coefficients will have the right standard errors and p-values because autocorrelation in the residuals has been eliminated. We can rely on the new p-values for determining which variables are significant.

SUMMARY

Everything described thus far belongs to what we can call the "traditional econometric analysis" of time series data. We can apply the same regression techniques that we use for cross-sectional analyses. The only differences relative to a cross-sectional regression are the following:

1. New candidates for regressors like a **time index**, **seasonal dummies** and **lagged X variables**
2. The potential problem of **autocorrelated residuals** (resulting in incorrect standard error estimates)

9.5 Time Series Analysis

We can also use a different approach to analyzing time series data, called **time series analysis**. Time series analysis, in its purest form, ignores ordinary explanatory variables and, instead, focuses on estimating the dynamic behavior of the dependent variable alone. In other words, time series analysis is the science (and sometimes art) of extrapolation from a series of numbers, Y_1, Y_2, ..., Y_T, without using any X variables except time and seasonality.

For example, one simple method of extrapolation (forecasting Y_{T+1} based on Y_1, Y_2, ..., Y_T) is linear trend extrapolation. You can do this by regressing Y against a time index. Another method, exponential trend extrapolation, is carried out by regressing LN(Y) on a time index. To make both models fit better, we can enrich them each with seasonal dummies. In what follows, we discuss more sophisticated, but similarly atheoretical (i.e., no underlying model or theory) methods.

There are at least three reasons for interest in such simplistic, naïve methods of forecasting. First, in practice, collecting data on potential explanatory variables to carry out a proper regression analysis is sometimes too expensive; the only data readily available may be a series of observations regarding the dependent variable. Second, even if we can obtain the extra information and build a proper regression model, time series forecasts are cheap, require little effort to produce and can serve as a useful benchmark for comparison purposes; running a time series analysis may uncover patterns that we will explain using regression methods. Third, a sophisticated time series forecast (for example, the ARIMA model, which we will describe below) may well outperform an unsophisticated (or incorrectly specified) econometric model. In the 1970s and 1980s, time series models became popular after several studies showed the superiority of ARIMA models over standard econometric models in particular applications.

Econometric methods have since improved (e.g., in handling autocorrelation) and are generally preferred over extrapolation methods when available.

The ARIMA model of time series analysis (also called the Box-Jenkins method after its inventors in 1970) has two building blocks: autoregression (AR) and moving average (MA).

A variable Y is a pth-order autoregressive series, AR(p) for short, if it can be written in the following way:

$$Y_t = \Phi_1 Y_{t-1} + \Phi_2 Y_{t-2} + ... + \Phi_p Y_{t-p} + \varepsilon_t$$

Φ_1, Φ_2, ..., Φ_p are the parameters of the AR(p) process, and ε_t is an independent error term.

In other words, the current value of Y only depends on its past values (up to p lags). A variable Y is a qth-order moving average series, MA(q) for short, if it can be written in the following way:

$$Y_t = \varepsilon_t + \theta_1 \varepsilon_{t-1} + \theta_2 \varepsilon_{t-2} + ... + \theta_q \varepsilon_{t-q}$$

θ_1, θ_2, ..., θ_q are the parameters of the MA(q) process, and the ε terms are independent errors. In other words, the current value of Y is a weighted sum of current and past (unobservable) disturbances.

The ARIMA(p,d,q) model is more general than AR or MA. First, we difference the original series d times. Differencing a series means that we replace Y_t with $Y_t - Y_{t-1}$; that is, we consider the increments of the series instead of the series itself. We call the original Y series an ARIMA(p,d,q) process if, after differencing it d times, the resulting series Y* can be written in the following way:

$$Y*_t = \Phi_1 Y*_{t-1} + \Phi_2 Y*_{t-2} + ... + \Phi_p Y*_{t-p} + \theta_1 \varepsilon_{t-1} + \theta_2 \varepsilon_{t-2} + ... + \theta_q \varepsilon_{t-q} + \varepsilon_t$$

ARIMA(p,d,q) can be thought of as a model where the dth difference of Y follows an AR(p) process such that the error term is MA(q).

There is no reason why a variable Y should follow an ARIMA process. ARIMA is not supported by any formal economic theory; it is a general class of random processes widely used in practice for forecasting without using explanatory variables. For example, if Y is generated by the famous "random walk" process, then it is ARIMA with p = 0, d = 1, and q = 0. If one decides to model Y as an ARIMA(p,d,q) process with a given p, d, and q, then a computer program can estimate the parameters Φ_1, Φ_2, ..., Φ_p, and θ_1, θ_2, ..., θ_q. Given these parameters, you can forecast future values or see how the past (observed) values of Y fit the ARIMA model.

KStat does not have an explicit module to compute the parameters of a general ARIMA(p,d,q) process, but you can easily fit an AR(p) model by regressing Y on 1, 2, ..., p times lagged values of Y. Differencing Y (maybe a couple of times) is useful because it reduces the chance of autocorrelated residuals, which cause problems (coefficient bias) when lagged Y variables are included among the regressors.

The main practical question that remains is how to choose the parameters p, d, and q for an ARIMA model and forecast. Time series analysts would probably say that this is the "art" part of forecasting. The most important guideline is to keep these parameters as low as possible (parsimony). In general, choose d, the number of times the series is differenced, to make the series stationary, which means that the mean, variance, and other properties of Y* must not depend on time. Usually d = 1 or d = 2 suffices.

To find the "right" parameters p and q, time series analysts usually look at a diagram called a correlogram. To create this diagram, for all k = 1,2,..., we compute ρ_k, the correlation coefficient between Y* and Y* lagged k times, and plot ρ_k against k. The correlogram should fall off to numbers close to zero as k increases; otherwise, Y* is not stationary and needs to be differenced further. A correlation coefficient ρ_k on the correlogram is called significant if it is greater in absolute value than $2/\sqrt{T}$, where T is the number of observations.

The pattern on the correlogram suggests the appropriate numbers for p and q. For example, if ρ_1 (respectively, ρ_1 and ρ_2) are significant but the subsequent ρ_k values look random, then Y* is an MA(1) (respectively, MA(2)) process. If the correlogram declines geometrically, then Y* can be modeled as an AR(1) process. If it exhibits a wave, then AR(2) or a higher order AR process is required. If the correlogram appears to decline geometrically but the sign of ρ_1 does not match the signs of the rest of the ρ_k values, then ARIMA(1,d,1) is suggested.

We summarize ARIMA by working out an example. The **Kodak.xls** file contains the annual gross revenues of Eastman Kodak Co. between 1975 and 1999 (in billions of constant 1982 dollars). Plotting the data in Figure 9.5, there is no visible trend, so we do not difference the series (d = 0). Next, we look at the correlogram in Figure 9.6.

Figure 9.5 Kodak's annual revenues.

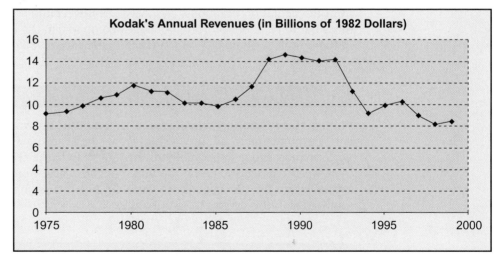

Figure 9.6 Correlogram of Kodak revenues.

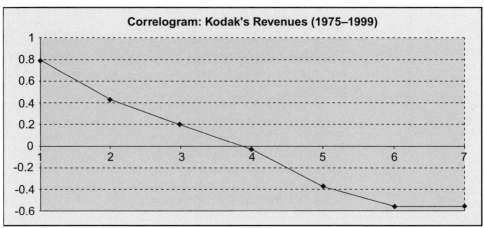

The decline in ρ_k appears to be steady (and approximately linear); the first two ρ_k values are significant (greater than $2/\mathrm{SQRT}(25) = .4$ in absolute value), but the rest do not appear to be random either (this is not an MA process). An AR(1) process seems to be appropriate. When we run the AR(1) regression in KStat, we find that the estimated AR(1) process can be written in the following way:

Revenue = 1.64 + .85*Revenue_1.

To check how well the AR(1) process fits the data, we can estimate Kodak's revenues for the years 1976–1999 and calculate the **mean absolute deviation** (MAD) from the actual observations, AVERAGE(ABS(**Revenue – fitted Revenue**)), which turns out to be about $0.76 billion. As a comparison, the average level of **Revenue** in the sample is about $11 billion (both in constant 1982 dollars).

SUMMARY

Though there is no theoretical reason why a particular variable might follow a linear or exponential trend, the techniques we have seen are useful. Predicting future performance using these methods has its drawbacks. However, the advantages mentioned earlier (including the value of the ARIMA model when the only data available are for the dependent variable and for establishing a baseline) make knowledge of this approach worthwhile.

NEW TERMS

Additive model A regression model using dummy variables to account for seasonality. Each season is assumed to have a fixed effect on the dependent variable

Multiplicative model A regression model which assumes each season affects the dependent variable by a certain percentage

Seasonal index An index used to seasonalize and deseasonalize the dependent variable and predictions in a multiplicative seasonality model

Time series data Consecutive observations of a set of variables

Time index A variable that increases by one every time period. Used to model a linear trend over time

Lagged variables Variables that use values from a previous time period to explain outcomes in the current time period

Autocorrelated residuals A problem where the error terms are not independent

Cochrane-Orcutt test A test for autocorrelation using the residuals

Linear trend extrapolation A time series method used to model linear trends in Y over time

Exponential trend extrapolation A time series method used to model linear trends in ln(Y) over time

ARIMA or Box-Jenkins method A time series method employing autoregression (AR) and moving average (MA) techniques

Stationary A model where the properties of Y* do not depend on time

Correlogram A diagram used to determine the proper time series parameters

CASE EXERCISES

1. Harmon Foods

Read the Harmon Foods case and prepare answers to the five questions listed in Section 9.3 of this chapter.

2. Paradise tax

The governor of the state of Hawaii is bound by the state constitution to budget no more funds then the amount projected by the State Council on Revenues. Part of this revenue is from the transient accommodations tax, which is a hotel tax. Forecasting the tax revenues from this and other tourism taxes are important to the state as well as the major businesses operating in the tourism industry. The data in the **hawaiiTAT.xls**[2] file contains information from 1990 through the summer of 2003 regarding the quarterly collection of this tax as well as statistics such as visitor days (the number of days spent by visiting tourists each quarter) and the average daily room rate. Furthermore, a seasonal index based on visitor arrivals by plane (no tourists swim or drive to the islands though a tiny percentage arrives by boat) has been constructed as well.

Develop an additive and a multiplicative model to forecast the state's collection of the transient accommodations tax. Which model do you feel is the better choice to make a prediction for the fall of 2003 when the room rates are expected to average $133 per night with 14,000,000 visitor days? Provide estimates from each model and justify your choice.

---

2. Derived from http://www2.hawaii.gov/DBEDT/

3. Restaurant Planning

The owners of Blue Stem, an upscale restaurant in a trendy area of Chicago, have gathered data on its nightly receipts. Over the year, the restaurant occasionally offers a free dessert promotion to ticket holders from the theater next door. The promotions occur mostly on the weekends, which are the most popular nights for dining out. The restaurant would like to separate the promotion effect from the weekend effect, so it can determine if the promotion is worthwhile. The data are available in the **bluestem.xls**[3] file.

An industry group has provided a nightly index reflecting the relative popularity of different nights for higher end restaurants in the city.

Develop two models, one using additive and one using multiplicative techniques, to test the effectiveness of the promotion. In each case, report how much, on average, the promotion boosts revenues on a Saturday night.

---

3. Source: Linda Hall, Co-owner Blue Stem Restaurant

CASE INSERT 3   NOPANE ADVERTISING STRATEGY

In this case, we will look at the advertising strategy for a drug, Nopane. The brand manager is faced with the choice of advertising level, copy, and region in the face of intense competition. The assignment is to read the case and answer the following questions. For the first three, you can use the regressions included with the case; however, you will need to conduct your own analysis using KStat to respond to the additional questions.

Questions to Prepare

1. What does Regression 1 in the case say about the merits of "emotional" vs. "rational" copy? What does Regression 3 say about the two types of copy? What is the interpretation of the coefficient on copy in Regression 1? Regression 3?
2. Assuming Alison Silk's hypothesis is correct, which of the regressions is most relevant for choosing an advertising strategy? Why?
3. Answer question 2, assuming that Stanley Skamarycz's hypothesis is correct.
4. Given the data from the case (in **nopane.xls**), what national advertising strategy (i.e., which copy and which one of the three levels of ad spending) would you advocate? Each additional unit sold per 100 prospects over a six-month period yields a profit (net of production and delivery costs, but not net of advertising costs) of $10. Provide support for your position.
5. Instead of a single national campaign, Ms. Silk knows it would be possible (though more costly) to have one campaign for the East and West Coast states and another for the middle of the country. Comment on the desirability of splitting up the campaign.

Hints: Remember omitted variable bias. For questions 4 and 5, you may want to think about using dummy variables and/or slope dummy variables.

The Nopane Advertising Strategy case is located in the packet of cases bundled to the back of this text.[1]

---

1. Nopane Advertising Strategy, Harvard Business School Case, Product #9-893-005.

CASE INSERT 4   THE BASEBALL CASE

Singha Field is home to the BK Lions professional baseball team. The team's new marketing director, Noelle Amsley, has been trying to develop a better understanding of the key drivers of attendance at the ballpark to increase ticket revenues, optimize concession inventories and staffing, and schedule the timing of promotional giveaways.

The stadium is capable of holding almost 41,000 fans. The exact number is hard to pin down due to the sale of standing-room-only tickets and VIP ticket comping. The data for this case are included in the file **baseball case.xls**.

PART A: REGRESSION ANALYSIS

Noelle's first model uses three concepts to predict attendance: time of day, temperature, and day of the week. Specifically, she has a dummy variable for **night** games, the day's high **temperature**, and three dummies indicating if the game takes place on a **Friday**, **Saturday**, or **Sunday**, respectively.

1. Use Regression 1 to estimate attendance for a Sunday afternoon game where the temperature is 82 degrees.

A quick look at the model analysis page on KStat shows six outliers among the 92 data points. Two of them are day games on very cold weekdays where the model predicts the lowest possible turnout. However, these particular games nearly sold out. Noelle kicks herself: They're both the opening day of the season, a special game for baseball fans.

Adding a new dummy variable called **opening day** that equals one on the first home game of the season and zero otherwise produces Regression 2.

2. Use Regression 2 to estimate the attendance for a Sunday afternoon game where the temperature is 82 degrees and it is not opening day.

Regression 1

Regression: Attendance	constant	night game	temp(f)	Friday	Saturday	Sunday
coefficient	19354.1844	2514.661736	186.114675	3572.41871	6451.25548	4313.77787
std error of coef	2716.61619	1381.218904	38.7590761	1458.08009	1641.43678	1488.04549
t-ratio	7.1244	1.8206	4.8018	2.4501	3.9302	2.8990
p-value	0.0000%	7.2144%	0.0007%	1.6309%	0.0171%	0.4750%
beta weight		0.1709	0.4232	0.2320	0.3722	0.2730
standard error of regression		4894.896069				
R-squared		34.26%				
adjusted R-squared		30.43%				
number of observations		92				
residual degrees of freedom		86				
t-statistic for computing						
95% confidence intervals		1.9879				

Regression 2

Regression: Attendance	constant	night game	temp(f)
coefficient	17143.6077	2766.43318	214.271986
std error of coef	2681.662	1317.87277	37.9907144
t-ratio	6.3929	2.0992	5.6401
p-value	0.0000%	3.8768%	0.0000%
beta weight		0.1880	0.4873
standard error of regression	4661.71554		
R-squared	41.06%		
adjusted R-squared	36.90%		
number of observations	92		
residual degrees of freedom	85		
t-statistic for computing			
95% confidence intervals	1.9883		

	Friday	Saturday	Sunday	opening day
coefficient	3265.07647	6723.67061	4626.66143	10892.1147
std error of coef	1392.08051	1565.65842	1420.67213	3476.048711
t-ratio	2.3455	4.2945	3.2567	3.1335
p-value	2.1333%	0.0046%	0.1620%	0.2371%
beta weight	0.2120	0.3880	0.2928	0.2721

3. Compare your results from questions 1 and 2. Explain why your estimate changes between the two models.

The team management recently began using a more sophisticated pricing structure to improve its revenues. Instead of charging the same set of prices for every game, there are two different pricing schemes: full-price tickets and cheap tickets. For games where management anticipates a lower level of interest, it charges the cheap ticket prices in order to stimulate demand. Regression 3 shows the significant effect of **cheap tickets** on attendance, but the coefficient is confusing to Noelle. She had expected the sign to be positive. Shouldn't the lower prices *increase* attendance?

Regression 3

Regression: Attendance	constant	cheap tickets
coefficient	35638.73418	-7957.34956
std error of coef	584.2965976	1554.374257
t-ratio	60.9943	-5.1193
p-value	0.0000%	0.0002%
beta-weight		-0.4749
standard error of regression		5193.341757
R-squared		22.55%
adjusted R-squared		21.69%
number of observations		92
residual degrees of freedom		90
t-statistic for computing		
95% confidence intervals		1.9867

4. Do these results violate the law of demand that says all else being equal, a lower price should increase the quantity demanded?

Noelle's colleague, Andrew Groden, is interested in learning how two other factors are driving attendance: promotional giveaways such as free hat day; and popular opponents, such as the team's historic rivals, the ML Tigers, as well as their cross-town rivals, the Pachyderms. To test these factors' significance, Noelle has added three dummy variables called **promo**, **Tigers**, and **Pachyderms**, which are added to her earlier regression to produce Regression 4. She quickly informs Andrew that the first two are significant, but the Pachyderms do not seem to be a big draw to the ballpark.

Andrew disagrees: "It's just because those games were all scheduled on days that were already popular. Five of the six times they played were on Fridays or the weekends, and all of the games were in the summer when the weather is usually perfect! Those games increased the interest in the games, but there just weren't enough seats available in the ballpark to see the effect."

5. Does Andrew's theory sound reasonable? Why would a team schedule games against a popular rival, knowing that it did not need to encourage attendance on those dates?

Regression 5 adds two more variables to Noelle's model. One is **school**, which equals one whenever the local public school system is in session (keeping thousands of potential fans away from many games), and zero otherwise. The other variable she adds is **Cheap Tickets**, as was used in Regression 3.

6. Is the variable **Cheap Tickets** significant in this regression? Interpret the coefficient and its significance in the context of this new regression.

Regression 4

Regression: Attendance	constant	night game	promo	temp(f)	Friday
coefficient	16564.31881	2325.53679	2429.938539	201.3943229	2717.848086
std error of coef	2580.76788	277.576756	994.7414743	37.09662168	1339.66775
t-ratio	6.4184	1.8203	2.4428	5.4289	2.0287
p-value	0.0000%	7.2366%	1.6723%	0.0001%	4.5729%
beta weight		0.1581	0.2074	0.4580	0.1765
standard error of regression		4411.275937			
R-squared		49.09%			
adjusted R-squared		43.50%			
number of observations		92			
residual degrees of freedom		82			
t-statistic for computing 95% confidence intervals		1.9893			

	Saturday	Sunday	opening day	Tigers	Pachyderms
coefficient	5487.208562	4180.384176	11109.54335	4010.041599	2848.318457
std error of coef	1579.429706	1357.819986	3300.049321	1701.465882	1931.134017
t-ratio	3.4742	3.0787	3.3665	2.3568	1.4749
p-value	0.0821%	0.2827%	0.1161%	2.0817%	14.4056%
beta weight	0.3166	0.2646	0.2776	0.1936	0.1205

Regression 5

Regression: Attendance	constant	night game	promo	temp(f)	Friday	Saturday
coefficient	23724.3827	2348.3121	1611.90762	136.000866	2312.42114	5222.543633
std error of coef	3713.75419	1378.057367	1031.80193	44.0172227	1359.57308	1592.26668
t-ratio	6.3882	1.7041	1.5622	3.0897	1.7008	3.2799
p-value	0.0000%	9.2249%	12.2182%	0.2755%	9.2857%	0.1539%
beta weight	0.1596	0.1376	0.3093	0.1502	0.3013	

standard error of regression		4286.660668				
R-squared		53.10%				
adjusted R-squared		46.65%				
number of observations		92				
residual degrees of freedom		80				
t-statistic for computing 95% confidence intervals		1.9901				

	Sunday	opening day	school	Tigers	Pachyderms	cheap tickets
coefficient	3709.76718	10272.16085	-2768.2469	4391.41594	2671.45663	-1792.01247
std error of coef	1414.02053	3266.218669	1272.0563	1672.61222	1879.94934	1656.933691
t-ratio	2.6236	3.1450	-2.1762	2.6255	1.4210	-1.0815
p-value	1.0418%	0.2332%	3.2490%	1.0364%	15.9196%	28.2714%
beta weight	0.2348	0.2566	-0.2204	0.2120	0.1130	-0.1069

Predicted values and residuals

15.2328	0.010%	Breusch-Pagan heteroskedasticity test
7.1979	2.735%	Jarque-Bera non-normality test
1.2094		Durbin-Watson statistic

7. Use Regression 5 to make a forecast of attendance for a Saturday night game against the Tigers that is not on opening day. Also, the temperature is 89 degrees, there are full-price tickets, a promotional giveaway, and school is out of session. Provide a 95% prediction interval for your answer. Do you have any concerns about your forecast?

PART B: NON-LINEARITIES

Noelle has been studying Regression 5. She is concerned about the Breusch-Pagan Test, which indicates a heteroskedasticity problem with the model. She becomes more concerned after conducting a semi-log model, Regression 6, which failed to fix the problem. Noelle suspects that a linear model may not be the most appropriate fit to the data; in particular, she is worried about the large number of games that are pushing the stadium's capacity limits.

Both linear and logarithmic models are unbounded, meaning they don't have an upper limit. Regression 1, for instance, predicts more than 42,000 fans for a Saturday afternoon game with a temperature of around 88 degrees (not unreasonable for a summer day) even though that exceeds the capacity of the stadium by

Regression 6

Regression: LN Attend	constant	night game	promo	temp(f)	Friday	Saturday
coefficient	10.0489864	0.073264282	0.05703051	0.00479724	0.07380671	0.159887464
std error of coef	0.12828648	0.047603076	0.03564216	0.00152051	0.04696456	0.055002639
t-ratio	78.3324	1.5391	1.6001	3.1550	1.5715	2.9069
p-value	0.0000%	12.7734%	11.3522%	0.2262%	12.0004%	0.4721%
beta weight	0.1481	0.1447	0.3244	0.1425	0.2744	

standard error of regression	0.148076734	
R-squared	50.50%	
adjusted R-squared	43.69%	
number of observations	92	
residual degrees of freedom	80	
t-statistic for computing 95% confidence intervals	1.9901	

	Sunday	opening day	school	Tigers	Pachyderms	cheap tickets
coefficient	0.11492838	0.325351455	-0.0766163	0.14849429	0.07921641	-0.07012413
std error of coef	0.04884537	0.112826984	0.04394142	0.05777806	0.06494024	0.057236471
t-ratio	2.3529	2.8836	-1.7436	2.5701	1.2198	-1.2252
p-value	2.1084%	0.5048%	8.5070%	1.2023%	22.6111%	22.4108%
beta weight	0.2163	0.2418	-0.1814	0.2132	0.0997	-0.1245

Predicted values and residuals			Regression: LN Attend
	26.7005	0.000%	Breusch-Pagan heteroskedasticity test
	26.8417	0.000%	Jarque-Bera non-normality test
	1.2770		Durbin-Watson statistic

more than a thousand people. A regression of ln(Attendance) using the same independent variables predicts more than 43,000 fans.

The problem as Noelle sees it is that none of the models she has learned about seems right for the pattern she observed in the dataset: attendance getting closer and closer to a maximum value as "conditions" improve. Taking temperature as the independent variable, Noelle plots Attendance versus Temperature with two different fits. These fits include one linear and one curving up toward the capacity. These plots are seen in Figures 1 and 2.

Looking at Figure 2 gives Noelle an idea. Though a semi-log model, $Y = a \cdot e^{bx}$ does not have a maximum when the constant a is positive, it does have a minimum. Y will never fall below zero.

Figure 1

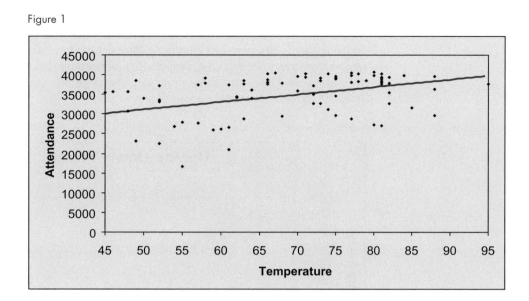

Figure 2

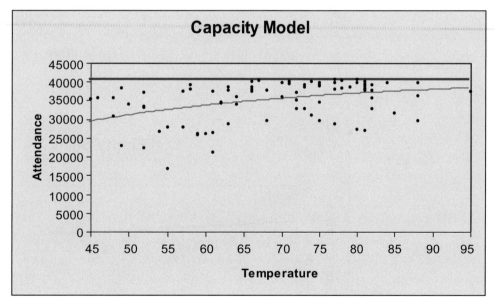

Flipping Figure 2 upside-down by plotting Empty Seats versus Temperature gives Noelle the graph in Figure 3, which looks just like the kind of graph where a semi-log model fits perfectly! Taking a log of the empty seats and plotting it versus Temperature gives her Figure 4. Empty seats were computed using 41,000 as the capacity. Regression 7 uses the same dependent variable but adds the entire collection of independent ones as Noelle had done previously.

Figure 3

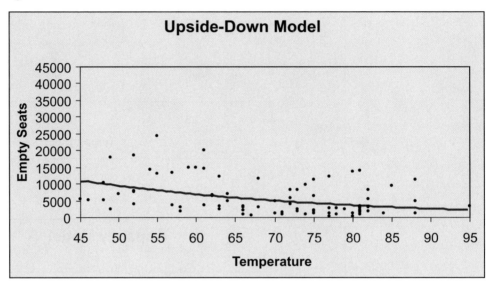

Figure 4

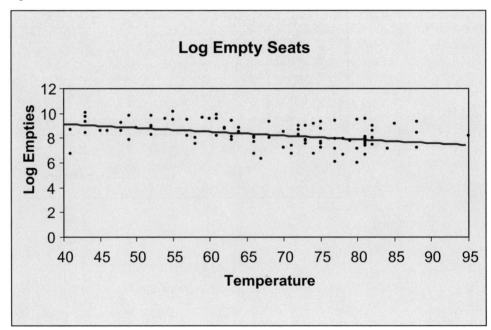

8. How does the semi-log model of empty seats used in Regression 7 compare to the models used in Regressions 5 and 6? Briefly discuss the pros and cons of using this last model.

9. Use Regression 7 to predict attendance for a Saturday night game against the Tigers that is not opening day. Also, the temperature is 89 degrees, there are full-price tickets, a promotional giveaway, and school is out of session. In addition to a single attendance number, provide a 95% prediction interval for your answer.

Regression 7

Regression: LN Empties	constant	night game	promo	temp(f)	Friday	Saturday
coefficient	9.63607376	-0.6626704	-0.1457834	-0.0171723	-0.5424369	-1.33806924
std error of coef	0.587088	0.21784989	0.16311218	0.00695845	0.2149278	0.251713121
t-ratio	16.4133	-3.0419	-0.8938	-2.4678	-2.5238	-5.3159
p-value	0.0000%	0.3179%	37.4131%	1.5727%	1.3589%	0.0001%
beta weight	-0.2622	-0.0724	-0.2274	-0.2051	-0.4495	

standard error of regression	0.67765579	
R-squared	60.26%	
adjusted R-squared	54.80%	

number of observations	92	
residual degrees of freedom	80	

t-statistic for computing 95% confidence intervals	1.9901	

	Sunday	opening day	school	Tigers	Pachyderms	cheap tickets
coefficient	-0.6943257	-2.061168	0.83040462	-0.4419581	-0.6054207	-0.02224734
std error of coef	0.22353512	0.51633944	0.20109273	0.26441453	0.29719137	0.261935991
t-ratio	-3.1061	-3.9919	4.1295	-1.6715	-2.0371	-0.0849
p-value	0.2623%	0.0145%	0.0089%	9.8538%	4.4943%	93.2526%
beta weight	-0.2559	-0.2998	0.3849	-0.1242	-0.1491	-0.0077

Predicted values and residuals

0.0075	93.091%	Breusch-Pagan heteroskedasticity test	
0.4532	79.722%	Jarque-Bera non-normality test	
1.0184		Durbin-Watson statistic	

APPENDIX

A KSTAT MINI-MANUAL

This KStat mini-manual is a complement, not a substitute, for the other resources available for you in learning KStat and Excel. Do not worry if some of the terminology used in this manual is unfamiliar. The purpose here is to instruct you on the mechanics of using KStat, not in understanding the statistics: this is what the text is all about!

KStat is a set of macros added to Excel and it will enable you to do the statistics required for this course easily. To start KStat, you need to open the Excel **KStat.xls** file, as you would open any other file. Your computer may warn you that the file contains macros and ask if you wish to disable or enable them. For KStat to work, you must have the macros enabled. The **menu bar** is the line near the top displaying the commands **File, Edit, View,** etc. After opening the file, note that the menu bar has an additional menu item called **Statistics**, which is not ordinarily there when you start Excel. This item is added to the menu bar by KStat. If the Statistics menu does not appear, it is because your Excel security is set on High and macros have ben disabled automatically. You can change this by clicking Tools > Macros > Security, selecting the Medium Box and then reloading KStat.xls. Throughout this manual, commands on the main menu and sub-menus will be separated by the > sign. For example, clicking **Statistics > Charts > Residual Plots** means doing this:

You can click on **Statistics**, then **Charts**, then **Residual Plots** (once each), or click on **Statistics**, hold the mouse button down as the sub-menus pop up, and release the button when you have gotten to **Residual Plots**.

GETTING STARTED

First thing you should do is to click **Statistics > Options** and to check all options in the Global Options dialog box that appears.

By checking the first box, you will tell Excel not to overwrite the results of one regression when you run another during your KStat session. Checking the second box will allow KStat to use the notation we will be using throughout this book. After you have checked both boxes, click **Done**. Now, you can click **File > Save**, and KStat will save these options, so you do not have to do this every time you start KStat.

Worksheets are for listing and analyzing data and displaying the results of your analysis. The names of the sheets appear on tabs at the bottom of the workbook window. To move from sheet to sheet, you click the sheet tabs. The name of the active sheet is always bold. You can rename the sheets, add and delete sheets, and move or copy sheets within a workbook or to another workbook.

Opening/Starting a Worksheet

When KStat starts, it will open a new workbook with only one worksheet, which is an empty worksheet called **Data**. This is where all data you wish to analyze must be entered. Usually, you will want to load a data file (which you have previously downloaded) into KStat. To do this, click **Statistics > Import data > File...** You will see a window like the one below. Choose the folder that your data file is in, choose the data file and click **Open**. For example, in the following window, by clicking **Open**, you can import the **Capm.xls** dataset into KStat.

Once your data are in place, the **Data** worksheet should look like this:

Microsoft Excel - kstat(1).xls

	A	B	C	D	E	F
1	date	sp500	smstk	crpbon	govtbon	tbill
2	2601	0	0.069863	0.0072	0.013756	0.003384
3	2602	-0.03474	-0.06019	0.008224	0.010037	0.006406
4	2603	-0.05186	-0.10171	0.014007	0.009737	0.008602
5	2604	0.015907	0.008508	0.000301	-0.00181	-0.00597
6	2605	0.023505	-0.00103	0.009987	0.006998	0.005715
7	2606	0.053215	0.045285	0.007891	0.011303	0.01095
8	2607	0.057324	0.020622	0.015134	0.009869	0.011677
9	2608	0.030559	0.031335	0.010114	0.00572	0.00825
10	2609	0.019444	-0.0058	-4.7E-05	-0.00198	-0.00347
11	2610	-0.03217	-0.02651	0.00589	0.006364	-0.00062
12	2611	0.030874	0.016954	0.001905	0.012202	-0.0007
13	2612	0.019593	0.033184	0.0056	0.007813	0.002778
14	2701	-0.01171	0.037133	0.013161	0.015033	0.010024
15	2702	0.061366	0.062345	0.014519	0.016397	0.010189
16	2703	0.014429	-0.04901	0.014058	0.031086	0.008717
17	2704	0.020101	0.057339	0.0055	-0.00049	0.002546
18	2705	0.05297	0.065657	-0.00882	0.003142	-0.00471
19	2706	-0.01629	-0.03987	-0.00528	-0.01647	-0.007
20	2707	0.086003	0.070554	0.019275	0.023945	0.021966
21	2708	0.057297	-0.01203	0.014103	0.013403	0.00856
22	2709	0.039203	-0.00109	0.009063	-0.00404	-0.00374
23	2710	-0.05598	-0.0717	-0.0003	0.004056	-0.00328
24	2711	0.074012	0.082749	0.008723	0.011629	0.004009
25	2712	0.029785	0.033563	0.008727	0.009078	0.004157
26	2801	-0.00203	0.0501	0.00463	-0.00168	0.004466
27	2802	-0.00285	-0.01395	0.016471	0.015791	0.012965
28	2803	0.110081	0.053051	0.0041	0.004545	0.002943
29	2804	0.032548	0.089037	-0.00055	-0.00231	0.000277
30	2805	0.013899	0.037939	-0.01365	-0.01356	-0.00261
31	2806	-0.03075	-0.07647	0.005352	0.011887	0.010874
32	2807	0.01407	0.005856	-0.001	-0.02174	0.003226
33	2808	0.078335	0.042231	0.006347	0.005694	0.001263

There are other ways to input data into KStat. If you have data in another Excel workbook, you can open that workbook in addition to KStat and then copy and paste the data to the **Data** worksheet of KStat. Occasionally, you may want to type in data manually. To do this, begin entering the data starting from the cell A1. You must ensure variable names are in row 1, each column is one variable, and the data is in consecutive columns.

Basic Statistics and Critical Values

With KStat and Excel, you can easily obtain some basic statistical quantities. Import the **adsales.xls** data file. **Statistics > Univariate statistics** will generate useful summary statistics for each variable on the **Data** sheet. The output looks like that in Figure A.1.

Statistics > **Correlations** finds the correlation coefficients between all pairs of variables in your dataset. Again, using the **adsales.xls** data, we produce the output in Figure A.2.

Here, 0.95549 is the correlation between exp and sales.

You can use the information provided in the univariate statistics output together with Excel's **TDIST** function to perform a **1-Sample t-test** (see Chapter Two). To compare the means of two populations using a **2-Sample t-test** (see Chapter Two), click on an empty cell. When you are done, Excel will put the result of the t-test in this cell. We will use the Excel function called **TTEST** that returns the p-value associated with a t-Test of the difference between two means. The syntax for this function is **TTEST(array1,array2,tails,type).** Here **Array1** is the first variable, **Array2** is the second variable, **Tails** specifies the number of tails to use for the test (If **tails = 1**, TTEST uses the one-tailed distribution, if **tails = 2**,

Figure A.1 Univariate statistics for the adsales.xls data.

Univariate statistics		
	exp	sales
mean	2.2900874	16.8873778
standard deviation	0.77765926	0.86660475
standard error of the mean	0.05929596	0.06607799
minimum	0.35679829	13.6289663
median	2.30022073	16.9419794
maximum	4.84897232	19.0247002
range	4.49217403	5.39573383
skewness	0.314	-0.826
kurtosis	0.568	1.996
number of observations	172	
t-statistic for computing 95%-confidence intervals	1.9739	

TTEST uses the two-tailed distribution), and **Type** is the kind of t-Test to perform. We will usually assume the variances of the variables in a 2-sample t-test are different so you will choose **3** as the type of test.

There are two ways to use this function in Excel. One way is clicking **Insert > Function....** In the dialog box that appears, choose **Statistical** as your function category and choose **TTEST** as your function name. The dialog box should look like this:

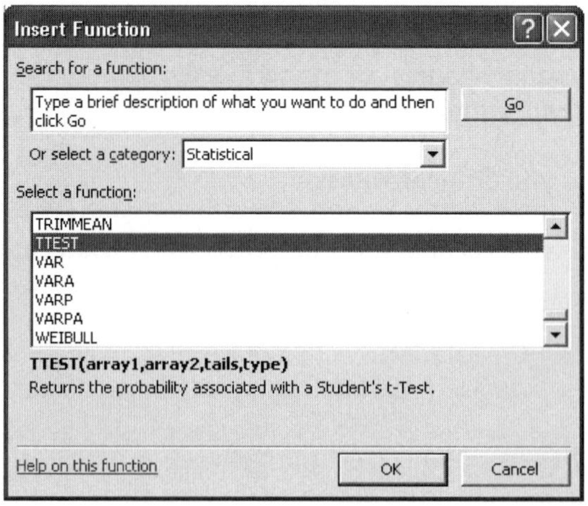

Figure A.2 Correlations for adsales.xls data.

Correlations		
	exp	Sales
exp	1.00000	0.95549
sales	0.95549	1.00000

When you click **OK**, you will obtain another dialog box. In the **Array 1** row, enter the range of the first sample, in the **Array 2** row enter the range of the second sample, in the **Tails** row enter **1** if you want a one tail test and enter **2** if you want a two tail test. Finally, in the **Type** row enter the type of the test that you want. Choose **3** (for unequal variances) as the type of your test. When you are done, the dialog box should look like this:

You can see the p-value associated with this test at the bottom where it says formula result. When you click **OK**, Excel will put the same result into the cell on which you clicked before starting the test.

Another way to do the same thing is typing **= TTEST(A2:A31,B2:B31,1,3)** directly into the cell.

Regression

In this section, we will use the **capm.xls** data .

The command you will probably use most frequently is **Statistics > Regression**. By using this command, you will obtain the following dialog box:

Choose the dependent variable from the list of variables and check the boxes for the appropriate independent variables. We will choose **smstk** as our dependent variable and **sp500**, **crpbon**, and **tbill** as our independent variables.

When you click **Perform regression**, KStat will create three worksheets: **Regression**, **ANOVA**, and **Residuals**. The active worksheet will be **Regression**, and you will get output as in Figure A.3.

Figure A.3 Regression of smstk on sp500, crpbon, and tbill.

Regression: smstk				
	constant	**sp500**	**crpbon**	**tbill**
coefficient	-0.0012814	1.36461728	1.5466021	-2.5374467
std error of coef	0.00452835	0.05101924	0.40357477	0.67671508
t-ratio	-0.2830	26.7471	3.8323	-3.7497
p-value	77.7450%	0.0000%	0.0163%	0.0223%
beta-weight		0.8455	0.1399	-0.1349
standard error of regression		0.06575673		
R-squared		77.31%		
adjusted R-squared		77.02%		
number of observations		240		
residual degrees of freedom		236		
t-statistic for computing 95%-confidence intervals		1.9701		

You may have noticed that some of the cells on the Regression worksheet and other worksheets have red dots on the upper right corner. These are called cell comments, which provide you a brief explanation of the cell content. To see a cell comment, put the cursor on the red dot in that cell and the comment will display automatically.

From the output above, we can see that our regression equation is, **smstk = -0.0012814 + 1.36461728*sp500 + 1.5466021*crpbon-2.5374467*tbill**. We get the standard errors, t-ratios, and p-values, and beta-weights for each coefficient, as well as the standard error of the regression, R^2 and adjusted R^2, KStat provides the number of observations, the degrees of freedom of the error term, and the t-statistic for computing 95 % confidence intervals.

Now, you can switch to the **ANOVA** worksheet. The output in this worksheet looks like Figure A.4.

Figure A.4 ANOVA worksheet output of regression.

Analysis of variance		
	sum of squares	**df**
regression	3.476071636	3
residual	1.020451604	236
total	4.496523241	239
F-ratio	267.9705	
degrees of freedom	(3, 236)	
p-value	0.00000%	

We obtained explained (regression) sum of squares, residual sum of squares, total sum of squares, F-ratio, degrees of freedom, and p-value. The p-value above is for the hypothesis test with the null hypothesis that all the coefficients are equal to zero. The p-value of zero says we can reject the null hypothesis with high confidence.

Finally, switch to the **Residuals** worksheet. This worksheet provides the predicted (or fitted) values and residuals for each observation in the dataset.

To make predictions using your most recently performed regression, click **Statistics > Prediction**. In the worksheet you obtain, you can make predictions and calculate confidence and prediction intervals. Suppose we want the predicted value for **smstk** where **sp500** = 0.05, **crpbon** = 0.01 and **tbill** = 0.02. Enter these numbers into the yellow cells corresponding to each variable and click **Predict**. You will obtain the following output:

On this worksheet, you can also obtain confidence and prediction intervals for the fitted values. To change the confidence level, type the confidence level you want in cell C12 and press Enter. The confidence and prediction intervals will then adjust to this confidence level automatically.

If you want to do predictions for more than one set of values, click the **Make multiple predictions** button. Suppose we want to make predictions for **sp500** = 0.05, **crpbon** = 0.01, and **tbill** = 0.02, as well as **sp500** = 0.02, **crpbon** = -0.02, and **tbill** = 0.03. Now you need to enter each set of values for the independent variables in a separate yellow column. After you click **Predict**, the worksheet should look like this:

After performing a regression, you can use some other advanced options by clicking **Statistics > Model analysis**. This option will expand the **Residuals** worksheet, and it will provide some useful statistics. (See below for an example of what the output will look like.) In particular, in addition to everything that was originally on the **Residuals** worksheet, you can obtain the test statistic and p-value for the Breusch-Pagan heteroskedasticity test, obtain variance inflation factors for the coefficients, and identify outliers and high leverage points, all of which are used in the text.

Graphs

In this section, we will use the **adsales.xls** data. Import this file into KStat using **Statistics > Import data > File....**

To plot one variable in your data against another, such as Y vs. X, click **Statistics > Charts > Scatterplots** and choose the variables from the dialog box that appears.

If you want the regression line to appear on your graph, you need to check the plot regression line box. By clicking **OK**, you can plot **sales** against **exp** and see the regression line as in Figure A.5.

If you want to save this chart as a worksheet, click on the **Save** button. You can graph any two variables from your data worksheet in this way.

In evaluating a regression, the graph of residuals versus predicted values will often be useful. Here is how to generate such a graph for a regression of **exp** against **sales**. First, run a regression where **exp** is the dependent variable and **sales**

Figure A.5 Scatterplot of sales vs exp.

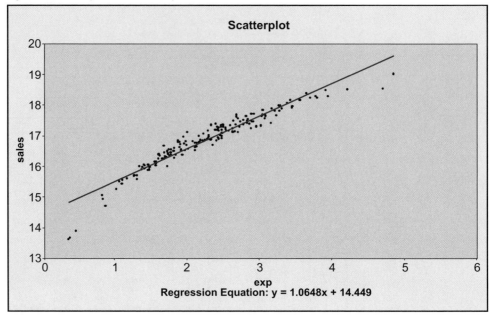

is the independent variable. Then, click **Statistics > Charts > Residual Plots**. You will obtain the following dialog box:

Choose predicted values as shown above and click **OK**. KStat automatically uses the residuals from the most recent regression you have performed in your current session. You will obtain the graph shown in Figure A.6 of residuals against the predicted values.

    To include the graph in a Microsoft Word file, first save the graph. Your graph will be saved in a worksheet named **Kept1**. (If you save more than one graph during a session, your later graphs will be saved in worksheets **Kept2**, **Kept3**, etc., in the order you saved them.) Switch to **Kept1** and click on the graph (in the white area not the gray area). Then click **Edit > Copy**. The graph will be copied into the clipboard and can now be pasted into Microsoft Word.

Getting P-values

In this section, we will use the **newspapers.xls** data. A regression of **Sunday** against **Daily** generates the output in Figure A.7.

    The p-value of 0.000% in the **daily** column of Figure A.7 is for one particular hypothesis test, where the null hypothesis is that β_1, the coefficient of **daily**, is

Figure A.6 Plot of residuals vs. predicted values from regression of exp on sales.

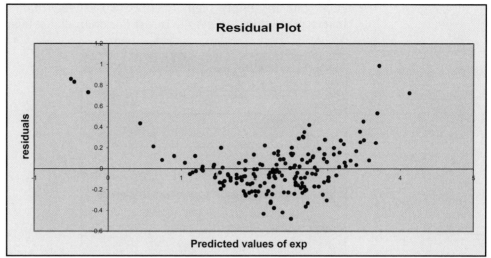

equal to zero. This p-value says we can reject the null with high confidence—we can be (virtually) 100% confident β_1 is not zero. If we wanted to test some other null hypothesis—for example, $\beta_1 = 1.1$—we would have to do the test manually. The t-statistic for this test is the following:

$$\frac{1.35117342 - 1.1}{0.09297695} = 2.7015$$

Figure A.7 Regression of Sunday on Daily.

Regression: Sunday		
	constant	Daily
coefficient	24.7631585	1.35117342
std error of coef	46.9866631	0.09297695
t-ratio	0.5270	14.5323
p-value	60.1701%	0.0000%
beta-weight		0.9300
standard error of regression		143.864401
R-squared		86.49%
adjusted R-squared		86.08%
number of observations		35
residual degrees of freedom		33
t-statistic for computing 95%-confidence intervals		2.0345

Now we can use Excel to look up the p-value corresponding to this value of t. First, click on an empty cell on the worksheet that you are in. Click on **Insert > Function...** to get the **Insert Function** dialog box:

Insert Function

Search for a function:

Type a brief description of what you want to do and then click Go   Go

Or select a category: Statistical

Select a function:

STDEV
STDEVA
STDEVP
STDEVPA
STEYX
TDIST
TINV

TDIST(x,deg_freedom,tails)
Returns the Student's t-distribution.

Help on this function   OK   Cancel

Choose **Statistical** from the **Function Category** window and choose **TDIST** from the **Function Name** window. Then click **OK**. You will move to the next step.

Function Arguments

TDIST

X 2.7015 = 2.7015
Deg_freedom 33 = 33
Tails 2 = 2

= 0.010812805

Returns the Student's t-distribution.

Tails specifies the number of distribution tails to return: one-tailed distribution = 1; two-tailed distribution = 2.

Formula result = 0.010812805

Help on this function   OK   Cancel

As shown in the screen shot, enter the t-statistic in the first row, degrees of freedom in the second row and, since we are talking about the probability associated with a two-tailed test, enter **2** in the third row. At the bottom of the dialog box, you can read the p-value associated with this test as the formula result. If you click **OK**, you will see **= TDIST(2.7015,33,2)** typed in the cell, which you could type directly into the cell. In any case, you should get the value 0.010812805.

Thus, the p-value for the test is 0.010812805; that is, if the coefficient on **daily** were 1.1, there would only be a 1.081% chance of obtaining a coefficient as far away from 1.1 as 1.35117342 because of randomness in the data. We would reject the null hypothesis at any confidence level up to about 99% (or any significance level down to about 1%).

We can also use Excel instead of a table to find critical values of t. To find the t-statistic corresponding to $\alpha = .10$ for our two-tailed test, click on **Insert > Function...**

to get the **Insert Function** dialog box. Choose **Statistical** from the **Function Category** window and choose **TINV** from the **Function Name** window. Then click **OK**. You will obtain the next window:

Type the sum of the probabilities you want in both tails, which is 0.10 into the first row, and enter the degrees of freedom into the second row. The formula result tells us the t-statistic is 1.692. So, we would reject the null with $\alpha = .10$ if we obtained a t-statistic greater than 1.692 or less than -1.692 (which we did). This additionally tells us that for a one-sided test with a 'greater than' alternative, we would reject the null with $\alpha = .05$ if we obtained a t-statistic greater than 1.692, and for a one-sided test with a 'less-than' alternative, we would reject the null with $\alpha = .05$ if we obtained a t-statistic less than -1.692.

We can also use Excel in place of a z-table. Suppose we want to look up the p-value corresponding to $z = 2.7$. First, click on an empty cell on the worksheet you are in. Click on **Insert > Function** to get the **Insert Function** dialog box. Choose **Statistical** from the **Function Category** window and choose **NORMSDIST** from the **Function Name** window. Then click **OK**. You will obtain the next window:

As shown above, enter the z value in the first row. Now, as the formula result, you can read $P(Z <\ = 2.7) = 0.996533$. If you click **OK**, this number will appear in the cell.

Suppose we wanted to find the z-statistic corresponding to $\alpha = .10$ for a two-tailed test. Click on **Insert > Function...** to get the **Paste Function** dialog box. Choose

Statistical from the **Function Category** window and choose **NORMSINV** from the **Function Name** window. Then click **OK**. You will obtain the next dialog box:

This time, we input the area and Excel gives us the z-statistic. In the following dialog box, when you enter the probability r, Excel will give you the number x such that there is a probability r of being less than x. We want the number x such that there is a 5% (i.e., $\alpha/2$%) chance of being greater than x, or, equivalently, a 95% chance of being less than x. Type 0.95 into the dialog box. The formula result tells us the appropriate z-statistic is 1.6448.

Creating new variables

Sometimes, you will need to make a new variable out of the ones given in a file. For example, you may want to use the logarithm of a variable as a predictor or response. As an example, create a new column, which includes the logarithm of the variable **exp**. To do this, first import the **adsales.xls** data and go to cell C1 on the data worksheet. Type the name you want to give to the new variable, say **lnexp**, into cell C1. Click on the cell C2, and click **Insert > Functions....** You will obtain the following **Insert Function** dialog box:

From the **Function Category** window, choose **Math & Trig**, and choose **LN** from the **Function Name** window. (There are different kinds of logarithms, LN stands for natural logarithm, and we will be using natural logarithms in this text.) Now click **OK**. You will see the following dialog box:

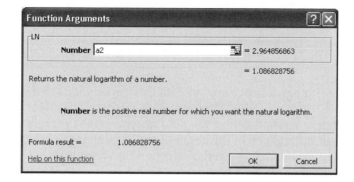

Click on cell A2 (the cell whose logarithm you want in the cell C2). Click **OK**. At this point in cell C2, you should have **= LN(A2)**. Alternatively—and this is much easier once you are used to it—you can type this formula directly into the cell. Now, copy and paste this formula into the rest of the column C, where there are corresponding observations in column A. When you are done, the worksheet will look like this:

	A	B	C
1	exp	sales	lnexp
2	2.96486	17.3135	1.08683
3	3.42961	18.1732	1.23245
4	1.70419	16.3328	0.53309
5	2.48654	17.2015	0.91089
6	1.90758	16.6317	0.64583
7	2.63043	17.2581	0.96715
8	1.78112	16.466	0.57724
9	1.82369	16.5027	0.60086
10	2.44622	17.2831	0.89455
11	1.3413	16.0042	0.29364
12	1.11347	15.5564	0.10748
13	2.50261	17.3702	0.91733
14	1.38603	15.9866	0.32645
15	1.02387	15.2672	0.02359
16	2.81939	17.6551	1.03652
17	1.96654	16.7589	0.67627
18	2.44776	16.9161	0.89518
19	2.54026	17.2237	0.93227
20	1.66775	16.2636	0.51148
21	2.47532	17.3489	0.90637
22	2.33189	16.89	0.84668
23	2.66398	17.1556	0.97982
24	1.27352	15.7223	0.24179

Now we are done. We created a new variable called **lnexp**. Each observation in **lnexp** is the logarithm of the corresponding observation in **exp**.

Many other mathematical functions are built into Excel that you can use to manipulate data, and we suggest you look and experiment with them.

Another type of variable we may want to create using Excel is a seasonal dummy variable. In the **soda.xls** dataset, we have the dummy variables **winter**, **spring**, and **summer**. **Winter**, for example, is a column with the following sequence of numbers:

$$1\ 0\ 0\ 0\ 1\ 0\ 0\ 0\ 1\ 0\ 0\ 0\ 1\ 0\ 0\ 0$$

There is a one for each row of data that corresponds to a winter quarter, and a zero for any other quarter. One way to construct a variable like this is to first type **winter** in the first cell of the column you want to create the variable in, type a **1** into the second cell of the column, and type three zeroes into the third, fourth, and fifth cells. Copy these cells onto the clipboard and paste them by choosing the appropriate cells as a destination. In the soda example, you need to paste this pattern three more times.

Everything else

Excel and KStat are capable of many tasks not discussed here. As you work through the problems in this book, you will become more familiar with the programs and their capabilities.

Prediction Intervals

What is a prediction interval?

A **prediction interval** is a confidence interval for a particular observation, rather than for the population mean, μ. In Chapter 1, you learned the formulas for confidence intervals for μ. The formulas for prediction intervals differ in two important ways from those formulas:

1. We can only calculate prediction intervals easily if we assume that the population is normally distributed.
2. For prediction intervals, we need to take into account the variance of an individual observation (the population variance) as well as the variance of $\bar{X}$. For confidence intervals concerning μ, it was only necessary to consider the variance of $\bar{X}$.

How do we calculate a $(1-\alpha)*100\%$ prediction interval?

Assume our sample of size n is i.i.d. and is drawn from a normally distributed population.

1. If we know the population standard deviation, σ, the P.I. is the following:

$$\bar{X} \pm z_{a/2}\sigma\sqrt{\frac{1}{n}+1}$$

2. If the population standard deviation is not known, then the P.I. is the following:

$$\bar{X} \pm t_{a/2;n-1}s\sqrt{\frac{1}{n}+1}$$

Correlation

Usually, the value of a random variable conveys some information regarding the value of another random variable. For example, if you know the height of someone, this gives you some idea about this person's weight. Typically, a taller person is heavier than a shorter person. This is not always the case, but it is fair to say that height and weight are positively correlated. Examples of positively correlated random variables abound, such as sales and advertising expenditures, the price of a Coke and the price of a Pepsi, inflation and the increase in the money supply, education and wages. In all these examples, the random variables are positively correlated because the probability of a high realization of one random variable is higher when the realization of the other random variable is high than when the realization of the other random variable is low.

A plot of two positively correlated variables may look like this.

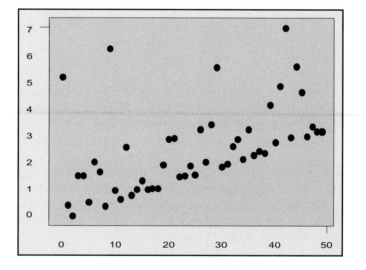

An extreme case of positively correlated variables is the case of two variables perfectly and positively correlated. In this extreme case, one variable is a positive linear transformation of the other, such as the price of a hamburger measured in cents and the price of a hamburger measured in dollars. One random variable is the other multiplied by 100.

Analogously, two random variables are negatively correlated if one is likely to be above average when the realization of the other random variable is low and below average when the realization of the other random variable is high. Examples of negatively correlated random variables also abound: inflation and contraction in the money supply, wages and poverty, and health and cigar consumption.

A plot of negatively correlated random variable may look like this.

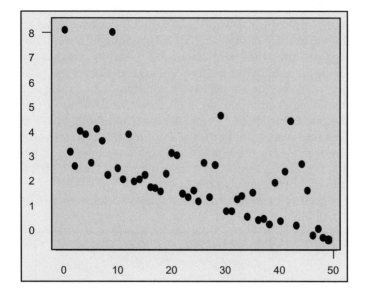

An extreme case of negatively correlated variables is the case of two variables perfectly and negatively correlated. In this extreme case, one variable is a negative linear transformation of the other.

Two random variables are independent if the realization of one random variable does not affect the probability distribution of the other random variable. A typical example of two independent random variables is given by tossing two different coins. Two independent random variables are not correlated.

The sample correlation coefficient of two variables x and y is obtained by dividing the sample covariance by the product of the sample standard deviation of x and the sample standard deviation of y:

$$r_{xy} = s_{xy}/(s_x s_y)$$

The components are as follows:

r_{xy} = sample correlation coefficient
s_{xy} = sample covariance
s_x = sample standard deviation of x
s_y = sample standard deviation of y

The correlation coefficient of two variables is always between -1 and 1. If it is -1, the two variables are perfectly negatively correlated. If it is 1, the two variables are perfectly positively correlated.

Using KStat, you can find the correlation coefficients between all possible pairs of variables in your dataset. To do this click **Statistics > Correlations**. For example, using the **adsales.xls** data, we produce the following output:

Correlations		
	exp	Sales
exp	1.00000	0.95549
sales	0.95549	1.00000

Here, 0.95549 is the correlation between exp and sales.

If your dataset contains more than two variables, KStat will return a table giving the correlation between any pair.

Properties of Logarithms

In this section, we outline some of the mathematical properties of logarithms, logs from here on, we will need to use in this text. In this book (as in most real-world applications), we will use only **natural logs**. Natural logs are called "natural" because they use the natural number $e = 2.71...$. We will use the notation **ln** for natural logs. Other common notations are log$e$ or log though the latter more often refers to a different kind of logarithm, i.e., log base 10.

Definition: the natural logarithm of a number x is the number y that satisfies: $e^y = x$.

So, $y = \ln x$ means y is the power you have to raise e to in order to get x. It's okay if the log of something is negative. It means you need to raise e to a negative number to get that value. On the other hand, there is no number you can raise e to and get -1; ln -1 is not defined. In fact, ln x is not defined for any negative x.

Fractional values for the log are possible:

$$\ln \sqrt{e} = 1/2 \text{ since } e^{1/2} = \sqrt{e}.$$

Negative fractions are allowed as well. ln x − -0.5 means that x is the -1/2 power of e or 1 over the square root of e. One general rule is that as x goes up, ln x goes up as well, but not nearly as fast as x does. In fact, as x goes up geometrically, ln x goes up linearly.

Raising something to a power 'undoes' the log as in this example:

$$e^{\ln x} = x, \text{ e.g., } e^{\ln 4} = 4.$$

The same holds in the opposite order as well:

$$\ln e^x = x, \text{ e.g. } \ln e^2 = 2.$$

SUMMARY OF PROPERTIES OF LOGS

There are a handful of properties of logs that get used a lot in general and in this book in particular. Here are some of the most important ones:

Property 1: Exponentiation and logs are inverses in that they undo each other. In particular, for any positive number x, the following is true:

$$e^{\ln (x)} = x \text{ and } \ln (e^x) = x$$

Example: $e^{\ln e} = e^1 = e$ and $\ln (e^1) = \ln (e) = 1$.

Property 2:   Logs of products are sums:

$$\ln (x*y) = \ln (x) + \ln (y)$$

This is true because you can add exponents in products as in this example.

$$\ln (e^2 e) = \ln (e^3) = 3 = 2+1 = \ln (e^2) + \ln (e)$$

<u>Property 3</u>:   Logs of powers are products:

$$\ln (x^y) = y \ln (x)$$

This is the same as property 2 above when you multiply the same thing together y times as in this example:

$$\ln (e^3) = \ln (e * e * e) = \ln e + \ln e + \ln e = 3 \ln (e)$$

Index